Exploring the Roots of Missions:

Personal, Biblical, and Spiritual

BOOK 1
Missions in a Coconut Shell

Esther Jones

ISBN 978-1-63961-008-2 (paperback)
ISBN 978-1-63961-009-9 (digital)

Copyright © 2021 by Esther Jones

All rights reserved. No part of this publication may be reproduced, distributed, or transmitted in any form or by any means, including photocopying, recording, or other electronic or mechanical methods without the prior written permission of the publisher. For permission requests, solicit the publisher via the address below.

Christian Faith Publishing, Inc.
832 Park Avenue
Meadville, PA 16335
www.christianfaithpublishing.com

Printed in the United States of America

Contents

Introduction 7

Chapter 1: Missions: Scope, Definition, and Practise 9
                What Missions Is 10
                Worldwide 10
                Discipleship 12
                Cross-cultural Barriers 13
                The Church 15
                Why we have missions 20
                Great Commission 22
                Where This Takes Place 1 26
                Tentmaking 29
                Life of Paul 35
                Preparation and Practise 38
                Cautions and Conditions 40
                      Where 2: The 10/40 Window 43
                Who Is Called 47
                When—Now and Pending 50
                      Summary 52

Chapter 2: Biblical Theology of Missions 53
                God's Nature and Character 54
                    God's Love 54
                    God is Light 56

        Old Testament 59
            Creation 59
            Covenant 61
            God's Call to Israel 62
            Prophets 67
            Exile 70
            Diaspora of the Jews 71
            Summary 72
        New Testament 73
            Gospels 80
            Acts of the Apostles 84
            Jerusalem/Judea, Samaria/ends of the earth 90
            Teachings in the Epistles 101
            Early Church 102
            Gifts 105
            Call of God 109
            Uniqueness of Message 111
            Gospel and Culture 113
            Religious Fulfillment 114
            Prayer: Necessity 116
            Summary 119

Chapter 3:   Forward to Missions 120
        Background 120
        To Stay or Not to Stay 123
        Esl Overseas 124
            1. Christum Suksa, Thailand 124
            2. Seoul, S. Korea 125
            3. Pohang, S. Korea 127
            4. Bangkok Christian College, Thailand 129
            Europe Experience 130
            5. Sungkyul University, S. Korea 130
        To Canada 2003 132
            Summary 133

Chapter 4:	Discerning Call and Preparation	135
	Calls in Scripture	135
	Being Called to Missions	138
	Practical Steps I	142
	Prayer and Missions	144
	Desired Qualities of International Workers	152
	Practical Steps II	156
	Summary	160
Chapter 5:	Spiritual Warfare	161
	Part 1: Understanding the Basics	161
	Old Testament Patterns	161
	Spiritual Grounding for International Workers	162
	Worldviews	167
	Kingdom Authority	171
	Deception	177
	Biblical History	180
	Armour of God	183
	Cleaning the House	191
	Breaking Chains	196
	Preparation	197
	Step 1: Counterfeit vs. Real	200
	Step 2: Deception vs. Truth	202
	Step 3: Bitterness vs. Forgiveness	204
	Step 4: Rebellion vs. Submission	205
	Step 5: Pride vs. Humility	206
	Step 6: Bondage vs. Freedom	207
	Step 7: Acquiescence vs. Renunciation	207
	Part 2: On the Field	208
	Wrestling	208
	Enemy Forces	209
	Areas Open to Attack	215
	Battle Lines	221

  Caution and Critique 225
  Practical Applications for International Workers 227
    Summary 231

Appendices 233
Appendix A: The Twelve Apostles 235
Appendix B: Otto Koning 238
Appendix C: The Hundred-Year Prayer Meeting and
      Subsequent Missions 240
Appendix D: Doctrinal Affirmation 242
Appendix E: Who Am I? 244
Bibliography 249

Introduction

The story of missions is complex and unique to each one involved. It begins personally but is universal. This is one kind of mission handbook set that would be useful to students just starting out. It is not exhaustive yet has enough depth to give a good bird's-eye view. There are four main sections to this writing: book 1, "Exploring the Roots of Missions"; book 2, "Crossing Cultures"; book 3, "Religions of the 10/40 Window"; and book 4, "Missions Throughout History."

The "Exploring Roots of Missions" book begins with a short introduction that summarizes the chapters in the book. The first root in chapter 1 is the definition and qualification of missions in scope and practise. This chapter comprises the answers to the questions what, where, who, which, and how of missions. This includes open countries with evangelism and closed countries where a myriad of ministries can be practised by the tentmakers to show to the nationals about God and His love.

The next root is the biblical theology of missions chapter that traces the theology of missions throughout Scripture in Old and New Testaments. The placement and influence of Israel among the nations as the light of God is emphasized. The New Testament shows the work of Jesus and the early apostles among the nations (both Jewish and Gentile).

The third root is the personal story of the author and her involvement in missions. As a young believer, she went to a youth conference and felt the call to missions. From there on, educational training in Bible college and subsequent overseas experiences confirmed her calling. This root is based on personal discernment and experience.

"Discerning Preparation and Call" in chapter 4 looks at biblical calls and how the individual can discern their call to missions work. Various aspects of the preparation are looked at, both spiritual and practical. From education and training to short- and long-term experiences, this root is a valuable part of the holistic preparation of the international worker.

The final root is the fifth chapter on spiritual warfare which is seen as the groundwork for missions because without the armour, the Christian cannot be the person Christ has called him or her to be, let alone do the task which is possible only in Christ's strength and power. Many insights are taken from various sources as well as personal observations and experience. Spiritual warfare starts out from a personal basis of who we are in Christ. Missionary application of spiritual warfare is under God's calling and work, and not in the animistic sense of some proponents that promote the workers to go and pray and believe that is all there is to the battle.

There are five appendixes at the end of the book. They cover the original twelve apostles, the Otto Koning story of growing (and keeping) pineapples, the one-hundred-year prayer meeting, a doctrinal affirmation, and "Who am I" relating to the spiritual warfare portion of the book.

1

Missions: Scope, Definition, and Practise

The contemporary idea of missions has changed incredibly from the days in the 1800s when Protestant missionaries went out to study the language and preach the Word. When the missionaries of the Roman Catholic Church, notably the Jesuits, went out, they also had ideas of how the church should be brought to the lost. A look at what is happening today shows how mission work is being done worldwide by the church of various nationalities and denominations.

> A South Korean computer technician working in Kazakhstan doing covert street evangelism and running a house group.
>
> A former Mexican street kid, now a Christian, who is part of a shop front ministry team in downtown Los Angeles.
>
> A fifty-year-old former long-time career missionary in Thailand now heading a small importing business in Vietnam.
>
> A Filipino couple working in Saudi Arabia, he as a gardener and she as domestic help.
>
> A Nigerian AOG pastor of 20 years' experience, now pastoring a church for African migrants in South Auckland.

> An Australian doctor setting up a whole series of low-cost medical clinics in rural Cambodia. (Christensen, 2001)

We're going to follow the pattern of the five Ws in this exploration of missions in this chapter. As we point out the main reasons behind missions, we'll discover what it is, why it is important, where this takes place, who is involved, and when this is to happen.

What Missions Is

Our first W is what missions is (as well as what it is not). Missiology is the study of missions—the work of the Christian church making disciples in cross-cultural situations. This is the work of bringing people to salvation in Jesus Christ through evangelism wherever they may be. Part of the process in bringing the gospel to people is making them disciples. This is the goal of mission strategy (Wagner 1983, p. 108) as the biblical passage that commands us to go, make disciples, baptize, and teach (Matt. 28:19, 20) contains only one imperative verb, "make disciples." A decision for Christ may be made in a moment, but the work of being a Christian, becoming Christ-like in every way, lasts a lifetime.

Nowadays we use the term "international worker" as this is less laden with negative cultural baggage that "missionary" is. Unfortunately, in some places, particularly the creative access countries, the term "missionary" has too much of a Christian content/history for governments that are opposed to the gospel. The abbreviated term for "international workers" is IW.

Worldwide

This discipleship also must be worldwide—all must hear of the gospel. The Lausanne International Congress on World Evangelization made a defining statement of mission as planting churches by a viable indigenous movement from within each culture (Dougherty 1988). This is the basis for Ralph Winter's emphasis in his mission papers and the U.S. Center for World Mission. Scripturally speaking, *apostello* means "to send." We get the word *missionary* from the Latin term *mitto*, which means the same thing. The apostles were called "sent ones." John 20:21 says that as God has sent Jesus, so Jesus also sends us out. We are sent out to the world to tell them of the gospel, the good news that Jesus Christ died for their sins. Later on in this section we'll look at what missions is not.

In the past, missions was seen mostly as Western Christian workers as pioneers crossing international borders to accomplish this task. Many international workers poured out from Europe to other parts of the world—Africa, India, Asia, South America, and eventually North America. Later on, North America became the prime sending force in missions. But now we have come full circle. Today IWs are going out from every nation to reach those of every nation. This is very exciting; it means that the rest of the world is getting involved in sending out people from the local church to fulfill God's plan of salvation for all. Nations that formerly received IWs are now participating in outreach themselves. Missions is a worldwide enterprise—Christians from every nation reaching out to their lost neighbours. This varies according to the ability of the sending church, but the results in the last few years are quite amazing. In 1983, Covell reported that three thousand IWs were being sent out by over two hundred non-western agencies. Wagner (Journey) reported 8,634 sent out the same year by 430 societies. By 1996, World Evangelism Fellowship reported the following:

> Pioneer work is the chief ministry of missionaries from Brazil (24%), India (29%), Korea (23%), Nigeria (36%), Philippines (23%), Singapore (28%) and the United Kingdom (21%). Church planting is the chief ministry of those from Costa Rica (25%), Ghana (24%) and the United States (21%). Working with national churches is the chief ministry of those from Australia (20%) and Canada (22%), and relief and development that of missionaries from

Denmark (25%) and Germany (30%). (WEF 1996)

Even the poorer nations are being dynamically involved in reaching their neighbours for Christ—a much needed thing for both them and their neighbours. Gospel for Asia, a third world mission, reports that 133 Bible schools have been established in the countries of India, Nepal, Bangladesh, Myanmar, Sri Lanka, and at the Bhutan border. There are over seven thousand men and women in training. These graduates minister in places where the gospel has not before been preached. They frequently establish a new fellowship within their first year (GFA 2005).

Discipleship

The matter of discipleship and the cost of discipleship is something that needs careful attention (Peters 1972, p. 186). The biblical phrase of taking up the cross is a part of our sanctification (Luke 9:23–24 cf. Matt. 10:38–39, 16:24–25; Mark 8:34; Luke 24:27). This includes all believers. Certainly, IWs the world over have been great examples of what it means to bear the cross. Peters contrasts it with two other issues that are often confused with it—burden of the flesh and thorns of the flesh. Cross-bearing is voluntary, daily, and includes self-denial for Christ's sake. A burden of the flesh that is common to all people are things like afflictions, trials, disappointment, and depression. These come from living in a sinful world. Thorns of the flesh, however, have affliction which is not voluntary. There is peace but no deliverance from the situation. It is generally something personal to the individual believer. Paul was afflicted so that he might be kept humble. Discipleship is a part of identification with Christ. Just as He identified with us, in becoming human and suffering, so we need to identify with Him in suffering and follow at any cost. Here Bonhoeffer reminds us that grace is costly and calls us to follow. Christ gave up His infinite nature in order to come and live on earth as a man.

> What has cost God much cannot be cheap for us… God did not reckon His son too dear a price but delivered him up for us. Costly grace is the incarnation of God. (Bonhoeffer 1967, p. 7)

Furthermore, Bonhoeffer asserts that one cannot have Christ without the necessary discipleship too. It is impossible to have Him and not take on all that He represents and encompasses.

> Christianity without the living Christ is without discipleship…and Christianity without discipleship is Christianity without Christ. (Bonhoeffer 1967, p. 11)

Every Christian is called to the same level of fullness of salvation as well as to the purpose of salvation. The lordship of Christ must be practised out in ordinary life. The gospel crosses all barriers and boundaries—the lordship of Christ must go everywhere. The discipleship of Christ is a path, not an achievement (Peters 1972, p. 189). Everyone, from beginners to the very senior saints, is a disciple.

Cross-cultural Barriers

Samuel Kim, himself an international worker from South Korea to Thailand, asserts that it makes a lot of sense, both culturally and financially, to send IWs across milder cultural barriers instead of the traditional extreme barriers. The extreme barriers are generally harder to deal with and more expensive. These cultural barriers can be from inner city work with street kids to working in a foreign culture like Mexico or Mali. Ralph Winter describes the cross-cultural barriers in the following way:

E1: Same culture. An IW going from one people group to another in the same cultural area. There is no new language to learn. An example of this would be a South Korean going to work with other Koreans—perhaps going from Seoul to Busan. There is no great cultural barrier to cross and no new language to learn. Another example could be a Canadian going from the east coast to the prairies, moving from a large urban area to a rural one.

E2: Similar culture. This time there is a slight cultural difference. An example of this would be a German person going to Switzerland. The shock of the new culture would not be as great as it would for a Caucasian North American. Another example of this would be a person going from Britain to Australia. The author calls this a "lateral cultural change" because some of the basics like language and culture are from the same root. There is some culture shock in this kind of change; personally I find it harder culturally in terms of expectations going from Canada to America or to Britain than Asia. I expect major differences in Asia from my homeland of Canada. Culture shock in Britain tends to be more subtle, but the difference is still felt. My husband, being from the United Kingdom, is fairly comfortable in many of the countries in Europe. He can speak French and German and therefore can adapt quite easily to the languages, even when he finds variations in Swiss German or Belgian French. For myself, I could sit in a French church service in France and pick out a few words I recognized. After six months, I could get 50 percent of the sermon. Lateral cultural shock is something unexpected and yet still a barrier to cross. Although the cultures in Europe are quite different from one country to the next, the same roots are there in terms of Western thought.

E3: Very different culture and language. The cultural change is large. A Swedish IW would have a lot of culture shock going to a traditional Muslim country. Muslim society is very conservative, especially from a woman's perspective. Sweden, on the other hand, is very liberal. The languages are very different, and there would be a lot of shock in adjusting. Another big change would be someone from South America, like Chile, going to Japan. South Americans tend to be very expressive and emotional. The Japanese tend to be fairly reserved. This would be a big change, in addition to the completely different language. In Asia, my European linguistically gifted husband found the languages just as difficult an adjustment as I do, as that is E3. In South Korea, the amount of time in church services did not help me with the language, unlike France. Without the cognates, I could decipher and understand little. Again, in an E3 culture, whatever your own background, there are major differences to be dealt with.

The Church

The church does the work of missions. The church is the sending agent of missionaries, now international workers, but missions is not all that a church does. Kirk states in the *New Dictionary of Theology,*

> The parallel between God sending Jesus and Jesus sending his disciples describes both the method and content of mission. The church's mission, then encompasses everything that Jesus sends his people in the world to do. It does not include everything the church does or everything that God does in the world. (Bosch et al. 1988, p. 435)

Some church organizations would say that the church and mission are the same. Wagner noted that the WCC (World Council of Churches) in 1973 Bangkok conference defined "lostness"

> as suffering under social oppression and "salvation" as freedom from torture or victory over enemies. (Wagner 1983, p. 36)

This is not a biblical definition of lostness. The church and missions are not the same in focus or in function. There are many good activities that Christians as part of the church body can get involved in that are not missions work. For instance, financially supporting a group that is working for political freedom in another country may be a good cause. But it is *not* missions. However, it only takes some effort to expand such steps into evangelistic focus. In nineteenth century, child labour was an issue. Many poor children were forced to work in factories all day long. It was dangerous and low-paid work. A Christian man started inviting them to study on Sundays; he taught them reading, writing, and the Bible. This became the first Sunday school. Those that did come to Christ through this work were saved as the result of a passion for souls. Eventually the laws were changed so that the children didn't have to work, and they had regular schooling. This was a good thing, but the implementation of education in and of itself was not missions. The concern expressed in the education work (as well as removing the children from a dangerous workplace) was a part of caring for the whole person. Teaching them the Bible was missions work. Both of these approaches can and do overlap, but they are not equal.

It is important here to define two terms that regularly occur in missions: *cultural mandate*—this is the general mandate for mankind as given in the first two chapters of Genesis to fill the earth (with human population) and to rule it giving wise stewardship of its animals and resources. This is often seen as a part of our loving our lost brothers and sisters and helping them out of their social problems (illiteracy, famine, sickness, and poverty). This is a general command that all people are to participate in caring for the planet as well as for humankind. This is needed to help build a wholesome culture. The second term is *evangelical mandate* (Matt. 28:19, 20) where Christ gives the command to preach the gospel to every creature, disciple them, and thus bring them into the kingdom. It includes things like evangelism, discipleship, and church planting. This is where the spiritual dominates the cultural. Both of these are from God, and both serve mankind. These two mandates are not to be confused, although we have artificially separated the two. The preaching of Christ should be in every humanitarian effort, whether directly or indirectly. Christians are to be salt and light. It was said in ancient Rome that the Christians cared for the others better than the pagans did, and so they should. The good deeds of Christians reaching their world holistically should not replace evangelistic work. These areas need to work together.

Church and mission are not separate ideas either. In the West, we have come to see them as two parties, two separate groups. In

EXPLORING THE ROOTS OF MISSIONS: PERSONAL, BIBLICAL, AND SPIRITUAL

a way, the separation of church and mission societies (that carried out missions) is abnormal (Peters 1972, p. 215). Part of this may have developed because of the Reformation itself. The theology of the Reformers in general was not very evangelistic in focus; in fact, Zwingli felt that missions work was for the apostles. But the Reformation did result in an ultimate mission focus on the world, albeit very belatedly. The church was very dependent on the state at this time. The majority of missions' work was done by mission societies. Within these societies were strong individuals who felt God's call on their lives to go forth in missions. Often, they were not accepted by sending agencies and went out independently. Church and mission are meant to be looked at quite differently.

Definitions of the church and mission will be helpful at this juncture. The term *church* is mentioned 115 times in the New Testament. The Greek word for church is *ekklesia,* meaning "called out ones." This is, as Peters says, not so much the idea of those who are called out but those who are called to God (Peters 1972, p. 200). The church proper was born on the day of Pentecost when the Holy Spirit came (Acts 2). It was made up of believers who expressed Christ's qualities (Eph. 5:25–27). Ephesians 2:20 says that the church is built upon the foundation of the apostles and prophets with Christ being the direct and immediate foundation. As the Father sent the Son, and the Son through the Holy Spirit sent the apostles out to the world. Christ is the Head of the church, and the church is His body, equipped with His gifts and calling. It is the church's job to make disciples (Matt. 28:18–20). Christ died for the church and bought it, cleansing it with His blood (Eph. 3:10–11). The true church is both salt and light, bringing God's health to a sick and dying world, showing the way back to God through Christ's redemption.

The church must teach the new converts and follow through on the discipleship according to the Great Commission. The church is also the agency that sends the apostles (2 Cor. 8:23). When the church sends out the international worker, it is the laying on of hands that gives the authentication, identification, and creation of a representative by delegation (Peters 1972, p. 221). The IW then goes out in the authority of the church and accepts the responsibility given.

There is responsibility and benefits on both sides. The mission society can be delegated by the church. Individuals (like William Carey and Samuel Zwemer) can be moved by God to go where the church had previously failed to go in its task. In Acts, Peter spoke to Cornelius. Francis of Assisi went to the Muslim leader Saladin. When there is disobedience to God, churches develop without missions, and likewise, there are many churchless mission societies (Peters 1972, p. 231). In the West we have made an artificial separation between the church and missions like this Diagram 1:

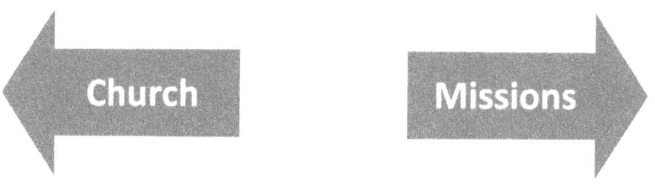

But in reality, the biblical picture is quite different see Diagram 2.

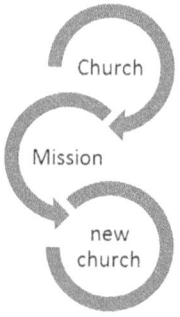

The church functioning as a body, a living organism, is involved in evangelism as a natural process. Evangelism is one of the spiritual gifts (1 Cor. 12, Rom. 12). This desire to communicate God's free gift flows naturally from evangelism into missions-crossing cultural barriers to tell others. Peter's epistle says that we are God's chosen people (I Pe. 2:9). We were called out of darkness to bring praises to God. Our gifts are for building up of the church (Eph. 4:11-13). We need to encourage each other through the gifts of teaching, preaching, and service. But let's not stop there. We also are to evangelize—that is also one of the gifts. We are to bring others into the kingdom (Matt. 28:18–20, Acts 1:8). The ultimate sending authority of international workers to the world is Christ Himself.

Some evangelicals, like Wagner, feel that the main issue is the spiritual factor (Wagner 1983, p. 47). Even if you manage to cure the cultural problems of mankind—famine, illiteracy, ignorance, disease—the main problem is sin. God did not provide a final solution to these issues at the time of the Fall except for sin itself. Man was ejected from the garden of Eden, and a flaming cherub kept Adam and Eve from returning to paradise. Sickness and death will finally be gone once Christ is established as King in the future kingdom. Now, there is salvation from sin—the evangelical mandate is to tell others. The rest will follow as the process of discipleship in a person grows in depth and breadth. In many cases, social and personal issues are resolved once people come to Christ and the Holy Spirit works in their hearts to change them. Some take a more concerted effort under personal mentoring and discipleship or counselling. Wagner's statement certainly applies to most individual sins and personal issues. As the light of Christ shines in our lives, we learn to change and grow. But for social sins and corporate injustices, Christians in the past have and should continue to work for justice. Part of God's desire for mankind is to see justice done for those who are wronged. Correcting wrongs is not salvation itself, but it is a valid expression of that salvation light. As the apostle James rebuked those who preached without action, so today we must act to show our faith.

The expression of the local churches may be quite different but they should still show Christ. The difference in Christ's presence in a situation is through proclamation to those that don't know Him. They may feel Him but not know who He is. The Christian presence must always be seen in the biblical context (because of what Christ has done for us) and not replaced with content that is not connected with Him (Peters 1972, p. 212). The redemption of Christ is for the whole of life, and His touch extends to every area of it. Thus, Christians can work in almost any arena of life and shine out the light that Christ has given. The work of the church as a body is to evangelize others, to tell others of the good news: Christ died to save sinners. A church sends out international workers, those dedicated to the full-time work of telling the good news to the nations. Once people begin to believe, they are discipled by the IWs and start a local body of believers. The local body is a church. This church then sends out IWs. One author on the Web even asserted that church planting was the only way to fulfill the Great Commission; the context given was in the Philippines (Missionary Training Service 2004). In a sense this is true. A believer grows best in the context of other believers, and a church plant can facilitate this very well.

Think of how a city works. It depends on various people and services to keep running. If there are financial problems, the whole city is in trouble. If the power breaks down, the businesses cannot run. We all need each other. Paul speaks in 1 Corinthians 12:12–31 of the many parts of the body. Each part is needed to do its task. A public task is no more important than a private one. A speaking gift is no less valid than a gift that uses faith. The gifts of the church also work this way; we need prayer, teaching, preaching, and administration. But if we leave out missions, we are hindering the church and the work of the gospel. A sad example of this is found in Africa. Western IWs were asked this question: "If the gospel is true, why didn't your grandfather come to tell my grandfather?" In fact, it seems that churches that hang on to their own survival and do not participate in missions also suffer and die. There is something vital missing if we do not all reach out to others.

Why we have missions

This is our second W—the all-important Why? Why is missions important? In Genesis 1 we have the record of God's creation. God made the world, and He made people to be in fellowship with Him (Isa. 45:18, 43:7). The Westminster Catechism says, "The chief end of man is to glorify God and to enjoy Him forever." We are made in God's image and we were made to have a relationship with Him. Communion with God is a part of our creation. But this communion and fellowship was broken when Adam and Eve sinned. Later when

EXPLORING THE ROOTS OF MISSIONS: PERSONAL, BIBLICAL, AND SPIRITUAL

God came walking in the garden, they hid from Him. Their wonderful fellowship was broken (Gen. 3:8, 9). They no longer trusted God; they were afraid of Him. We are God's because He made us. We put ourselves under Satan's power when Adam sinned. Adam's sin is also our sin. We became lost to God and His fellowship. Our sin did not mix with His holiness. God drove Adam and Eve from the garden (Gen. 3:22–24) so they would not eat of the tree of life. But God made them a promise: though the serpent shall bite your heel, you shall crush his head. One day the serpent, known as Satan, would be destroyed. When Adam and Eve ate of the forbidden fruit, they died spiritually. They became separated from God and His life. They lived for themselves independent of God. They were lost from their relationship with the Eternal One. This is our number one reason for missions: *man is lost* (2 Cor. 5:20). To Peters, it is nothing short of an emergency situation or a malady that has but one cure (Peters 1972, p. 15). No "upgrade" of mankind is sufficient to mend what ails man; he is a willful sinner in a state of rebellion against God. Worse than that, he is enslaved in his sin so that he cannot possibly fix what is wrong. Born into sin, he is condemned by that sin to die. Sin has taken away his purpose and destiny as a child of God, thus making his life meaningless and empty. The book of Ecclesiastes takes great pains to point out that unless one takes God into account in the pleasures and work of this life, it is rendered meaningless. It is a futile chasing after the wind, and the only one to give it purpose and reality is God Himself, for He designed it that way. God made us to look after the eternal; the "God-shaped" vacuum can only fit Him.

Sauer expresses it this way as an example using the religions of the world (adapted from Olson, p. 42).

> The Greek says: Man, know thyself.
> The Roman says: Man, rule thyself.
> The Chinese says: Man, improve thyself.
> The Buddhist says: Man, annihilate thyself.
> The Brahman says: Man, merge thyself with the universal sum of all.
> The Moslem says: Man, submit thyself.

> But Christ says: Without Me you can do nothing in Him the Christian says I can do all things through Christ who makes me mighty. (Phil. 4:13)

It is only in Christ and through His power that we can know who we are, people made in His image. We can then also control ourselves by the Holy Spirit. People want to live for themselves, independent of God. They think of themselves first, not Him. This is sin, the wages of which is death (Rom. 6:23) and that penalty means separation from God forever. When you sin, you are living your own life in your own way, not God's. We fall short of His glory (Rom. 3:23) of perfection. We are condemned because of disobedience to God's law.

Salvation comes when someone pays the penalty for us (1 Tim. 2:5, 6). God sent Jesus, His Son, to earth to take our place on the cross (John 3:16, Rom. 4:25). Because He was sinless (2 Cor. 5:21) and obeyed all of God's commands, Jesus is able to give us a new life. He gives it to us as a gift. Sinful man is condemned to eternal punishment (Matt. 25:43, 10:32). Being separated from God is the worst punishment because we were made to worship Him. The only way we can become real is by submitting to God Himself, not the annihilation of our beings as in Hinduism. We become made into His image, and yet in the process, we do not lose ourselves—just the selfishness and sin that has attached itself to our nature.

Great Commission

God has given to us, His children, a part in the task of the Great Commission (Matt. 28:19, 20). God has chosen to give us the task of being co-labourers with Him (1 Cor. 3:9). God has given mankind the ability to rule over the earth. God created man last of all creation; people were God's masterpiece (Gen. 1:26, 27). Part of our being made in God's image involved being able to rule, like God does, on a smaller scale. We are to make disciples from all nations (Acts 1:8). We are to work together as God's partners in sharing the good news (Rom. 10:14–15). It is tragic that the Great Commission has been more debated than obeyed (Peters 1972, p. 173). The natural outflow of the character of God is revealed in the Scriptures as missions first and foremost. All four "snapshots" in the gospels of the Great Commission pronouncements taken together form a good balance of what Christ's intent was. From Matthew come the authority, time, and extension of the work. Mark stresses the urgency and geographical scope and Luke the Christocentric message to all the nations. The gospel of John gives the spiritual equipment and nature of the work. The process of making disciples includes the gospel message in all its entirety, so that the people experience God's grace through Christ's work on the cross and in His resurrection. The building of God's people into a new life, the use of the spiritual gifts, and dependence of the Holy Spirit—all these are a part of the scope of making disciples.

Christ declared His sovereignty (Matt. 28:18, Phil. 2:9–11, Rev. 3:7) and told His disciples to take the gospel to all people (Acts 1:8). The nature of the gospel was Christ's sacrifice (Acts 26:15–23, 1 Cor. 15:2–4). The work was to be done by the power of the Holy Spirit—they were waiting for this in Jerusalem (Luke 24:48). The Holy Spirit and Word together balance God's work in us and through us. The more we, as Christ's disciples, have His Word in us, the better we can interpret what the Holy Spirit is saying to us. The Great Commission is repeated in Scripture for this very purpose, to break through into life from the written page.

Piper asserts that since worship is the goal of the church, it will go on forever. All the tribes and nations will gather around the throne of God in glorious worship. Thus, in that context, missions are temporary. When we worship God, then we will be motivated in our desire for missions. It was during worship time in Acts 13 that Paul and Barnabas were set aside to go out from Antioch in response to the leading of the Holy Spirit. Dillaman makes the link between worship and the release of God's power and provision (Cowles 1996, p. 87). Paul and Silas praised God in prison, and the doors were opened. Jehoshaphat sent his worshipper-priests into the battle in 2 Chronicles 20.

Our worship stems from knowing how great God is and wanting to tell the nations of His greatness. When we look at God's glory, at the things which He did for the sake of His name in Scripture, we get a picture of Who our God is, great in mercy toward us and desiring to save us for Himself, just as He did with the Israelites. From creation (Isa. 43:6, 7) to calling Israel out of the nations (Isa. 49:3, 9, 11), the rescue of Israel from Egypt (Ps. 106:7, 8), forgiveness for sin (1 Sam. 12:20–22), restoring Israel from exile (Ezek. 36:22–23, 32). All through the Old Testament God is working out salvation for His own glory and name. In the New Testament, this pattern continues as Jesus does work for His Father alone (John 7:18). God answers prayer for the sake of His glory (John 14:13), and the ministry of the Spirit is toward that end (John 16:14). God wants us to see and enjoy His glory (John 17:24). Our service to God is for His glory (1 Cor. 10:31), and our good works honor Him (1 Pet. 2:12). Ultimately all the earth will enjoy His glory (Hab. 2:14).

Dillaman gives seven benefits of a worshipping church (Cowles 1996, p. 90ff).

1. God's power is released (Luke 24:49).
2. Our love for God is sustained as we focus on Him. In John 21:15, Jesus's question for Peter was if Peter loved Him first and foremost. When Peter affirmed this love, he was given the instruction to feed the sheep.
3. Our faith is strengthened (Ps. 100:4, 3) as we enter into the courts of praise; we acknowledge who God is. We are His sacrifices because we are His sheep. Yet as living sacrifices, we are challenged in this every day, not just once.
4. The focus of our shift then goes from ourselves to God.
5. Our sensitivity is to God alone (Ps. 22:3).
6. Our enemy is hindered as we engage in spiritual deliverance, counsel, and prayer.
7. When people see God's holiness, they are convicted of sin. In this way, legalism can be avoided.

EXPLORING THE ROOTS OF MISSIONS: PERSONAL, BIBLICAL, AND SPIRITUAL

Thus, our zeal for God imitates His zeal (Rom. 15:8, 9) and will bring many into the kingdom. It is more than just getting more labourers.

> Missions is not a recruitment project for God's labour force. It is a liberation project from the heavy burdens and hard yokes of other gods (Matt. 11:28–30). (Piper 1993, p. 32)

Paul says that he received grace for the sake of the nations (Rom. 1:5). Psalms declares that the nations should be glad and sing for joy (Ps. 67:4).

The purpose of the Great Commission was to ensure that the gospel would be preached. Jesus declares Who He is and passes on the authority to take the gospel out of all nations, knowing that He would go with them (Matt. 28:18–20). Mark stressed belief and baptism as a part of the message (Mark 16:15–16), while Luke speaks of repentance and forgiveness of sins, as well as the suffering and death of Christ (Luke 24:46–49). The emphasis on being sent is brief in John (John 20:21–22), while Luke records the specifics in Acts 1:8. Paul has his own commission Acts 26:17–18. Paul established many churches and provided an example for us to follow in the way he worked with them. He considered them his partners; they were his resources for his work as well as his fruit (Rom. 15:20, 24, 30–32; Phil. 1:5, 2:25, 4:14–17; Eph. 6:18, 19; Col. 4:2–4). He asked them to pray for him and the work as he continued to go to various places. The relationship was from the fellowship in the Spirit, in the suffering they went through as the body of Christ (Gal. 4:12, 19; Eph. 2:25–28; 2 Thess. 1:5). Paul recognized the gifts of the Holy Spirit from each church. In certain ways, Paul had the advantage over modern international workers. He worked as if in a home mission field and had no language or cultural barriers to overcome. Paul was a Roman citizen but raised as a Jew, so he spoke both Greek and Hebrew. There are many factors in the Graeco-Roman world that are not the same as missions today.

The history of the early church from Acts onward was that of missions. We go to tell others because we ourselves know the freedom from sin. It's been said that Christians are like beggars who have found bread telling others where to find it. Jesus is the bread of life. We need to tell others about Him. This is the history of the church. It is God's command that we go to tell others. It is His desire that we go to tell as many as possible (2 Pet. 3:9). When God gives a command, He enables us to do it. He has made us co-labourers with Him. We sow the seed, and God's Holy Spirit makes it grow and take root in their hearts (1 Cor. 3:6–9).

Christ is returning soon. But He will not return until all have heard the gospel (Matt. 24:14). There are many people who have not heard yet. The hope of Christ's return is what we look forward to. He will come back for us as He promised (John 14:3). This is the completion of the work begun at Calvary. Jesus's coming will bring us our blessings in full (Eph. 1:14, 1 Thess. 4:13–18).

Where This Takes Place 1

Our third W comes in two parts but with the same word where. Where 1 has to do with the general type of area you want to go to in the world. Where 1 looks at two general areas where you can serve this aspect of missions. Let's look at the avenue of obedience first.

Obedience is not geographical, but it is important. There are times when God desires us to minister in certain places, with certain people. God calls us to obey Him first; *where* we obey Him is secondary. I want to serve God wherever I am, wherever that may be in the world. I don't want to be a Jonah. Jonah ran away so he didn't have to go to Nineveh. He didn't want his enemies to repent and escape judgement. I want to obey God by staying or by going. In 1986 I worked in a church in Hawaii. In 1987 I felt I should go home again to Canada. If I had stayed, I would have disobeyed God. In 1994 I worked in Thailand teaching English. I went home to Canada because it was the best place for me to be. I went home and learned many things. I committed myself to obeying God in Canada. I prayed a lot about my future. At the right time, God opened the doors for me to go to Korea in 1995 for a few months. In 1996 I returned to Korea to teach in a *hogwan* (after-school academy) in the city of Pohang. I felt called to go to Thailand, but instead the door opened in Korea. After six months, I began praying for Thailand and looking for a job there. When the right job came, it was so obvious God wanted me in Thailand. So I went to Bangkok to teach English again. I left Thailand after my marriage, and we moved to Europe. (This turned out to be not such a good idea for many reasons. We did not wait for God's leading on that occasion. It was a difficult time.) Eventually God opened the doors for us to teach in a university in Korea, and I taught a missions course as well as ESL there. Obeying God is more important than going somewhere or staying somewhere. If God tells you to go, you go. If He tells you to stay, you stay.

How is this done? There is a great variety of the ways in which missions work is approached. Some Christians see missions as evangelism only, the preaching of the gospel directly. Those people at the Lausanne Congress felt that they did not want to see the preaching part ignored in favour of other issues, social, moral, and educational.

This can happen when the IWs are involved in multiple kinds of ministries.

International workers based in Thailand like Mo Bradley and Daniel McGilvary accomplished many valuable things (medical, printing publications, translation of Scriptures, tracts, and education), and at times, evangelism seemed to get crowded out of the schedule. Smith declared of missions in Thailand that when the focus is on education, then the church growth was slow. Kim (another IW worker in Thailand) felt that when a lot of energy was poured into the avenues of education and medical work, that little time and energy was left for direct evangelism (Kim 1980, p. 118). If the focus was on evangelism, then the church grew better (Smith 1982).

However, the need for education and medical help opened the doors for the IWs to make their presence and consequently their faith known. The Thai kings at the time of the early pioneer IWs remained open about the messengers and their work, if not the message itself. In this way, evangelism is seen as a part of a broader work-developing nations being helped in the name of Christ, so that the gospel can be heard. It is difficult to hear the gospel if your basic needs are not met. Medical missions, literacy work, feeding the poor, teaching English, and introducing self-help programs are all ways in which the doors can be opened to hungry hearts. Samaritan's Purse is an organization that meets the physical and emotional needs in the name of the gospel. They have a yearly Christmas project whereby they send shoeboxes of gifts to children in many poor countries with practical gifts of toothpaste and pencils and also small toys to children who otherwise have very little. Likewise, Bible translation in itself is a great work but is not directly involved in disciple making. Someone must use the translated Scriptures and give them to the listeners and teach them the Word. The ideal ministry is a balance of meeting felt needs of people and presenting the gospel in that context as meeting the ultimate need, that of salvation. Christ Himself met both needs in His teaching, preaching, healing, and casting out of demons.

There are two basic ways in which you can serve God overseas:

1. Open countries—these are countries in which IWs are accepted to work in open evangelism. Places like Mali, Cote d'Ivoire, Philippines, Peru, Brazil, Taiwan, and France. The international workers in open countries are free to evangelize, plant churches, and teach the people spiritual truths of God. Medical and literacy programs are also common ways of ministering in open countries. Associate organizations also help the IWs themselves. MAF (Missionary Aviation Fellowship) works in Mali, an associate organization that helps the mission groups themselves function better. Robinson and Vincent reported that a missionary pilot working for JAARS (Jungle Aviation and Radio Service) saved five years of work (by cutting down travel time on poor roads, bringing in needed supplies, etc.) for the missionary translator. Without the ready assistance of JAARS, the job would have taken much longer because of the logistics of the situation.
2. Closed countries—these are also called creative access countries. These ones are not presently giving visas to IWs.

Examples are Saudi Arabia, Iran, China, India, and North Korea. This is where tentmakers come in. They teach in schools and work in many professions such as engineers, businessmen, doctors, and nurses in that country. They are Christians who show through their lives the true light of Christ.

Tentmaking

This brings up the whole avenue of *tentmaking*. The concept of tentmaking takes into account the shortness of funds from churches and other sending agencies. Money is tight, and churches are having a hard time supporting those that are going out. Delayed departures for mission work overseas are the result of those waiting on God's people to supply their needs. The necessary support can be supplied by those who are involved in tentmaking. These tentmakers are workers going out across the world to spread the gospel through their occupations.

Siemens recounts the story of Joe as an example (Siemens, Tentmaker Stories, 2001). Some years ago, Joe and five other students from his college went to China on an exchange program. Since Joe had a degree in physical science, he was assigned to teach at a college of physical culture on the outskirts of Beijing while he studied Mandarin. Eventually some of the other Americans left for various reasons: expulsion for immorality, restricted freedom, and poor behaviour—China was a tough place to live for them. By the middle of the year, Joe was the only American left. Then three Chinese students approached him to find out what made him so different. "You're not like the others. Why is that?" Joe invited the students to come to his dorm room, and several others showed up as well. Joe explained the difference Jesus made in his life. Over several weeks, Joe led three of these students to Christ. When Joe's contract ended at the end of the school year, Joe had to leave and was concerned for his new friends in Christ. Shortly after he returned to the United States, a letter arrived asking if he would return for the next school year. One of his new Christian friends, Chao, met him at the plane, along with two recent believers. Chao had been busy witnessing during Joe's absence. Later Chao asked for materials to disciple new believers on his own. In addition, the school Joe was teaching at wanted Joe to teach a course on American holidays, Christian roots and all. Apparently sixty Chinese exchange students were going to America, and they needed to know about American culture. More than just those sixty showed up. Joe still lives in China and has married a Chinese Christian. He has also been asked to recruit others for English teachers; teachers like himself, the implication being that Christians were good teachers.

Tentmakers work in the workplaces of the world in order to reach those around them. They are Christians working in other cultures with the intent of reaching others for Christ. They are often self-supporting, using their vocation as their springboard of contact and connection for evangelism in a low-key manner. The term *tentmakers* was used of Paul because it was his way of supporting himself as he evangelized. Now the term *tentmaking* refers to finance and strategy of mission work in many countries. When Joe went to China to teach physical science, that was his job, but he also went there as a witness in the context of his work and lifestyle.

Tentmakers are similar to the familiar mission worker supported by donors in that their focus is on evangelism where they are. How they differ is that they form their relationships not by church outreach but in working alongside the people themselves. This helps greatly in the bonding process and the trust of the people to the tentmakers. They are godly workers who use their integrity, quality of work, and caring relationships to build a witness for Christ (Eph. 6:5–8, Col. 3:23–25). We are all lights shining in the world (2 Cor. 4:6). At work or play, we are to show Christ in our lives. We are to use our gifts in the church for the ministry. Where we work as a tentmaker is important, and determining where God wants us is part of our spiritual task. This process will be dealt with in more detail a little further on.

Siemens mentions several aspects that make tentmaking a viable option today (Siemens, "Why did Paul Make Tents," 1996). Usefulness:

EXPLORING THE ROOTS OF MISSIONS: PERSONAL, BIBLICAL, AND SPIRITUAL

1. Never enough personnel—it takes too long to train the traditional international worker and raise support. IWs take several years to train and educate. By then they are usually in debt, and by the time they have paid it off, they are too comfortable in their lifestyle (Western) to leave the comforts of home. In the Christian and Missionary Alliance, it takes a minimum of six years to train, four years of Bible college or university, two years of home service or practical experience, and finally a year or so of seminary training. People that have to raise their own support "faith missions" may even have a harder time getting backing before they go.
2. Cost—mission budgets rise with living costs. Tentmakers cost much less, even if they are partially supported. It depends on the country and the profession. Some full-time jobs overseas do not pay well. English as a second language is a popular job in many countries, but the pay is usually poor compared to working for a company or business. In Thailand, ESL is rising in popularity, and although the teachers are paid eight times what their local counterparts make, it is not much compared to foreign businessmen. In France, ESL is poorly paid too; one has to work two or three jobs to make ends meet. It is best suited to a single lifestyle, as a family would have difficulty finding quality time together.
3. Closed countries—80 percent of the world's people live under restrictive governments for missions-related work but want vocational expertise. These are great doors for Christians to come in and share Christ in the workplace.
4. In open countries, many people are best reached in a professional way such as in Japan (1 percent evangelized) and Europe. Europe has grown cold to the gospel and needs a fresh touch in the way it looks at religion and Christianity. Traditional evangelistic methods are not very successful.
5. Growing global market—God's door to evangelism worldwide. The 10/40 Window has a lot of openings—many in urban settings.

6. Tentmaking encourages lay involvement, especially in reaching unreached people groups.
7. Reduces the attrition rate of IWs.
8. Evangelise as a learner—useful in language study! When your whole "lifestyle constitutes bait," your verbal witness is essential backup. People need to understand why you believe as you do.
9. Tentmaking can supplement Christian radio to secret believers.
10. Good for poor emerging nations—they can catch up economically and yet receive the benefits of the gospel.

Especially in sensitive countries—ones that are not open to the gospel—one must be careful how one shares about faith in Jesus Christ. Here are some tips on how to proceed. Morris says:

1. Holiness in broadest sense—distinguish between our cultural values and supracultural standards. Keep in mind that we are the salt of the earth; use the scriptural attitudes of servanthood and dignity. Emphasize the values of simplicity, encouragement, and co-operation.
2. In your honesty, work for company as a Christian. The quality of your work is important.
3. Wholeness and integration—don't departmentalise and leave your ethics at home or for the Bible study. Morris has noted that professionalism doesn't have to show a lack of servanthood, where self-confidence and competence are valued above humility. Don't witness on the job per se. Bible studies during work hours may or may not be okay. People should come to us to find out what makes us different. Do your job and use the opportunities to talk about your faith. Those who are interested in your life and beliefs are "fished out" by wholesome non-judgemental conduct. Their questions are answered in free time with Bible studies. In sensitive countries, you should be discreet and answer their questions in a non-confrontational way.

EXPLORING THE ROOTS OF MISSIONS: PERSONAL, BIBLICAL, AND SPIRITUAL

> Let the seekers pace the conversations (1 Pet. 4:14–16; Col. 4:5, 6). The idea of a silent witness doesn't work; "silence is never an option." In spending daily time with others, you take on a spiritual responsibility. In this way, evangelism can lead to church planting.

Ginter speaks of the wise use of time that is a perpetual problem with those in ministry. He mentions three types of ministry time: vocation, intentional, and serendipitous. The vocational time is the one we are all given to work with. This is the professional occupation for which you are paid. Intentional ministry is planned time used in Bible studies and discipleship ministry. The third time is the hardest of all to work with; this is God-arranged time that is unplanned and spontaneous. Something happens, and you need to answer the need of the moment. These are often inconvenient times, but they are the times when the Holy Spirit is working, so you need to answer to His summons. Sometimes life just happens, and ministry has a powerful impact at these times. A family emergency, an accident, or any trouble in life may cause a co-worker to turn to you for help. These are times when you can plant the seed of Christ's love and compassion for others.

Many do not always think of it this way, but the ancient world was evangelized by those travelling due to flood, famine, migration, trade, persecution, and government edicts. Acts 8:4 says that the Christians were dispersed, and they preached the Word more than ever. This was God's way of getting the gospel out in the world. It wasn't what the apostles may have wanted, but it was definitely that which was used by God.

1. One Old Testament example was that of Daniel in Babylon. He was captured when Judah fell to Nebuchadnezzar. Daniel was deported along with many others to live and work in Babylon under the secular government of King Nebuchadnezzar (Dan. 1:4.) He worked as one of the wise men that served the court. Now that was a secular-based job if ever there was one, for these wise men turned to spiritual help that was not of God. Daniel sought God

three times a day in prayer (6:10). He risked his life to be a godly man in the midst of a nation that did not know Him. Daniel did not compromise his food standards (1:8). He was following the eating of clean and healthy foods that God had given to the Jews. The alternative was to eat the rich food of the Babylonians, which was not following Jewish law and custom. Daniel trusted God in his troubles (2:18), being a light to those around him, even to the lions' den (6:22). After his rescue, he bore eloquent witness to God's faithfulness and power. Daniel continued to witness to all the kings over him, even the king of the Medes and Persians who conquered the king of Babylon.
2. The New Testament example of Paul and his fellow workers. In Acts 18:3, "and because he was a tentmaker as they were, he stayed and worked with them." Paul was one of the greatest examples of an international worker and servant of Christ that has been graphically portrayed for us in Scripture. It's as if God used Paul just to show us what was possible if you put your life in God's hands.

Paul's example was that working for a living was the standard of a godly Christian life (1 Thess. 2:9; 2 Thess. 3:7–8; Acts 20:31–35; 1 Cor. 4:12, 9:6). He showed that work is central to life. Paul used work to identify with the people whom he witnessed to. He states that he was free from all people—as a slave to all to win more (1 Cor. 9:15ff). In Acts 13:16–41, Paul contextualized the gospel (to Jews and God-fearers), Acts 17:22–34 to philosophers, and in Acts 24–26 to local rulers. The gospel travels along the network of relationships—invitations are usually personal—tentmakers share personal work and interests. Paul told his disciples and his churches to imitate him. He was the example (Phil. 3:17). His work materials (aprons and handkerchiefs in Acts 19:12) were used by people and healings occurred as they touched the sick. He taught during the afternoon time break. People tend to do what their leaders do—Paul was a positive example of leadership. His example continues to be one that we as international workers need to follow.

Life of Paul

English gives a brief introduction on tentmaking and the apostle Paul's role in it (English, "Missions for a New Millennium," 1999). He includes also the team-mates that Paul worked with. There were many people on Paul's team (2 Thess. 3:7–10). Paul didn't want to do all the work himself. He wanted others to be involved in the work of the gospel. The more people involved, the more the possibility of reaching the lost. Paul was born in a Roman province (Acts 21:39) of the city of Tarsus to Hebrew parents (2 Cor. 11:22). He was also born a Roman citizen (Acts 22:25–39). He sat at the feet of Gamaliel for Pharisaic instruction (Acts 22:3). Paul persecuted the church, believing that the Christians were against God. He even went so far as to hold the cloaks of those who were stoned (Acts 7:57–58). Paul ended up going to Damascus to imprison more believers (Acts 9:1–2). Jesus meets Paul and sends him on to become a witness to many (Acts. 26:16–18). Eventually Paul is commissioned by the church in Antioch to go out as an international worker in 44 AD to bring money to those in need. He went with Barnabas as a fellow worker (Acts 11:30). Barnabas and Saul are sent off by the church at Antioch (Acts 13:1). On his second missionary journey, they end up in Corinth where Paul joins Priscilla and Aquila in making tents. Paul preaches in the synagogue on the Sabbath to reach those there (Acts 18:3–6). The Jews reject him. From then on he goes to the Gentiles.

Gentiles

It appears that Paul followed the pattern laid out in Acts 1:8; with Jerusalem being first, then Judea, on to Samaria, and finally to the ends of the earth. Paul went from Jews to Gentiles. Jews went to Jews first until Peter's vision in Acts 8 where God told him that all things were clean and that the door of salvation was open to the Gentiles also. Paul made Antioch his headquarters (Acts 18:6). The churches Paul planted were self-supporting and not dependent on foreign funds (Eph. 4:11, 12). It says in 1 Timothy 3:7 that the pastor was the example in the workplace. Paul's churches were to provide well for pastors (Galatia, Ephesus; Gal. 6:6, 1 Tim 5:17–18).

Financially, Paul could charge his listeners as philosophers of the day did, receive from friends and church, or he could support himself. There are several verses that give evidence of this:

1. 1 Corinthians 9:12–15, 18—Paul worked to put no obstacle in the way of the gospel to the Gentiles.
2. 1 Corinthians 9:6—Paul and Barnabas had gifts from the church.
3. 2 Corinthians 11:12—Paul worked night and day; he was not a workaholic. Those were the two shifts available at the time before and after the afternoon siesta. He even paid for meals (2 Thess. 3:7–9, 1:1; 1 Thess. 2:9). Judaizers gave trouble about support in Ephesus (p. 27; 1 Cor. 4:11, 12; Acts 20:3; 1 Cor. 6:10–11). In 1 Corinthians 9, Paul makes a case for his right to church support but then says three times that he never took any (stated at the end of the third journey). Paul "robbed" the church; this was said to shame the Corinthians (2 Cor. 11:8 cf. Phil. 4:14–16).

Biblical reasons for working from Paul:

1. Working gives Paul and his message creditability, even under persecution, proof of no financial gain. Thus, he was not beholden to the churches.
2. Paul identifies with working class (as one of them) and lets them spread the message (Phil. 3:7–9).
3. Model of the work ethic for the new converts. They needed to see discipleship and godly living in action. The Roman Empire had poor work ethic; many converts were thieves, idlers, drunkards, adulterers, and prostitutes (1 Cor. 6:9–10). We must be able to trust each other to get any work done. Max Weber said,

EXPLORING THE ROOTS OF MISSIONS: PERSONAL, BIBLICAL, AND SPIRITUAL

> Society needs a critical mass of Bible believing Christians to produce at successful market economy. (English, "Missions for a New Millennium," 1999)

They needed to know that a worker is worth his hire (1 Cor. 9:14). Paul showed them by example (1 Thess. 3:8) how to live, how to give generously (2 Thess. 3:6–15; 1 Cor. 6:10, 11; Eph. 4:8; 1 Tim. 5:8). Paul was also the example meant to establish patterns of lay evangelism (2 Thess. 1:5–8; 1 Cor. 7:7–14, 3:10–17). Paul didn't earn a lot of money by working (2 Cor. 11:8, 9). He received gifts from the Philippian church (Phil. 4:15, 16).

Christians have always been involved in tentmaking as they lived and travelled, but Paul emphasized it because he was a prominent leader in evangelism. It became necessary during a missionary trip, and thus it was noticed as such. The early international workers were poor; donor-funded work has only been around for the last one hundred years. In history, almost all IWs were tentmakers until the postcolonial era! English is now the trade language because of the massive US influence through the Internet and computerized (with Microsoft English) globalization.

There are many famous examples of tentmakers in church history. We'll look at only three. During the latter half of the fourth century, an IW by the name of *Ulfilas* (311–380) went out to evangelize his own people in Goth. He had been sent to Constantinople for domestic service from Goth and became involved with a bishop who taught him the scriptures. Ten years after he left, he returned to Goth, which was in a barbaric region outside of the Roman Empire. He stayed there for forty years, translating the scriptures into their tongue—the first of the many translators who have worked with new peoples since. Missions work in China had a difficult beginning. In the late thirteenth century, some IWs arrived and planted many churches. But the Chinese expelled the IWs about seventy-five years after, and Christianity died out. *Matteo Ricci* (1552–1610) came with the Jesuits and began a mighty work. He used his mathematical learning to open a door to the scholars. He adopted their culture and dressed as one of them. Ricci worked there for twenty years. Eventually in the early 1700s persecution rose against the church. The Protestant *Hudson Taylor* (1832–1905) pioneered mission work in China on a great scale. His training as a doctor was part of his preparation to go to China. He depended on God alone to answer his needs financially. In Shanghai he studied Chinese and was determined to adopt Chinese ways to more easily reach the people. He dressed as they did and dyed his hair. He ran into much opposition from local doctors who were jealous of his work. He married another IW teacher named Maria who taught at the mission school for girls. Taylor went on to found the China Inland Mission based on the principles that he himself believed in concerning finances. The Chinese people were hostile to the foreigners; they called them barbarians. Nevertheless, the mission continued and converted many people. Over six hundred IWS were in China by 1882.

Preparation and Practise

Siemens gives several practical suggestions for preparing for tentmaking ministry (Siemens and English, "Tentmaker Preparation…," 2000).

Work mindset: Get out of the very secular mindset that work is the result of sin. It was there before the Fall of man. Work is the way we fulfil our cultural mandate (Gen. 1:8). Ask God to help you choose your vocation. Skills that are useful or helpful for your work are best. (Exotic majors or specialized ones are not good for transferring overseas; they won't even be recognised.) Education should be of good quality for that reason. A bachelor's degree is good; a master's is even better. For instance, I have a Bachelor of Religious Education and a Master's degree in Missiology. I have taught English in both Thailand and Korea, anywhere from public schools to private ones and in university level as well. Get some work experience right after graduation or look around for "practise" experiences. There are lots of mission agencies that let you find out what you can do overseas. Mennonite Central Committee, for example, has many opportunities in practical situations. Alliance Men builds school buildings, church buildings, and other projects in the practical realm that are a short-term experience of working in a different culture and environment.

Find work by *networking* and contacts, including international students. The largest areas in need of workers are education, health care, computers, science and technology, business and finance, and agriculture. My specialty was religious education, and I used both my ESL skills and my theological background in my last job in South Korea. My resume is full of jobs obtained overseas through the following connections:

1. Contact of sister in seminary in LA. This was my first job teaching ESL for ten months at a Thai Christian school in Bangkok. This came directly after I completed seminary.
2. Bible college contact for Korea. This job gave me the experience of working in the denominational headquarters of a Korean church in Seoul, South Korea. I taught ESL and also developed a mission course (ESL level) for Korean international workers going overseas.
3. Bible college contact for Pohang, South Korea. A former student from the same college was looking for more teachers for the after-school program in an English academy. This job was ESL ages four to fifteen.
4. IW contact for schoolwork in BCC Bangkok. A IW I knew of in Bangkok informed me of this school position teaching ESL in the English immersion department. I had informed her I was actively looking for work in Bangkok.
5. University contact (Seoul) for job in Anyang. This was the case where I felt the prompting of the Holy Spirit to write the university of the same denomination where I had worked earlier. It turned out they did need English teachers, and both my husband and I were accepted. In addition to teaching English, I also taught a course on tentmaking as well as a single class on contextualization (with translation).

Research: Once you've decided and have been accepted, you should research your field or area—both for history and culture in general and any spiritual work that's been done. The Internet has lots of general information as well as books from local libraries. Johnstone's *Operation World* has a good synopsis of what the spirituality is like around the world. Talk to other tentmakers; see what it's like and what they found helpful. You need to know what you are getting into. It is costly in terms of commitment; count the cost for your work and ministry.

Language study: Many overseas jobs are done in English, and some employers even pay for language study. Studying the local language helps in winning respect, helping in cultural adjustment, and sharing the Gospel sensitively. It is ideal to learn a language and culture at the same time. Brewster's LAMP method is good for that.

Salary: The pay for most jobs overseas is modest to high. Some of the poorer countries may not be able to afford to pay well. In this case, it is a good idea to supplement your income with support.

Cautions and Conditions

Norrish gives several cautions about tentmaking as an individual or with a team. For a tentmaker to work as an individual may be easier in some ways—for example, security is easier—you have to educate your prayer or financial supporters, not to mention your work and ministry in closed countries. Some people may lose their jobs if the government hears that they are Christians. Again, without a Bible college on the resume, it gives one a little more creditability in the eyes of the secular authorities, especially those in Muslim countries that are hostile to the gospel. These are some of the pitfalls in working as a tentmaker. However, the team concept is probably better for you in terms of support—both locally and from those overseas. You may also have access to ongoing training through your support group.

One of the problems in being a donor-supported international worker is that a lot of time is spent in the mundane tasks of living—shopping, cleaning, cooking—which takes away from language study and church outreach. These can be very time-consuming, especially in poorer countries where less technology is available for these tasks. The tentmaker already has a place of sorts in the community by virtue of their job. This is a good place of contact for the people they want to reach; they don't have to win their audience over in the same way that a "preacher" evangelist might. The network of support (professionally and logistically) is already set up, and the business often helps the newcomer tentmakers to settle in. Sometimes an evangelist can be suspected of ulterior motives—such as being one of the CIA—but a paid worker will gain some creditability in the familiarity of his work. Money is a powerful motive in many places, and people may have a hard time believing that someone would evangelize or preach for their own good.

Siemens has several other practical suggestions: *Learn* practical skills—they come in handy working overseas. You never know when you'll need them yourself or when you can teach them to others. DIY, cooking, baking, carpentry, or car repair—these can be good for you and be a bridge to reach others by teaching or helping. Recreational skills and hobbies are also bridges.

Test your calling and make sure that this is God's will for your life. Becoming a tentmaker is a difficult calling, for in order to do it, you must leave much that is familiar and go somewhere where things are very different and sometimes very difficult. Being a tentmaker does not mean that you must be perfect, spiritually or otherwise. But it does mean that you must be spiritually aware and in tune with what God wants and what is happening in your life.

Take some Bible and missions training—Biblical basis of missions, in Old Testament and New Testament, history, geography (where missions is strong and weak) trends, issues and strategies, cross-cultural shock, and language learning, know what your mission expects and does. Firsthand experience in another culture can be a great eye-opener in learning what it will be like. Education in a Christian ghetto is a danger. In some ways, a secular university is the best real view of the world and how to live in it. Take Daniel in Babylon as an example, studying the Babylonian liberal arts. "All truth is God's truth." Learn to relate to others in a natural way. The biggest problem with the biblical or professional training is the high attrition rate.

Don't go to school endlessly so that you never go overseas. Go with a learner attitude, not a know-it-all. Know yourself before you go.

Learn to study the Bible for yourself—see it with eyes of those looking for answers. Memorize passages to help you know the Word better. Learn doctrine—what you believe and why. Use the narrative Bible passages for teaching. These are really good in oral-based cultures where the story itself can be a powerful tool. *Evangelism*—learn to fish, not hunt, says the GO website authors. Most Christians hunt; they tend to press questions on people which can make them feel defensive. Fishing is answering questions of seekers (Col. 4:5, 6; 1 Pet. 3:14, 16). This approach is also called friendship evangelism. It can grow into a church planting work by extending the evangelistic Bible study into a discipleship Bible study. *Get some experience* in the spiritual work too before going overseas. This is where the C&MA has a good plan the idea of practical home service where the IW learns about church work, leadership, and essentials for a church. Get involved in drama, children's work, singing, Bible studies, men's group, etc. Be accountable to a local church—field team is invaluable for good support. Learn to communicate to those at home about your work. If you are unable to speak clearly about your ministry overseas, tell this to those at home and let them know how to pray for you. You can lose a job if it becomes known that you are evangelising.

One thing I noticed being a student in seminary and Bible college was that the foreign students always seemed to huddle together around mealtimes. I didn't understand why. Once I went overseas myself, I understood. The feeling of belonging is integral to our sense of well-being. Even if at home you never would have become friends, there are ex-pats you meet overseas that you connect with. You have something in common. You are bonded by the strangeness of the culture you are in. Likewise, when you return home, there is another kind of bonding. Others will not understand you except perhaps those who have cross-cultural experience themselves.

"Toto, we're not in Kansas anymore," says Dorothy in the Wizard of Oz, looking around her where animals talk and things were so different. Being overseas is much the same. The rules are different, and you need to adjust to them accordingly. That is the challenge. That's a hard feeling to shake. You go through alternate feelings of love-hate in dealing with the culture that you are in. As a tentmaker working in this environment, the intensity may be a bit different than for the regular IW. Working with familiar concepts and tools may ease the shock and help in the bonding process with the nationals. Plunging into language study, as many international workers do, both increases and lessens the shock. It lessens it because understanding grows the language learning. It increases it because learning a new language is hard and frustrating. Learning to "ride out" the culture shock is part of the process.

English comments that our discipleship and example to the world, too many fall and fail. Many IWs throughout history have unwittingly imported their culture as a part of their faith. Don't make that mistake. We are the salt; don't let the world go bad on us! Western enlightenment confuses other cultures. We depend on science and what is factual for our take on reality. We dismiss spiritual reality that isn't our "own." If a sickness or problem is blamed on a spirit, we have trouble believing in curses against us or anyone else. (The chapter on spiritual warfare has more on this.)

When we do go in God's name, we need to know that He is willing—and able!—to answer our needs. This applies to personal as well as professional issues.

> It is good to know the rumours about God's love and power but he wants us to experience it firsthand. (Ruth Siemens, GO, "The Story Behind GO")

Where 2: The 10/40 Window

Now we'll look at part 2 of our Where. This is a special part of the world that needs extra and prayerful attention. This special area of consideration is what is called the *10/40 Window*. This is a block extending from ten degrees north to forty degrees north of the equator, from West Africa to Asia. This area is where most of the world's population is located. Ninety-seven percent of 3.2 billion people live here. Three main religious blocks are located in this area: the Muslims (706 million), Hindu (717 million), and Buddhist (153 million). There is a lot of ancient history in this area, including that of the garden of Eden. The Fertile Crescent where the garden of Eden was located is in ancient Mesopotamia. There are fifty-five of the most unevangelized countries in the world. According to Culbertson, many of the people here have never heard the gospel even once. Howard Culbertson (2002) has the following information regarding the unreached people groups

> 865 million unreached Muslims or Islamic followers in 3330 cultural sub-groupings
> 550 million unreached Hindus in 1660 cultural sub-groups
> 150 million unreached Chinese in 830 groups
> 275 million unreached Buddhists in 900 groups
> 2550 unreached tribal groups (which are mainly animistic) with a total population of 140 million

However, it is not impossible for ministry to happen here. God is working for the establishment of His kingdom in traditionally "hard" areas. For example, in 1989, there were four Christians in Mongolia; by 2002, there were ten thousand (Culbertson 2002). Missions researcher David Barrett says the country with the most rapid Christian expansion ever is China, which has ten thousand new Christian converts every day.

The 10/40 Window is also an area of great poverty. Eight out of ten of the poorest people live here. Culbertson also reported that when rain fell in a hostile North African country after an Easter service, that the Christians were credited with having brought rain to the desert (Culbertson 2006). However, only 8 percent of the international workers work in this vast area. Attempts to evangelize in the 10/40 Window have had very slow progress. This is a satanic stronghold which prevents the people from coming to Christ and true spiritual freedom.

The stronghold of the 10/40 Window is due to several factors. Many Christian leaders believe that Satan's angels hold a tight grip on the area and that this grip must be broken. Moreau feels that naming of the spirits (in order to bind them) may not be a spiritually balanced approach, as some of these leaders claim. Also, much of their spiritual warfare work is done through prayer only and not any evangelism or practical work done to help the people. This falls short of a thorough approach. Another way of looking at the stronghold's grip is through the deception of the false religions. The grip is increased because of the devotion expressed in daily, monthly, and yearly rituals. These rituals increase the bondage so that even when IWs do reach this area, they cannot break through easily. The very words of the IWs do not make sense in terms of worldview to the hearers, but the allegiance to the false gods prevents any forward movement toward Christ.

A brief summary of each of these main groupings of false allegiance follows with an assessment of their spirituality.

Islam—the *Shahada* is said five times a day during salat. It is the first thing you hear on birth and the last thing you say before you die. "There is no God but Allah and Mohammed is his prophet." The basic creed is what the Muslim believer puts his faith and trust in—the revelation of Allah (in the Quran) and in Mohammed who received it from an angel and put it into writing. This closes the mind to the idea of a loving, caring God so different from Allah and of Jesus's righteousness and atonement as His messenger and Son.

Buddhism has daily offering of flowers, lighting of candles in worship. This is done in every monastery, temple, and home. They also make merit by giving food to monks every morning and evening (Theravada) or to Buddha (Mahayana). There is chanting done in schools daily (Theravada). Part of it runs as follows:

> The Exalted One, far from defilements, perfectly Enlightened by himself, I bow low before the Buddha, the Exalted One… Honour to him,

> the blessed one, the worthy one, the fully enlightened one. (Sriwittayapaknam School website)

Daily commitments and worship to Buddha hinder devotion to Christ.

Hinduism also has a daily ritual of offering fruit, flowers, and cooked food in worship to the family gods. Part of the worship is eating the food. This ensures that the eater has a part of the god's power too. There are also special rituals only the Hindu Brahmin priests perform.

Animism: There is no one ritual that fits all the kinds of animistic beliefs. Since everything is seen in the light of the spiritual world, then all actions are governed by the spirit world. There are rituals for all of life as fear of the spirits is very important. They must be appeased. One ritual, for example, can be an offering to the spirits that guard the homes. Other rituals are for casting spells or curing sicknesses or diseases.

Each prayer or chant is an offering of oneself in bondage so that the gospel cannot even be heard—keep on praying for God's freedom to break through.

Atheism (China): This is officially an atheistic country since Communism took over. But it is still influenced by its roots in Buddhism. Also present are folklore, animistic and occultic practises. As with Western countries though, it struggles with materialism and secularism.

Other ways in which the bondage is kept and maintained are also mentioned in Robb's article on the topic (Robb 1993, p. 178). This is done through animistic practises in which the spiritual world is controlled or tapped into through rituals as mentioned above: political leaders, spirit mediums, or shamans. Political leaders, as seen in the Old Testament, can lead the people into God's truth and ways or away from it. King Saul started out on good footing with God but then started disobeying (1 Sam. 15:22–26). This disobedience cost him his kingship. Other spiritual leaders in Israel followed in his wake. Human examples can also be found throughout history—the Marcoses of the Philippines, Mao Tse-tung of China, Idi Amin, and

Pol Pot, to name a few. These leaders were all involved in the destruction of life and property to some extent, just plain greed in others. In all cases, the people were not led into a good relationship with God, their Creator. This is one reason why Paul encourages us to pray for our leaders—it is necessary for the good and proper welfare of the nations (Rom. 13, Tit. 3:1, 1 Pet. 2:17). The leadership of shamans or priests that tap into these powers is also a control over the people leading them to grab for the power they can have now in a dramatic way. This leads into syncretism as the people may believe the Christian leaders as well as the traditional ones. The bondage is still to the spirits, and the trust is not ultimately placed in God. Bondage can also be maintained through certain objects and places dedicated to the spirits. This is why in every revival in ancient Israel led to the breaking down of old altars that were not dedicated to God. Gideon's first act was to break down the altar his father had built to Baal (Judg. 6:25–26). He could not worship the true God and leave the old altars standing. A final aspect in maintaining control in the 10/40 Window is that of blocking God's people. Since they are so few in these areas, it is a relatively simple matter for this to happen from Satan's point of view. Blocking God's people may simply come about through discouragement, infirmity, disunity, and discrediting ministers and ministries. Unfortunately, these incidents are all too common, and the possible spiritual source is not dealt with properly.

The practise of warfare prayer for God's light to break through these imbedded kinds of strongholds cannot be underestimated. God will work in people's hearts, but it is a time-consuming process. The Word must soak into their hearts, and as they see it lived out in the lives of believers, then the truth of the gospel can be comprehended.

Who Is Called

Who is our fourth W. The natural question at this point is of course, Who shall go to do this great work of God? We have answered it in part—those who are called in obedience. Let's look briefly at what the Scriptures say about this matter. In the gospels, it is interesting to note that the call to the harvest (which is ready now) is mentioned in all four books. In Matthew, Jesus has compassion on the crowds who were harassed and helpless like a sheep without a shepherd (Matt. 9:36–38). So Jesus goes on teaching and healing for the need of workers is great. The passage of Luke (Luke 10:2) it was to the seventy-two. He said this—sending them out in teams to minister in God's name. Here, they were preparing to go out in person to practice with the multitudes what Jesus had been teaching them. When Jesus was talking to the Samaritan woman at the well (John 3:34–38), he told the disciples that He was obeying His Father's command to reach the unreached, and that included the Samaritans, the lowest of the lowly, on the Jewish scale. The disciples could not imagine that. But it was all a part of Jesus's plan to reach the nations.

Paul continues on Jesus's refrain to the disciples that all may be included, Jew and Gentile into God's kingdom. Paul calls for those who are sent to go.

> How, then, can they call on the one they have not believed in? And how can they believe in the one of whom they have not heard? And how can they hear without someone preaching to them? 15 And how can anyone preach unless they are sent? As it is written: "How beautiful are the feet of those who bring good news! (Rom. 10:12–15 NIV)

All are called to obey Christ. The church is made up of the people called of God. God gives all of us gifts to use for the working of His kingdom (Rom. 12; 1 Cor. 12). We are all lights shining in the world (2 Cor. 4:6). At work or play, we are to show Christ in our lives. We are to use our gifts in the church for the ministry. A. B. Simpson, founder of the Christian and Missionary Alliance, felt God's call on him to missions. He even dreamed about the Chinese in a dream that seemed to portray the anguish of the lost. He then tried for a long time to go, but the door did not open. It was not until years later that God revealed to him that the whole point was obedience and passion for the lost, wherever he was (Thompson 1960, p. 120). Although Simpson stayed at home, his passion for the lost did not waver, and he raised up mission work to go to the lost and, ultimately, a denomination with the same desire at heart.

We say again, Who is it that shall meet this great need of the lost? Certainly those that are trained in many skills can go to answer this call through tentmaking. The computer programmers, the medical teams, those in construction, education, literacy, and in English as a second language—all these specialists can fulfill a need in the world that calls to us to step in and answer. The world needs these skilled hands. Hands that can meet many needs in many places. But even more, the world needs the gospel that speaks to every heart and truly fulfills the longing of the soul for fulfillment in God.

Some are called to go cross-culturally. We need the support and the prayers of those who stay at home. But we are called to go; someone must go and tell others (Rom. 10:14). This is a conviction we cannot shake. It must not be shaken. Our call is to obedience. As with any of the gifts and call of God on one's life, we must test this call and sift it out from our own fears, hopes, and imagination. The very background and experience in life of a believer may prove invaluable in answering this call. Professionals are needed in many countries. Retirees as well as young people also can go out and work. Many possibilities are there; you only need to explore the opportunities available through the many missions services.

There are those who can go more directly—that is, they can give themselves to public ministries that speak of the Word of God and of His Son, Christ Jesus, who died for them and rose again. These include the preachers, the teachers in Bible schools and seminaries, as well as those in translation of the Word into indigenous languages. Preparation for ministry such as this takes a great deal of time, especially with language study in the beginning. (This will be dealt with further in detail in chapter 4.) But with every step gained in the language and the learning of the culture, one is a step closer to the fulfillment of the Great Commission.

The Great Commission doesn't belong to any particular era or region of the church; rather, all churches at all times and in all places must endeavor together in making disciples of all nations. Our opportunity in light of these global trends is not only to send from our congregations but to partner with international churches in sending, supporting, and serving missionaries among the nations. (King, 2016).

When—Now and Pending

The last W we are to talk about is when. When is this to be done? When will this be completed? This is a more ambiguous a question than it seems. Of course, we should say, "Now, right away." But getting the message out to all the nations is not an instant thing, not even in this day and age when we can send a text or an e-mail virtually instantly. To be sure, the internet and modern communication devices make communication across great distances easier in a way. But communication goes two ways—how do we know the message has been received and understood correctly? I can have a lesson over Zoom with my students, whether they be in Calgary or China. But whether they actually understand my lesson is another matter. Some explanations are harder to comprehend. A few years ago, I had a student in my classroom who when I asked if he understood my point answered, "I'm still downloading." True enough, some aspects take some time to consider before you *think* you understand. Sometimes it takes several repetitions of the question in different ways before the meaning is understood. Communication is a challenge especially when some of the aspects are cultural. It took a student several tries the other night before I understood her question. Then suddenly it made sense to me what she was asking. Then I could answer it properly.

Technology aside, the communication of the gospel *takes time* to sink into the heart and mind of the hearers. Whether the issues are cultural, linguistic, or spiritual the Holy Spirit has His way of moving at the right time to show His love into the hearts of those who seek Him. Seeking the truth, the Truth, itself is the goal who all who seeking meaning and purpose in life. Jesus said in John that He was the Way, the Truth, and the Life. The way to heaven is through the cross. The cross stands for all time, for all peoples, for all sin.

So when is when you can. When you are on the road to answer the call, when you are aligning your life in response to God's command, you are answering the call. Also, when the person listening is listening with all their heart, is seeking the answer to their questions—that is when. The convergence of God bringing the obedient one in answer to the call and the one who is seeking, who is calling unknowingly for what their heart desires. This is God working out His good will for His good purpose (Eph. 1:11).

Bill Bright, the founder of Campus Crusade for Christ (now named Cru), says this about fulfilling Christ's last command,

> If the Great Commission is to be fulfilled in our generation, now is the time for action.
> We must begin now and dedicate ourselves daily—as a way of life—to communicate God's love and forgiveness to everyone we meet. From the time we awaken in the morning until we go to bed at night, our number one priority should be sharing "the most joyful news ever announced." (Bright)

The charge given to those preaching the good news was that they continue *until the end of the age* as Kane says (Kane, 252). Christ is sending His people out to the ends of the earth. They will continue until the age has ended. No one knows when this age will end, but Revelation 7:9 says that every tribe and nation is represented before the throne of the Lamb. This is a part of the urgency of missions. We want to have people of every group and nation in those before the throne.

> As long as one people group is unrepresented before God's throne, we have an ongoing responsibility. People need to hear the message of a Saviour… (Smith 1996, 272)

The need is urgent. People do need to hear the gospel of a Savior who loved them so much He came to earth to die for them. But it takes time to train people, time to get permits and visas, time to gain skills to use, and time to learn how to deal with people, listening to a heart that cries out for God. Somehow in the midst of all these things that take so much time, God is moving among His people, preparing hearts and minds as they prepare to go. God is also moving among the lost, calling them to Himself, calling them to see a need beyond what their eyes can see, to the God-shaped void in their hearts.

Summary

The story of missions covers the five Ws thoroughly. From here to there, from inside your country to another place, missions is evangelizing those who have not heard the gospel, whether in an open country or one closed to open preaching of the gospel. Now we'll look at the biblical theology of missions—a deeper look at what Scripture considers the lost.

2

Biblical Theology of Missions

Having covered the basics, we now turn to Scripture where we see the biblical foundation for everything we do in mission. Biblical theology of missions is the study of the scriptural basis for missionary work. The Bible is where we get our knowledge of God and His revelation to us. It is in the Scriptures that we see His desire to reach people and call them back to fellowship with Himself. Biblical theology of missions is a strong concept found throughout Scripture—the light of God's saving grace to the nations of the world through various means. In the Old Testament, the work of God was through Israel to reach the nations around her. The Old Testament seeks to draw people toward God through Israel's holy example. (Although Israel was not the only means which God used. There were many individuals and nations that God used to call people to Himself in repentance and love.) Israel was meant to be a specific example of a people called to God. In the New Testament, the disciples were sent out to all the world in spreading the Gospel, following Jesus's example of commitment and sacrifice. Establishing a people called out for Himself was a part of His salvation plan for the world. This salvation plan is an integral part of God's nature and character.

God's Nature and Character

The foundation of mission rests in God's nature. It is because of His love and forbearance that we are invited to fellowship with Him. Because He is good and loving, He desires the best for mankind. This is the crux of salvation and, thus, our basis for missions. It is God's nature that makes this possible, and it is His work that brings it about. God's love is outgoing; He is relational. Not only did He create a universe, but He put man in it (Isa. 45:18). With this man, He desired a relationship of the holy God to His people, as a parent to a child. God connected with Abraham, Isaac, and Jacob in a personal way. He actively seeks people to worship Him. We see that God loved the world enough to do something drastic in Jn 3: 16. He sent His only Son to die. It is an infinite, all-encompassing love that is unconditional and unchangeable. God loves us no matter what. No matter what we do or say, we cannot stop His love. He will love us forever. No matter what our personal background or country, we are loved by God. Only in Christ is this love expressed for the world. No other religion talks about love for mankind without conditions. This love is outgoing and dynamic, sacrificial and active. We love Him because He first loved us (1 John 4: 8–10, 16).

God's Love

Under the love of God, we see six areas in which this is expressed (source unknown):

1. *Creator*—God is the Creator of everything in the universe (Gen. 14:19, Deut. 32:6, Isa. 43:7, cf. Col. 1:10, Rev. 4:11). He is the Creator of mankind (Gen. 1:27; 5:1, 2). It is in the nature of a creator to love that which he has made. When you or I make something, we love it. When an artist paints a picture, she loves her creation. When a carpenter builds a house, he enjoys it. So it is with God. He loves because He made us. He has made us in His image. The image of God is not physical but spiritual. We are like God

in our personality, will, and emotions. We have the spiritual nature He has given us.
2. *Provider*—God cares for us and sustains us; the universe is upheld by His power (Ps. 68:10, 145:13–17; Isa. 46:4; cf. 1 Tim. 6:17; Heb. 1:3). He provides for our physical, spiritual, and emotional needs. When you buy a car, you take care of it. You buy gas, put air in the tires, and keep the motor in good condition. God's care is for all people—both the just and the unjust (Matt. 5:45). God provides for all people so that at the right time they too may see His hand in their salvation. God's love is unconditional and is poured out freely on His creation. As a loving Father, He is always waiting for us to ask for more than just food and drink. He is willing to give us salvation (Ps. 145:18, 19).
3. *Redeemer*—God also has a Redeemer's concern for His people. To redeem something in the biblical sense means to buy it back, to set it free. When God's people are in trouble, He comes to rescue them (Gen. 22:8; Isa. 43:1–3; Ps. 44:26, 49:7–15; cf. Rom. 3:24; 1 Cor. 1:30; Eph. 1:7; Heb. 9:12). He provided a ram for Abraham instead of sacrificing Isaac. When Israel was in Egypt under bondage, God came to rescue them. The judges were raised up to save Israel from their enemies. God sent Jesus to redeem us by dying on the cross (John 1:14). In His deliverance, He shows His faithfulness and mercy.
4. *Faithfulness* is standing by someone in good times and bad. Parents are faithful to their children when the children listen to them and when they don't. God showed His faithfulness by continuing to help His people when they didn't deserve it (Deut. 7:9, 32:4; Ps. 145:13; cf. 1 Cor. 1:9, 10:13; Heb. 2:17). Over and over again God kept His promise to His people. He didn't leave them to die in their sin. He proclaimed His faithfulness to them over the generations.
5. God showed His *mercy* to them in their sin by providing a sacrifice, a way for them to get right with Him again (Deut.

4:31; cf. Heb. 4:16, 2:17; 1 Pet. 1:3). Mercy is not getting what is deserved. When the people of Israel should have been destroyed because of their disobedience, God showed mercy and did not harm them (Gen. 32:9–14). His mercy was expressed in His provision in the extreme sacrifice of Jesus Christ.

6. Finally, God has shown His *holiness* and *justice*. His holiness is shown by His distinct separateness from sin. Holiness is moral and spiritual purity. He hates moral evil and must act in judgement upon it (Ps. 77:13, Exod. 19:6, cf. 1 Cor. 1:30, Eph. 4:24, Heb. 12:14). When the Israelites sinned by grumbling against God in the wilderness, God sent snakes among them for judgement (Num. 21:5–7). God is undefiled by sin and allows no sin in heaven. The Ten Commandments show the standards of God's holiness. God's justice is shown in the penalty for breaking His commands (Gen. 18:19, Deut. 32:4, Ps. 37:28, CRF John 5:30, Heb. 2:2, Rev. 15:3). The wages of sin is death as it says in Romans. Adam and Eve died spiritually and physically. God rewards those who seek Him and His ways.

God is Light

Another characteristic of God is that He is light. Peters sees this as being an expression by implication of God's missionary character too. God's holiness renders Him unapproachable; He is a consuming fire. Light is something we are still trying to understand in the realm of science. It is necessary to our existence and so is God.

> Light is diffusive, penetrating, searching, spreading itself all over space, and entering into every nook and corner… Light makes life and action possible. (Peters 1972, p. 59)

In John 1:3–5, the light of God was that which shone in the darkness. It was God in Genesis who said, "Let there be light." It was light which made life possible. When plants grow in sunlight, it enables them to make their food by photosynthesis. The light is absorbed by chlorophyll (the green pigment of the plant). Plants actually turn and lean toward the light. It is a natural response to something they need. When plants breathe, they take in carbon dioxide and breathe out oxygen. It is oxygen that we need to breathe as humans. God does for us what light does for plants. God shines into our hearts bringing His life into us when we put our faith in what Christ has done for us.

Christ came to earth to share His life freely as a part of the Father's light and love (John 10:17, 18). The Father and Son were unified in their purpose to redeem mankind. The only way this was possible was through the incarnation of Christ. This

> event is the cosmic divide that separates the darkness from light, the temporal from the eternal, the carnal from the spiritual, death from immortality, perdition from life, condemnation from presence, and hell from heaven. (Peters 1972, p. 62)

It is salvation that is a spectacle to the world and a mystery to angels. Jesus was the seed of the woman spoken of in the garden of Eden. It is God who initiated salvation—when Adam and Eve fell; it was God who came walking in the garden asking questions. God also came to Noah and to Abraham to make his covenant for the redemption of man. Noah's covenant was a temporal one that promised a flood would never again make such destruction of God's creation. But Abraham's covenant was that of blessing to all the earth. It is through Christ alone that we have salvation, and each of the gospels takes great pains to focus on the death of Christ on the cross and of His resurrection later. The sacrifices of the Old Testament thus gave way to the ultimate sacrifice in the New, and the new covenant was made. Jesus Himself said that if He was lifted up that He would draw all men to Himself (John 12:32).

The Trinity is involved in the salvation of man from beginning to the end—the Father had a plan, the Son was slain as a lamb to enact it, and the Holy Spirit works in us to apply it by faith when we believe. So it is that Paul speaks of salvation as God's gift to us (Eph. 2:8, 9). Faith is man's personal response to the grace of God. Romans 5:6 says that Christ died for the ungodly. It was He who destroyed the works of the devil (1 John 3:8), and Satan is also included in that destruction (Heb. 2:14). As Christ became sin for man, so He died and did away with death. It was not the sin of man, says Peters, that is the measure of redemption but the sacrifice. Thus, salvation is the outpouring of God's richness and mercy upon us (Rom. 8:19–21, Col. 1:19–20, Rev. 21:22). The sacrifice is an effective countermeasure against the sin that had infected all of mankind (Rom. 5:12–21). All who call on God for salvation will be saved—but only if they call on Him. The cosmos too is restored in the ultimate redemption at the end of time, and the scene in Revelation 21–22 is a part of the new creation.

Peters refers to the two main redemptive outgoings of the Godhead as the incarnation and Pentecost (Peters 1972, p. 76). Not all the ministries in which God is involved in are soteriologically oriented. The general work of the Holy Spirit is providential. Mankind in his fallen state is "pathetic, miserable and dangerous." Yet still there is something of God's image in him, for he searches for God in religions and philosophy. John 1:9 speaks of God's light that shines in men's hearts. Man's ability to heed the light means that the depravity has not taken away God's image in man. The opportunity to respond is still there—the work of the Holy Spirit in conviction of sin, righteousness, and judgement shows that His work has a purpose. The Holy Spirit desires repentance and turning to God for salvation. Peters says the world is preserved as a mission field so that the seasons of high potential for salvation will appear and that those responsive to God's grace will partake of it.

EXPLORING THE ROOTS OF MISSIONS: PERSONAL, BIBLICAL, AND SPIRITUAL

Old Testament

Creation

The history of the Old Testament starts right back at creation when the world began. Here a perfect man was created and placed into perfect surroundings. But despite all these natural advantages with no physical, spiritual, or mental weaknesses, he falls into temptation and sin. This changes the original raw material to a different nature. The Old Testament repeatedly shows God's concern for redemption of His wayward people since the Fall.

The problem is that mankind's fallen nature is not compatible with God's. Humankind was created *perfect* by God (Gen. 1:31). Made in God's image, humankind was given a cultural mandate: to subdue the earth and fill it. He had the ability to think, create, rule, love, and make valid sound decisions. But as a result of listening to the serpent, man fell into sin. Man was no longer perfect, no longer able to worship God the way he used to. Mankind could not even see reality correctly and did things his own way. God's rule and direction were ignored and reviled. The result was that God sent a flood because of his extreme sinfulness (Gen. 6:5). Man was bent on being sinful. The New Testament describes what man's nature was like (Kane 1989, pp. 155–60): Man was dead in trespasses and sins (Eph. 2:1), making him alienated from the life of God (Eph. 4:18). His sin made him ignorant of God's truth (Rom. 1:25) so that he turned away from truth and sought instead falsehood. This state of deadness makes mankind hostile to the law of God (Rom. 8:7) and disobedient (Tit. 3:3). Thus, lost man tends to love darkness rather than light (John 3:19). Mankind is enslaved to sin (John 8:31–36), being born in its clutches (Ps. 51:5). As a sinner, he cannot help but sin (Rom. 7:18, Jer. 17:9), thus putting him under God's wrath (Acts 17:30–31, Rom. 2:3–5) and destined for hell (Matt. 25:41, 7:13–14). Thus, we see that sin has changed and warped the whole of mankind's life, from the cradle to the grave. It has affected his thoughts, actions, and motives. There is no area of life that has not been touched by sin's influence. Sin has pervaded and corrupted what God originally made to be good. Man's focus has gone from God to himself. Furthermore, there is no one who has escaped the effects of sin. No one can claim to be sinless (Isa. 64:6).

The early section of Genesis 1–11 is meant for all mankind. Adam is representative of the human race as well as an individual. Thus, Paul argues in Romans 5 that he (Adam) is the head of the human race. But the promise of redemption in Genesis 3 is for all mankind. Peters here lists six facts about this promise (Peters 1972, p. 85): (1) This promise is of God, not man. (2) God (and therefore good) will triumph ultimately. There is no cyclical history that repeats itself endlessly. (3) Salvation is intended for more than just a family but for all of mankind. (4) Mankind will be involved in salvation, for the seed is from the woman. (5) There is suffering in redemption, for the serpent shall bite his heel. (6) This salvation is within our history, a certain thing we can point to. When God makes his covenant with Noah, it is in the plural—that is, Noah's descendants are included (Gen. 9:1, 8, 9).

Salvation may be for all, but not all people will receive it. Steeped in sin, they cannot rescue themselves. In the religions of the world, there are many ways to God, yet they are all man-made roads. Progress and science have not eradicated it. The search for God is a need deep within mankind. It is an irony and sadness that although every people has a religion of some kind, only Western man has detached himself from it. Secularism and humanism have replaced worship of a god on a shelf, yet they are every bit as pervasive and entrenched. If the focus is not on the true God, then it is not salvation. The opposite of no god is in this sense animism, where at least the sacredness of life is recognized. As far as the Old Testament goes in the realm of religion, the belief and faith system of the people known as the Israelites was similar to other cultures in its institutional structure. There was worship and sacrifices to the gods of the land. Many variations were present in the ancient near eastern cultures around the nation of Israel. They all had their myths of the world's origin (the Babylonian Epic of Gilgamesh included the flood), gods, religious literature, rituals, priests, prophets, kings, covenants (suzerainty treaties with the Hittite kings and their peoples), law (the Hammurabi code of Babylon), sanctuaries, and festivals of worship. It was the content of the Israelite worship that differed the most drastically. It was God's revelation of Himself to mankind, and He did not, as the other religions, desire human sacrifices. The perfect lamb was the sacrifice required, and the meaning for this became clear in the New Testament.

Although the Israelites were a specific nation called out to worship God in this way, it was not meant to keep this worship to itself. As Abraham was the beginning of this culture-specific blessing, and he was the father of Israel physically. Romans 1:18–32 is the theological interpretation of religious history of the nations after Babel in Genesis 11:1–9. Religion, morality, and philosophy came under God's judgement. Since man has chosen to turn away from God, then divine intervention is needed for salvation.

Covenant

But God did not forget man in his sin and leave him there. He promised that He would bless them and send a deliverer. In the garden, God promised that "your offspring shall crush the serpent's head." Cain's sacrifice was a self-made redemption; he depended on his idea of sacrifice and did not heed the warning he was given. This is where the concept of religions separating man from God flows from, for they are apart from what He has revealed about Himself. An inadequate view of God leads to an inadequate view of all else—sin, mankind, and nature. So Cain slew his brother instead of heeding God's advice. God's judgement fell on the succeeding generations which grew worse and worse into evil. To Noah he said he would never again send a flood (Gen. 9:9–17).

God called Abraham out (Gen. 12:1–3) saying that He would bless him and all peoples through him. God freely made a covenant with Abraham (and Israel also); He ratified it Himself by passing through the sacrifice pieces (Gen. 15:17). He had bound Himself to keep His promise. It was a one-sided faithful act of God to His people (Deut. 4:31, Gen. 17:7). When God called Abraham out, He started a counterculture to the religions around him. There was degeneration, decay, and disintegration in the worship of the nations. The Old Testament regulations given to Moses were quite different in their details which condemned divination, soothsaying, necromancy, witchcraft, idolatry, human sacrifices, and temple prostitution. Breaking the law of God often ended in death to clean out the contamination among the people of God. The Ten Commandments were God's ideals. The people of Israel called to God by His relationship to their ancestors, Abraham, Isaac, and Jacob. The blessing on Abraham is for his obedience. The promise was that he would have numerous seed (Gen. 12:2) and inherit the land (Gen. 12:7) and on the peoples of the earth (Gen. 18:18). This promise was passed on to his descendants too.

When God revealed Himself to Moses (Exod. 3:6–17), He showed his nature in the "I Am that I Am" statement. This showed He was like no other. It was by God that Moses was able to rescue the people of Israel: God's great power accomplished it. The testimony of God in Deuteronomy 6:4 was that God was like no one else. The nature and character of God were defined according to His nature and actions. His love and concern for Israel were plain. So was His holiness. Moses stood before the bush that burned, and he quaked. He knew he was in front of a holy God. At Sinai, the smoke and thunder scared the people. God was too awesome for them. At Sinai, God stated His covenant stipulations to them in the Ten Commandments. The people of Israel also bound themselves to keep the covenant (Exod. 24:7, 8). The law was given to enable the people to keep the covenant (Exod. 31:16, 34:28).

God's Call to Israel

But God had not forgotten the rest of the world. The nations had decided to forget Him, reject Him, and follow other ways. God declared in Scripture His ownership over them still, even though they had abandoned Him. The Jewish prophets themselves stated that God's rule was over all the earth. Amos declared God's rebuke in the first two chapters of his book. In Isaiah 13–23, God rebuked many of the nations for their sins.

EXPLORING THE ROOTS OF MISSIONS: PERSONAL, BIBLICAL, AND SPIRITUAL

God's call to Israel was to be His witness among the nations.

1. *Purpose*: He began with Abraham; He called him out of Ur to follow Him. The descendants of Abraham were the nation of Israel. One family was chosen to bless all other nations. *Through your seed shall all the nations be blessed.* Stott says that the blessing was not physical in nature but spiritual (Stott 1983, p. 10). The first part of the fulfillment of the promise to Abraham was in Abraham's children—Isaac was the child of promise. Kane specified three purposes for Israel's call (Kane 1989, p. 23). (a) Hebrews 1:3 states that Israel is the special one through whom God revealed Himself and was to be a guardian of that revelation. General revelation was not sufficient. Something different from the other gods had to be evident. The law of God was different because God demanded holiness. God showed Himself to Moses in the burning bush (Exod. 3) and to Israel by stating "I AM." At Sinai, she received the law, and the ark was made to keep it. (b) Israel was God's servant and witness in the midst of the other nations (Isa. 44:1–2, 43:10). Israel was to be the means by which God reached the world. God's working in Israel was a witness to the other nations around her. Various incidents in the Old Testament support this. In Egypt, God sends plagues, not only to deliver the people but also to show His power and glorify His name (Exod. 9:14–16). Joshua declares this in his opening address to the people (Josh. 4:23–24) that the opening of the Red Sea and the Jordan was a display of God's power. When David faces Goliath, David slays him for the glory of God among the peoples (1 Sam. 17:46).

The psalmists state that all nations should come to worship God on His holy hill (Ps. 33:8; 67:2; 102:21, 22). The Psalms contain over 175 references to the Gentile nations, many of them speak of God's reign overall, according to Peters (Olson 1994, p. 29). I've added another example here: In looking at the book of Esther, one can see that although she was Jewish, she was caught in her times and found herself winning a beauty contest and married to a foreign king. That certainly is a witness of the most unusual sort. Yet God used Esther's devotion to Him to save her people in Susa. So in her own way, she too was a light to the nation in which her husband ruled. God's providence was in placing her to save her people. This is remembered in the memorial of Feast of Purim. Although this book is about the salvation of the Jews, it is also a light to the Gentiles. (c) Israel was the channel through which the Redeemer was to come: from the tribe of Judah (Mic. 5:2, Isa. 49:6, cf. Rom. 1:3). Through Israel, God would be able to fulfill the new covenant through Jesus's coming. Jesus's death made the new covenant possible.

The redemption of Israel from slavery in Egypt was a major theme in its history and literature. This deliverance was a witness to the nations around them that God of Abraham was holy and powerful. This was a significant and focal event in Jewish history. References to it come up time and time again in national addresses and spiritual liturgy. The Passover was their victory celebration of what God had done for them. God delivered them from their political enemies many times; from Haman (Esth. 3–7), from the Midianites (Judg. 6–7), and from the Assyrians (2 Kings 19). They were the apple of His eye (Zech. 2:8). However, the spiritual dangers were more of a problem. If Israel disobeyed God, the world would see God's judgement on them and be afraid. Israel was to witness through her presence; she was different in her worship than other nations, not immoral or dishonest. There were strangers who were allowed to be in their midst (Num. 9:14; Lev. 17:8, 19:33–334). The story of Ruth was an example. God was not just a local god, like the Baals who were territorial in nature (gods in certain areas only). In the future, Israel would not be the only nation worshipping the true God. Other nations would come and proclaim God's glory (Hab. 2:14). Jerusalem would no longer be the worship centre, but everyone could worship wherever they were. (Jesus refers to this when He speaks to the Samaritan woman in John 4:21).

However, God had a conditional requirement. In Deuteronomy 30:15–20, He stated that obedience would bring blessing but disobedience, cursing (or ruin). God rescued the people out of His love; He bore their rebellion with patience and forgiveness and judged them too. There was a direct relationship between their sin and suffering as a result. Judgement fell on the people as a collective unit and as individuals. But suffering is not only linked to sin, as Job learned. It can be substitutionary or for other purposes. In Isaiah 53, the suffering was of the voluntary substitutionary sort. Thus, it has a part in salvation, not only in repentance but also in obtaining redemption. The atonement in the Old Testament is one of the things that sets it apart from the other religions of the Middle East. The lamb slain for the sinner was a key component in the complex sacrificial system.

As a people called out from among the other nations, Israel's role was to be of a light to the nations. She was called to draw the nations around her to God by virtue of her uniqueness. In this way, the people of Israel were called to be priests (Exod. 19:4–6). It was the covenant with Moses that made the people a nation and servant. The responsibility they had also came with a privilege. During the Passover, even strangers were allowed to take part (Exod. 12:48, 22:21). The revelation of God was for those who chose to follow Him (Deut. 1:16, 29:11).

2. *Privilege*: The effect of the call was a privilege and a responsibility. Because Israel failed to keep God's law, she was rejected and disciplined through exile and scattered abroad. God did keep a remnant: those who believed (Isa. 1:9, Rom. 11:5) in Him. These people continued to be a faithful witness for Him. But many failed because of their sinfulness. They followed after the gods of the nations around them: Baal and Ashtoreth, for example. They worshipped the gods of these nations and forsook the God who had redeemed them.

The judges and prophets both stood for God's law. But God continued to repeat His promise of faithfulness to them over and over even in the time of the judges (Judg. 2:1). The time of the judges has been noted for the fact that each one went his own way (Judg. 21:25). It records the obedience of the tribes to God (Judg. 1:2, 19, 22) and of their disobedience (Judg. 1:27, 2:1–3). God's angel told the people that because they had not persisted in driving out the pagan nations, that they would be ensnared by them. After Joshua died and those of the generation who had seen God's deliverance out of Egypt, the next generation arose who did not acknowledge God (Judg. 2:10–15). They fell into God's wrath for their disobedience. Their failure to follow the judges God gave them (Judg. 2:16–18) only made their situation worse. The pagan nations were left there to test Israel and see if Israel would keep to her covenant. The judges that came and went showed the fickle hearts of the people—Othniel, Ehud, Shamgar, Deborah, Gideon, Tola, Jair, Jephthah, Izban, Elon, Abdon, and finally, Samson who was the last. Some judges have gone down into history—for example Deborah, Gideon, and Samson. Their stories were more detailed than most of the others. But all of them were mighty for God. Sadly, the ups and downs of these early leaders were to be repeated in the reign of the kings to follow them. God remained faithful even though His people did not. Thus, their ability to be a drawing light to the nations for God's glory was poor at best.

God was also faithful to the kings (1 Kings 8:21–24, 1 Chron. 16:15) despite their faithlessness to Him. To King David, God made a special promise that He would bless him and be faithful to his descendants (2 Chron. 13:5, 2 Sam. 7:11ff). During David's reign, there was a high emphasis on worship. When Solomon built the temple, this gave the kingdom a politico-religious centre to focus on. The worship of the Psalms is among the richest literature and was based on the experiences of the saints, used both in public and private worship. There are 175 references of universalistic note where salvation was to be for the nations (Ps. 33, 66, 98, 117, and 145). Psalm 33:8 commands the earth to fear the Lord. He is watching all they do (33:15). All the earth worships God (Ps. 66:4) and praises Him (66:8). All the earth has seen the salvation of God (98:3), and He comes to judge it in righteousness (98:9). God has great love toward His people (117) and all that He has made (145:9, 10). Verse 18 of Ps. 145 speaks how God will save all who call on Him in truth, and the whole psalm rejoices in God's goodness in provision and salvation. Solomon's prayer was significant in what he prayed on behalf of the people. Solomon desired that all people would know who God was (1 Kings 8:43) and that they would know Him only (1 Kings 8:60).

Prophets

Peters looks at the world religions of that day with the image of four concentric circles (Peters 1972, p. 118). In the innermost circle are the authentic prophets of the Old Testament. Then come the false prophets (for example the 450 prophets of Baal). Next are the prophets of the neighbouring countries and finally the prophets of the major world religions, most of who are from a similar timeframe as Judaism. All of these have certain ways of looking at the world, life, and religion.

- Zoroaster (600–583 BC), founder of Zoroastrianism—Persia
- Mahavira (599–527 BC), founder of Jainism—India
- Gautama Siddhartha (560–480 BC), founder of Buddhism—India
- Lao-Tzu (604–517 BC), founder of Taoism—China
- Confucius (551–479 BC), founder of Confucianism—China

Although these are roughly contemporary, a look at the authentic marks of the prophet of God is to be noticed (Peters 1972, p. 119,). The prophet depended totally on God and had great integrity. Even when he did not understand the content of his message, he went forward in faith. As a spokesman for God, he was aware of his divine commission and calling. (Freeman notes that these often came with miracles and signs.) The message was Messianic in nature for the Messiah was to come from the people of Israel. Freeman adds too that the message was certainly in harmony with what God had previously declared, and the predictions themselves were to be accurate (Freeman 1981, p. 110). A final aspect on Peters's list is the sense of unworthiness and conflict in service. These prophets knew their worth and background and did not feel that they were adequate to pass on that message. Yet God still used them.

The prophets continued to repeat to the people of the faithfulness of God (Jer. 33:19–22; Isa. 42:6–7, 61:8). In Isaiah, the book addresses Judah among various other nations (1–39) all under the sovereignty of God. The prophet calls down judgement on the surrounding nations. This means there is some element of divine concern. Isaiah 25:8 says that God will wipe away tears from all faces and remove the disgrace of His people from all the earth. There is an element that reaches beyond Israel here. In the next chapter, he talks about the people learning righteousness. God's blessings are on the peoples (Isa. 2:1–4, 11:9–10, 25:6–9). But He would do it through the nation of Israel. Just as she was called to be a witness (Isa. 43:10, 12; 44:8), Israel was also called to be God's servant (Isa. 40–55). In fact, He became very specific as to how the blessing/fulfillment of the covenant would come. It would come in the Messiah, foretold in the Messianic passages of Isaiah 42–53 (Olson 1994, p. 31). The Servant would bring justice to all nations (Isa. 42:1). The latter half of the book focuses on the servanthood passages. The phrase "my servant" occurs thirteen times. The Servant Songs in chapters 42, 49, 50, and 52 all talk of aspects of Israel as servant (Peters 1972, p. 124). Israel is a messenger and witness in 42:19, 44:26, 43:10–12, and 44:8. Israel did not come about as a result of their own work; they were chosen by God (43:12). As those chosen by God, they were to uphold monotheism in the midst of idolatry (44:6; 45:5, 6, 21). God is the only Creator, Redeemer, and the One who makes true prophecies (41:22, 43:10). The idea of Isaiah's message was to take the attention off idols and back onto God (Peters 1972, p. 124–126). This is done by remembering God's great redemptive deeds, the irony (and utter folly) of idolatry, and the judgement on the idolatrous nations, such as Babylon. In the midst of all the judgement is God's unchanging love and promises (Isa. 40–48). God's unique sovereign rule is established (Isa. 41:4, 43:13, 44:8–10, 45:22–23, 46:9–11, 48:12). But the true meaning for Israel, declares Peters is in missions to the nations (40:5; 42:1, 6–7; 44:6, 26; 51:4, 5; 52:10, 15).

    The description of Isaiah goes beyond Israel; it touches on the Ideal Servant. This servant is publicly rejected and suffers voluntarily. He dies as an atoning sacrifice and is resurrected in triumph (Isa. 52:13–53:12). He is the justice and light to the nations in Isaiah 42:4, 6, 7. The Servant also will be a light to all nations so the salvation would go to the ends of the earth (Isa. 49:6). The Servant startles the nations in Isaiah 52:15. The final section of Isaiah (55–66) is the restoration of Israel, which is a blessing for the nations. In 55:4–5, the nations are told to seek God. In 56:2–7, God will not reject any who do so. They have come to Him, and He accepts them, for He has called them. In Isaiah 59:19 and 60:10–16, the nations flock to God's call and light. The prophet talks about the year of God's favour where good news, healing, and freedom are proclaimed in Isaiah 61:1–11. The nations come to the light of Zion's dawn (Isa. 60); the Saviour comes to Zion as salvation is proclaimed to all the earth (Isa. 62:11). Isaiah 65:1 declares that God is found by those who have not sought Him. God's glory is proclaimed among the nations (Isa. 66:18–21).

Through the prophet Jeremiah, God stated that He would make a new covenant with the people of Israel (Jer. 31:31–34). Each time the covenant is repeated in Scripture, it becomes richer and fuller in its promise. Because Israel consistently broke the covenant (Jer. 31:32, Hos. 6:7), the prophets also talked about the coming of a Redeemer, God's ultimate fulfillment of the promise (Isa. 9:2–7). Just as God used the nations as instruments for His judgement, so He also had care and concern for them as seen in the book of Jonah.

Jonah is an unusual example of a prophet in Scripture. The prophets tended to be very obedient in the face of dire circumstances, with no encouragement for their hard work. But as Samson was an example of how *not* to judge, so Jonah was the example of how *not* to run away from God. Jonah was sent to preach to Nineveh, a city of an evil people who were renowned for their cruel treatment of enemies (Nah. 3). Jonah did not like the idea of preaching repentance and salvation to his people's enemies and so rebelled. It is impossible to run away from the Almighty Infinite God, however, and after spending some time in a great fish, Jonah decided obedience was a better option! Even so, his lesson was not taken to heart, for when he did arrive and preach, the people repented, much to his disappointment. He was not glad they repented and had a hard heart for a servant of God, even after his earlier fishy rebuke.

Pain—The disobedience of Israel through her apostasy brought pain through her exile. Nebuchadnezzar destroyed Jerusalem in 600 BC and carried the Jews away to Babylon. They were there for seventy years before a remnant was allowed to return. This time forced the Jews to stop taking God for granted. Taken by force into a nation of idolatry, they learned the lesson of their blessing as God's children. They stopped being idolatrous and realized who God really was. They became good representatives of Him in their faithfulness.

Exile

During the exile, one prophet stands out as a witness to those around him among the foreign nations. Certainly Daniel and his three friends—Shadrach, Meshach, and Abednego—were witnesses to their captors in Babylon. They stuck to their principles, even in the face of danger (Dan. 1). They honoured God and God blessed their witness to Nebuchadnezzar. Daniel interpreted a dream for him (Dan. 2), and they were all promoted instead of executed, even though the dream predicted dire things. In Daniel 3, the three face the fiery furnace for not bowing down. God is with them in the fiery furnace. Another dream in Daniel 4 from the king presents Daniel with another test. The dream comes to pass, and Daniel's God is honoured. Nebuchadnezzar honours God and lets other nations know as well. King Belshazzar, Nebuchadnezzar's son, also has a problem which he brings to Daniel in Daniel 5. Daniel interprets the writing on the wall, and this king is overthrown. In Daniel 6, he is tested by his loyalty to God by the new king Darius. Darius's advisors were jealous and so plotted to put Daniel to the test. After this king, it seems that the time of testing for Daniel in this fashion was over, and the rest of the book was given to visions of the future which did not directly relate to the kings he served. There are no tests recorded for his service under King Cyrus. Daniel lived for a long time and was used by God in his close proximity with the kings he served.

The missionary thrust of the prophets was over a span of 175 years (from 800–625 BC). Obadiah, Jonah, and Nahum had non-Jewish messages. Joel, Amos, Hosea, Isaiah, Micah, Zephaniah, and Habakkuk all had a note of universality. The judgements of the day affect all the nations (Zeph. 1:2–3). All the nations shall revere God (Zech. 2:11; 3:19, 20) and bow to His saving power. In

Habakkuk comes the verse where "the just shall live by faith" (Hab. 2:4) which Luther later used. The book of Amos refers to God as the universal judge and saviour. Although Israel too is judged, she is restored in the last bit of the book (Amos 9:7–15).

Diaspora of the Jews

From that time, the Jews have spread throughout all the earth. The spread of the Jews is called the *Diaspora*. They began to gain converts to Judaism, both proselytes (circumcised) and God-fearers (Gentile believers uncircumcised). There were six aspects of Jewish worship that developed during the time of the Diaspora:

1. Synagogue—wherever there were ten men, they set up a synagogue for teaching purposes and worship. There were no sacrifices at synagogues as at the temple, and converts were allowed to be involved. The people of Israel were too widely dispersed to gather at the temple as they used to do. The synagogue made local worship possible. With the rise of greater cities, certain feasts could not be observed as in the rural beginnings of Judaism. The synagogue was a social centre for the Jews and was where the children were instructed in the law and history. The study of the law took the place of the sacrifice, and the rabbi functioned instead of the priest.
2. The Sabbath was strictly observed. There was no regular work done that day for it was a day of rest. There were certain prescriptions for what was allowed—certain distances travelled, etc. It was a day for worship, prayer, and study of the Scriptures.
3. Hellenization of the Scriptures—Hebrew was forgotten in exile, so they learned Greek from the nations around them. The Jewish Scriptures were translated into Greek in the third century before Christ in the city of Alexandria. This translation is called the Septuagint because it was the work of seventy scholars.

4. Monotheism was a chief trademark of the Jews in the Graeco-Roman world. Many of the other peoples worshipped a profusion of gods, up to thirty thousand in the Greek world. These gods were very immoral. The God of the Hebrews was certainly different than the gods of the Greeks and Romans. His standards for worship and lifestyle were quite different.
5. Morality—pagan cities were very immoral. Divorce and infanticide were common, and so was fraud and corruption. Jewish family life was exempt to a large degree of these vices.
6. Promise of the Messiah—other nations couldn't solve the world's problems. Philosophers and kings did not have the answers. The Jewish Messiah was a prophet, priest, and king; only He would have the solutions. The Messiah would take the Jewish people out of their present situation and lead them to victory in a political as well as a religious sense.

Summary

Missions begins in God's heart and is a repeated theme throughout the Old Testament. Man's nature was created perfect but became corrupt because of sin. This showed itself in unfaithfulness to God and mistreatment of fellow man. God desired that all men should worship and have fellowship with Him. God made a special covenant with Israel that showed His faithfulness. This was to be an example to all nations of God's care for people. He also made a covenant with Israel at Sinai which Israel did not always keep. Throughout their history, God is always calling them back to Himself. God is concerned for the lost. The result of their sin of unfaithfulness was exile, and afterward they spread out to many other nations. During exile, they learned to worship God wholeheartedly again and became a good example of purity in religion. This paved the way for the true spread of the Gospel in the New Testament and beyond.

The New Testament talks of the covenant being made by God's Son, Jesus, who died as the sacrificial Lamb (Matt. 26:26–28, Mark 14:24, 2 Cor. 3:6, Gal. 4:21ff, Heb. 9:13ff). Jesus mediates the new covenant. In the covenant as originally given, it is clearly stated that there is blessing for obedience and punishment for disobedience. The exile of Israel was because of their disobedience. But God never forgot His people; He was always calling them back to Himself. He wanted them to worship Him with a pure heart as Malachi stated.

New Testament

The New Testament has several themes that will be covered before the content of books is looked at in more detail. Foremost is the whole idea of *prophecy*. The prophets in Scripture saw fulfillment of prophecy in triplicate—they saw the past fulfillment in the history of Israel, the present fulfillment in the church shown by the gospels, and finally the complete fulfillment in the worldwide representation of tribes around the throne (Rev. 7:9). Jesus and His ministry were a fulfillment of the Old Testament scriptures. Matthew talks about the prophecies that referred to the people living in darkness (Matt. 4:15–16). The Jews, the people of Israel already had the light of God's truth, in the Law, the prophets, and the covenant they received. Matthew, as a Jew, picked up the thread of Jesus's royalty, fulfilling all the visions and prophecies of the Old Testament. Both Luke and Matthew record the fulfillments quite specifically—Luke 3:6 cf. Isaiah 40:5—all mankind would see God's salvation. It was to be located in Galilee, a very nondescript place (Matt. 4:15, 16; Isa. 9:1–2 cf. Luke 2:32; Matt. 12:21; Isa. 42:4). This light, a particular servant of the Lord, was to be a revelation who were to the Gentiles. Jesus Himself was the fulfillment of over three hundred prophecies. Sixty of these prophecies were Messianic in nature. These prophecies were made over four hundred years before Jesus's birth (remember the Septuagint was written in the Greek in 200 BC). The Old Testament typology is no longer an idea, but a Person. The spiritual shadows flee in the presence of his reality (Peters 1972, p. 37). It was the Gentiles who had no written revelation to show them who God was. This revelation originally was to be shown in Israel's obedience in the Old Testament, but it was sadly lacking in many cases.

McDowell traces a succinct line of descent running through the books of the Old Testament that complements the passages in Matthew and Luke. In the very first book of the Bible (Gen. 3:15), Jesus was the one to be born of a woman—the one that should crush the serpent's head. From the time of the flood and Noah's sons would come the line of Shem (Gen. 10:22–25 cf. Luke3:35). Abraham was chosen to be the father of many nations, yet of his line, only one was to be of the Messiah (Gen. 12:17, 21–22). When Isaac in turn fathered twelve sons, it was of Jacob's line that was next (Num. 24:17). Finally, out of the tribe of Judah came David, the son of Jesse (Isa. 11:1–5). Thus, Jesus, out of the many possibilities, came out of David's lineage (Matt. 22:44, Luke 1:69, 2 Sam.7:12–16, Ps. 89:3–4), born of a virgin (Isa. 7:14, Matt. 1:23). His birth in Bethlehem was also known (Matt. 2:6, Mic. 5:2). A prophet like Elijah would announce His coming (Matt. 3:3, 11:10–14; Isa. 40:3–5; Mal. 3:1, 4:5). His rejection was foretold (Ps. 69:4, 118:22). Not only was Jesus to be rejected by His people, He would also be betrayed by one of His friends for money! This was in Zechariah where a description of two shepherds is the background for this passage (Zech. 11:11–13). The ultimate betrayal of Jesus to His archenemies was to the Jews (Ps. 41:9). This too was the final straw, that the Messiah would be betrayed by His very own people, to the common enemy of the Jews, the Romans.

Another theme developed is that of the *kingdom of God* beginning with Jesus's ministry. Jesus begins His ministry much as John the Baptist did—focussing on the kingdom of God. The missionary thrust of Christ was on the kingdom of God; this phrase is mentioned over sixty times in the gospels (e.g., Mark 1:14, 15). The kingdom has an increasing narrowing point from creation on down to Israel itself. While God is king over creation in the providential sense and of the nations in a general sense, but He is king over Israel in a particular way. The New Testament adds to these dimensions, that of king of the inner man (Peters 1972, p. 40). This makes the kingdom personal as well as spiritual, moral, and social. Thus, the kingdom begins in man's heart as he takes in God's love and forgiveness and spreads outward to those around him in concentric circles. Just as Zacchaeus gave back to others money that he had wrongfully taken, the morality of believers touched others' lives as they themselves were reformed by God's Holy Spirit. Paul continued this theme in his preaching in Acts 14:22, 19:8, even when he was on trial and imprisoned for it (Acts 23, 28:31). With the birth of the church, Christ became its Head—giving gifts and sending His people out as His ambassadors (Eph. 1:23, Col. 1:18, Rom. 12:5). Peters adds that the Christian conscience in society is a judgement on some and the enrichment on the order of society too (Peters 1972, p. 41). All relationships are regulated according to God's will and purpose. The kingdom of God is local, both in the believer and church, but it is universal in that the focus is that the gospel is to be preached to the nations. The church is indeed made up of many peoples of the world.

A prime focus of the gospels is the *fatherhood of God*. As it is the Son's purpose to make His Father known (John 1:18) so that we can have a good relationship with Him. Matthew's gospel uses the term *Father* 44 times, Luke mentions it 16 times, and John surpasses them both with 109 references. Only in Mark does this concept not play a significant role, being mentioned only five times. The "children" of God is more personal in application in the New Testament than in the Old (just as the Holy Spirit is more personal there too). Jesus goes out of His way to point out that He is God's Son in John 5. But He does not limit God's fatherhood to the Israelites only. God is the Father of all who believe. This was difficult for the Jews of His day to understand.

Another unusual designation Jesus used was the term *Son of Man*. In fact, it is used eighty-four times in all. Jesus affirmed His identity as the second Adam. Both began as perfect men of God, but only Christ resisted sin. He was the promised Messiah (Ps. 80:17, Dan.7:13–14). The term *Son of Man* was what the Jews called the Messiah. Jesus used the term when speaking eschatologically (Matt. 16:27, Mark 8:38), soteriologically (Mark 10:45, Luke 9:22), and of his Messianic authority and missions (Matt. 13:37, Mark 2:28, Luke19:10) (Peters 1972, p. 45). Jesus's purpose was not just to live and teach, though His example was important. Jesus not only claimed to fulfill the Old Testament promises, He was its true interpreter and content. The baptismal formula in all of the gospels notes that the Trinity is involved in salvation. But Jesus's life was more than that; John the evangelist says in his gospel, "Behold the Lamb of God who takes away the sin of the world" (John 1:29). Jesus did not die for the Jews alone; He died for the world. His messiahship was not for them alone but so that all the nations would be blessed (Gen. 12:3). The commission of Christ to reach the world with the news of this salvation came *after* His resurrection.

In the gospels, the references to the *universality* of the gospel are few compared to the references of the work being to the nation of Israel. But they are certainly present in the passages—as a hint as to what was to come. The announcement of Jesus's birth was a part of this plan. The angels announced that Jesus's birth was a joy to all people (Luke 2:10–12). Simeon prayed his prayer in Luke 2:25–32 before the people, and John the Baptist said that all flesh would see God's salvation (Luke 3:3–6). Jesus Himself said to the Samaritan woman in John 4 that salvation is from the Jews. When Jesus cleansed the temple in John 2:13–17, it was an act of worship for the nations. The temple court divisions were concentric with the Gentile court being on the outside, the court of Israelites (men) next, and the court of women. Last came the inner court for the priests. It was in the court of the Gentiles where the buying and selling were done. Jesus, in His wrath, emphasizes the original purpose of the house of prayer—for all the nations (Mark 11:17 cf. Isa. 56:7). So not only were the sellers/priests likely extorting the Gentiles, but they were preventing them from worshipping God appropriately by their actions.

Jesus declared that the believers were the *salt of the earth* (Matt. 5:13–16) as well as the *light of the world*. In fact, He predicts that the rejection of the Jews for the gospel will result in their losing the gospel message to the Gentiles. (Paul explains this in more detail in Romans 9–10). This idea was incredibly offensive to the Jewish leaders, that they could actually lose their privileged position. What they had forgotten was the reason for their privilege—to be a light to the nations. Luke further says that many peoples (from other places), the implication was that it would not just be the scattered Jews, who would sit at the banquet table (Luke 13:28, 29). The universalist activity of God is shown in John in the following passages: 3:16, 17 (where God's love is for the world), 1:29 (He takes away its sin), 6:33 (He gives life to all), and in 8:12 (His light is to the world). Just to be sure the Jewish listeners did not miss the point, Jesus threw in some parables in His teaching to illustrate the international focus. The parable of the Good Samaritan was shocking and effective because the good and upright example was the Samaritan, not the pious Jewish leaders. In the great feast of Luke 14:10–24, many others not of the "upper crust" of society were invited since those who were first invited (the Jews) were too busy to come. They gave their excuses. Imagine turning down God's great offer of salvation for business reasons or marriage! Yet it was the normal everyday things of life that were given as reasons for not attending God's great banquet. In Matthew 13:36–43, the description of the wheat and tares is another example of the weeds of evil growing in the world. The prodigal son can also be seen as a portrait of those who had salvation (Luke 15:11–24) and yet threw it away. The elder brother, who was self-righteous in his obedience to the law, was the one who didn't truly understand salvation (the Jews). Salvation was exclusive in one sense—that one must enter the narrow gate (Matt. 7:13–14, Luke 13:22–30) and the wedding banquet (Matt. 22:11–14 cf. Luke 14:15–24). Although many were invited to the banquet, not all were able to enter. They had to be wearing the correct clothes (that of Jesus's righteousness). Without Jesus's death on our behalf, all our own righteousness is as filthy rags in God's eyes. The world religions could not fulfill this requirement, and so the necessity of missions. In the book of John, Jesus declares in the "I am" passages that He is the only way (John 1:14, 18, 36; 17:3; 14:6). John the Baptist referred to all of mankind being saved (Luke 3:4–6). Salvation would be there for those who repented. John the Baptist even points out that the Jews would be judged for their laziness in trusting Abraham's faith (not their own) a few verses on.

Paul remarks later on in the book of Romans (1–3) the development of the gospel was to the *Jews first, and then to the Gentiles.*

Certainly, Jesus said He was sent to the Jews and told His disciples not to minister beyond the borders but to Jews only (Matt. 10:5, 6; 15:24). Peters explains this by stating that before the cross, there was no salvation for the Gentiles. Jesus was a Jew working with Jews—His focus then was to draw the interested Gentiles to Himself as the Jews were to have drawn the nations to them by their example of holiness. Although Jesus was rejected by the Jews (John 1:11), He did draw some. The disciples who later became the apostles, along with Paul, were significant converts who carried out Jesus's ministry. It was Jews who were the first converts, who gave the rest of the world the Bible, the first missionaries, and the first churches (Peters 1972, p. 53). But throughout the gospels, we see hints that Jesus did not intend the ministry of God to stop with the Jews.

The New Testament begins with the advent of the *Messiah's birth*; the Redeemer has come! Both Matthew and Luke spend considerable portions of their writings on this, to give a good background for the events to come. Matthew mentions the prophecies that have been fulfilled in particular by Jesus's birth (ch. 1–2) as well as Jesus's human bloodline. (We have already discussed the prophecies mentioned.) The early chapters of the gospel in Luke begin with the prophecies that refer to the covenant of Abraham (Luke 1:72–79).

It is interesting to note that the history of the *Gentile bloodline* is in Jesus. The first one noted was Tamar, a daughter-in-law of Judah and had a child by him through subterfuge (Gen. 38). Legally she was within her rights, as he had refused her marriage to another son of his, after the first two died. They had been wicked, and God judged them. Next was Rahab of Jericho. She was accepted into Jesus's bloodline as a result of her role in saving the spies in Jericho (Josh. 2:1, 6:22 cf. Matt. 1:3–6). A third Gentile was Ruth, who, although a Moabite, first married a man of Israel (Kilion), then after she became a widow, travelled with her mother-in-law back to Israel and found a new husband, Boaz. Boaz turned out to be a kinsman of Naomi, her mother-in-law, and sought to redeem Ruth (Ruth cf. Matt. 1:5). The final Gentile blood was through Bathsheba, the one whom King David lusted after in 2 Samuel 11:3. Jesus was of the line of David, but he was not strictly a pure Jew. Jewish heritage is commonly passed down through the female line, and it is interesting to note that all the Gentile blood in Jesus came from the females in His history.

This says several things about God. It says that He was not concerned that the bloodline be only of Levites and priests so as to assure His purity, for the heritage was not of Jews only; it was also Gentiles! It also says that He was not too proud to include women in His lineage, for most of the lineages in Scripture seem to be of men only, with exceptional women occasionally showing up. Jesus's genetic history is full of people who were not necessarily the purest of folk. Tamar and Rahab certainly had shady moments in their history. Rahab was a prostitute before the fall of Jericho. Tamar resorted to trickery to get her plight noticed by her father-in-law. Ruth was the prime example of purity, who wholeheartedly devoted herself to her mother-in-law's people and accepted the redemption from Boaz. Bathsheba came at King David's call, and whereas she may not have had a choice, she was involved with complicity in the immorality that followed. God was concerned enough about the Gentiles to bring them, even through Jesus's bloodline, into proximity with the coming kingdom of heaven.

Foreign kings are a part of Jesus's reception, a hint of the true intent of the gospel (Luke 2:1–12). Luke goes into more detail by also talking about a forerunner too: John the Baptist. Angels make the announcement to the shepherds that Jesus's birth will be good news for all people (2:10). Simeon blesses the light of the Gentiles as he holds Jesus in his arms. The gospel writer of John makes reference to Jesus's divine origin (1:1–3, 14). The Son has been sent. The gospel of John also refers to the ministries of both John and Jesus and stresses both of their unusual origins and purposes. Jesus and his parents must hide in Egypt, from Herod's wrath. Galilee itself was an area near Decapolis and Samaria; Jesus grew up in this area with Gentiles surrounding his native Palestine.

Peters sees that the beauty of the gospels is not in the harmonization of their perspectives but in their systemization (Peters 1972, p. 36). As each writer has a different viewpoint and purpose, then it is most fitting to see each snapshot of Jesus's life in the way in which it was intended.

Gospels

Jesus's ministry as recorded in *Matthew* begins with "fishers of men in" (4:19) in His call to the disciples. Matthew includes the directive to be salt and light as well (5:13, 5:14–16). Jesus has a concern for sinners and the hurting both. By Matthew 8:5–13, Jesus heals a Roman centurion's servant. The Romans were enemies of the Jews, so why should He even have bothered? However, this Roman had helped build the temple and so was loved by the Jews. This Roman in particular seemed to have understood who Jesus was and what kind of authority He really had (in contrast to the Jews who couldn't or wouldn't see it). He told Jesus to just say the word, and he *knew* that his servant would be healed. Jesus commended him for his great faith.

Later in chapters 11–12 (cf. Luke 13:28–29), Jesus rather blatantly points this out—that God indeed raised children up from Abraham, not from stones but from Gentiles (Stott 1983, p. 13)! This was a major shock to the Jews who felt that *they* were the heirs of the promise. However, as Stott remarked, "Election is not synonymous with elitism" (Stott 1983, p. 9). This was indeed the error that the Jews had fallen into through their long association as the chosen people of God. They forgot that they were chosen to share the news of God's love to other nations too. It is interesting to note that in Matthew 9, the passage starts with the healing and forgiveness of a paralytic, call to sinners via Matthew's conversion, then moves into healing ministry and ends with a call to labourers for the harvest. Jesus sees that the people are hungry for God's touch and work in their lives. In chapter 10 he sends out the twelve, almost as if in response to what He has seen in chapter 9.

Matthew 15:21–28 records an interesting story of Jesus and the Canaanite woman. At first, He treats her rudely and tells her she doesn't deserve that which was meant for the Jews. Her quick response said that even dogs got table scraps—and her faith was rewarded. Again, Jesus commends a Gentile for having great faith!

The court of the Gentiles was to be used by the Gentiles in their worship. The Jews were to pray for them, that they too would be brought into God's kingdom. But in Matthew 21:12, Jesus found that animals sold for sacrifice were there, and the place of worship was desecrated for commercial purposes! No wonder He was upset! He responded by stating that the temple was to be a house of prayer for all nations (21:13) quoting Isaiah 56:7, and that the Jews had made it into a "den of robbers" (Jer. 7:11). (For other gospel references, see earlier discussion.)

In the final chapters of Matthew, Jesus includes a call to the Gentiles in 21:33–43 and 22:1–14. Those who did not treat the landlord's son correctly were subsequently punished. They were also replaced, and the vineyard was rented out to other tenants. The wedding banquet was the same; those who were chosen did not want to come, so they were punished, and others invited. The curse on the fig tree (21:18, 19) was a foreshadowing (Richardson 1981, p. 185) of God's wrath on Israel for not being a light to the world. Since the Jews had not done as God asked, then it would be to the Gentiles to take a turn in obedience to God (Richardson 1981, p. 186). The Jews had an invitation, but it is not limited to them alone.

Matthew closes with the Great Commission: go to all nations and make disciples. Christ has the authority from God to send the disciples out to accomplish His purpose. He promises that He would not only send but also go with them to enable them to accomplish this incredible spiritual task. In Romans 14:9, Paul asserts that Jesus is the Lord of the dead and the living. There is no higher authority than this. This fact means that nothing could stop Him from accomplishing His purpose in them. He can open and shut the doors (Rev. 3:7) that no one else can. God calls and takes the responsibility for His obedient servants. He provides what they need in the process of carrying out His orders. In the Great Commission, Christ has told us to make disciples; this is being made into His image (2 Cor. 3:18, 1 John 3:2). Christ has told us to follow Him, and He called the original disciples—Simon, Andrew, James, John, Matthew, Philip, Peter, and the others (Matt. 4:19, 21, 9:9, 16:24, 19:21; Mark 1:17, 20, 2:14, 8:34, 10:21; Luke 5:27, 9:23, 18:22; John 1:43, 12:26).

One of Richardson's tenets is that Jesus meant to change the disciples' minds from ethnocentrism. This was certainly unsuccessful in the case of Judas, who felt betrayed by his master's strange behaviour and sold Him to the Jews (Matt. 27:5 cf. Acts 1:18), committing suicide in remorse.

Mark sees Christ as God's servant with the summary of his life's work in Mark 10:45—Christ's purpose was ministry to others. He was to give His life as a ransom for many (Mark 10:45). There are a lot of references to the urgency of what was happening. Mark does not spend time in discussion; action is always present in the story he is telling. This writer talks about Jesus's desire to go into other towns (1:38). He quotes the passage from the Psalms in 11:17: "A house of prayer for all nations." Many of the passages in Mark are similar to that found in Matthew, except that Matthew's version is more expanded. Even in the short book of Mark, there is considerable attention given to the passion of Christ in the last week of His life. The Last Supper, Jesus's agony in Gethsemane as well as His arrest and trial are all given a good deal of attention. Mark closes with the commission to preach the gospel to every creature in 16:15–20. His focus there is on belief and baptism, although he also has an emphasis on the signs which is not included in the other gospels.

After his view on the nativity, it is the compassionate doctor *Luke* who not only sees the sin of mankind (and therefore points out the priesthood necessary for salvation) but also the saviourhood of Christ. The history of God's work properly begins with Adam and back at the beginning of creation; God is working to save His creation, mankind (Luke 3:23–37). He begins his next section with the startling statement that "Today this scripture is fulfilled in your hearing" (Isa. 61 passage of God's redemption coming to the sick, the imprisoned, and the broken-hearted) and concludes with a warning that God goes to the receptive and that will be the Gentiles (4:17–28)! Jesus follows this one with another missionary line, saying that the widow in Sidon was the one who received help in the famine of Elisha's day, not the surrounding Jews. Then there was Naaman the Syrian, who, although an enemy, was healed of his leprosy through the witness of a *captive* Jewish girl. At this His listeners were furious and made to kill Him, but He went out unharmed.

From there periodic comments are made about ministry to Gentiles and sinners (as in Matthew and Mark in chapters 5–10).

EXPLORING THE ROOTS OF MISSIONS: PERSONAL, BIBLICAL, AND SPIRITUAL

Although His disciples wanted Him to destroy a Samaritan village (Luke 9:51–56) because it did not welcome Him, Jesus rebuked them and went on. He didn't assume the Samaritans should be destroyed because they were non-Jews. Shortly after that He sends out the seventy-two to preach and teach. Early in chapter 10 Jesus makes the startling declaration that certain cities in Israel (namely Korazin, Bethsaida, and Capernaum) were not as open to the gospel as the ancient cities of Tyre, Sidon, and Sodom would have been! These were Gentile cities, and the ancient condemnation of them in prophecy was well known. Yet the modern cities saw miracles that the ancient ones had not and remained hard. Then Luke repeats the warning closer to home: the parable of the Good Samaritan in 10:30–37. Not even the Jews could miss the idea that a *Samaritan* was capable of doing good, better than a priest or a Levite! The parable of the narrow gate summarizes the series of kingdom parables (13:23–30). The focus on the lost is repeated again in chapter 15: the lost sheep, the lost coin, and the lost son. God's concern is being expressed and emphasized.

Luke caps his book off with a command to preach to all nations (24:46–49). The content of Luke's commission is the death and resurrection of Christ. This is to be carried by the witnesses to the nations about them. The promise of the Father and the Holy Spirit are present.

John is full of how God relates to the world (cosmos). He is benevolent in His contact with the world showing bountiful love. It is the Holy Sprit that draws the nations to Christ (12:32). The world is on His heart and purpose. The redemption of mankind here is both personal and universal.

> Time and eternity, heaven and earth, are spanned in Christ, and God and men become reconciled. (Peters 1972, p. 39)

The gospel of John is full of references to believing, sending (or sent), the unique words of Jesus and the work of the Holy Spirit. They are mentioned more here than anywhere else in the gospels.

Jesus tells Nicodemus he must be born again (3:3–7). He speaks to the Samaritan woman in chapter 4 reaching out beyond the Jews to others who ask. She was both Samaritan and sinful, but that didn't bother Jesus. Jesus never turned away anyone who asked of Him. He mentions Himself as the bread of life and the living water (6:28ff and 7:32ff). He declares Himself as the light of the world (8:12). Jesus inflamed His listeners by saying that that Abraham saw Jesus's day and was glad. He even went further and proclaimed Himself "I Am" and was nearly stoned in response (John 8:56–58). In the good shepherd passage, He says there are other sheep that He must go to (10:16). In 12:20–22, the disciples bring some Greeks to see Jesus. This causes Jesus to break forth in a praise-prophecy that His hour was soon come. In John 15–16, He tells of the work and ministry of the Holy Spirit. This is key to the success of missions, the conviction of the Holy Spirit. Finally, in the high priestly prayer, He includes prayer for those who will come to belief—us (John 17:2–20). This is definitely a missionary prayer. Again the gospel closes with the phrase "so send I you" (John 20:21–23). The forgiveness of sins is key in this gospel as well as the Holy Spirit. The church's obedience to God is in preaching the gospel—the news that Christ has come and reconciled man to God. Forgiveness is a part of that reconciliation.

Jesus was crucified on what appears to be the ancient Mount Moriah, where Abraham nearly sacrificed Isaac in obedience. The angel interceded at the last minute, and the ram took Isaac's place. Here there was no intercession by an angel, although they were standing by. The Lamb Himself died on the cross as an intercessor for the guilty sinners.

Acts of the Apostles

The gospels show the steep learning curve of the disciples while the epistles and Acts are a record of what they did and wrote. Beyond Acts, we do not have any firm accounts, although tradition says that many of them died as martyrs. Acts is a historical record, with the epistles written afterward to the churches established during that period. The tradition of the apostles is that of missions itself. Romans

10:14–15 were Paul's questions for the necessity of missions. The book of Acts takes the horizontal aspect of the believers reaching other people for the gospel, and the epistles that followed were focusing on the vertical aspect. Every church in that time was surrounded by multitudes who did not know Christ (Phil. 2:12–16). The believers were commended by Paul for their evangelization and witness (Rom. 1:8, 1 Thess. 1:8). The Philippians were also active in ministry (4:10, 2:5). Paul encourages them to follow his example (1 Cor. 11:1, 4:16; Phil. 3:17; 1 Thess. 1:6; 2 Thess. 3:6–7). His goal was missions itself (1 Cor. 1:17, 9:16–18). Paul argues eloquently for the need of missionaries (sent ones) in Romans 10:12–18, Ephesians 3:1–12, 1 Corinthians 9:16–18, Philippians 2:14–16, 1 Timothy 2:1–7, 2 Corinthians 5:19–21, and Romans 1:13–17.

In the book of Acts, missions really begins to take off with the *coming of the Holy Spirit*. The power of the church is given to the one hundred and twenty gathered in the upper room. The gospel spreads like fire, and many come to the Lord. Acts is a book of believers; there are at least eleven references to "believers," more than anywhere else in the New Testament. This makes it, by definition, a book of action by the believers. The directive is given to them in Acts 1:8 (NIV), "But you will receive power when the Holy Spirit comes upon you and you will be my witnesses in Jerusalem, and in all Judea and Samaria, and to the ends of the earth." This will be our guideline in looking at the work of missions in the book of Acts.

Power of the Spirit: One thing we notice first about this verse is that Jesus tells them to wait for His power before they begin to witness. It was the coming of the Holy Spirit that changed the weak disciples into men of power. They were no longer afraid to proclaim that Jesus had risen and given them His command. The power of the Holy Spirit is what makes missions possible. It is His voice that convicts the sinners of sin, righteousness, and judgement. He is the one who leads the apostles, the early believers, and us in this present day and age to go to those who have been prepared to hear the gospel. There is a good deal of teaching on the work and role of the Holy Spirit in John 15–16. Without Him, the gospel is empty words falling on deaf ears. The Holy Spirit leads both the speaker and the listener and opens hard hearts to the truth. Since Christ could not be everywhere Himself because He had a physical body, He sent the Holy Spirit to be omnipresent and effectively carry out and thus multiply His work among the believers by indwelling each and every one.

The motivation of the apostles has been the key to understanding what they did. The redemption by Christ was made possible by His death and resurrection. It was God's purpose and plan long ago that such work was for the benefit of mankind (Acts 2:23, 4:28 cf. 1 Pet. 1:20). Contrary to what many liberal theologians have proposed, Christ's death was not a surprise or a horrible accident that ended His life while young. It did not frustrate God's plan but rather accomplished it. God acted in Christ to save people and bring them back into fellowship with himself (2 Cor. 5:19, 1 John 5:12). Salvation is for those who called on God (Acts 2:39, 3:18–19; 1 John 2:2, 4:14). Those who call on God must repent and believe in Him (Acts 2:38, 17:30). Obedience to God was not optional; it was an occupation (Acts 4:19). The Holy Spirit gave them courage to obey God in spite of consequences from their enemies. Peter stood up and defended his actions based on the power of Christ (Acts 4:8–12). The Holy Spirit gave them power to endure and continue (Acts 4:31).

Jerusalem: It was God's desire that the gospel be first preached in Jerusalem, where Jesus had been condemned to die. Jerusalem had killed many prophets, but now it was her turn to hear first of the gospel of salvation (Luke 13:34 cf. 24:27). The gospel would be preached in Jerusalem first. God still had Jerusalem in His plan, the gospel to the people there (stiff-necked and hard-hearted as in the past) first. This is where the Holy Spirit comes upon them as fire and gives the gift of tongues so that all of the different races in Jerusalem were able to hear the gospel in their own tongue (Acts 1:8–11).

There were several reasons for beginning in Jerusalem. Jerusalem was the centre of trade and religious gatherings. Religious pilgrims came from all over the world to worship in Jerusalem. In 2:9–11, there are people present from most of the then modern world. From Mesopotamia to Asia Minor, Egypt and Libya (North Africa), from Rome to Crete, and Arabia (from area east of the Red Sea and Euphrates)—all are included in the list of peoples present from other countries and that of the Diaspora. This covered a good deal of the area around the Mediterranean spreading west to Rome and Libya, east to ancient Persia (modern Iran), north to the Black Sea, and south to Egypt. All these places were represented by someone in Jerusalem. Thus, reaching anyone in Jerusalem would be an automatic bridge to these other places. Eventually the gospel would travel along these routes to the birthplace of the visitors. It is much the same today. By beginning in Jerusalem, not only would the gospel reach the Jews, both native and that of the Diaspora, it would also reach people of other races where the Diaspora were located.

The apostles had their centre in this city as Jerusalem was the hometown of the Jews. This was the place they knew best. This was where Jesus had preached, suffered, and rose again; it was the first witness to who He was. They knew the culture and background of their city the best. They knew the problems and open hearts. The apostles often started in the temple since that was where the people were used to hearing religious teaching. Paul also began much of his ministry in the temple until he faced too much resistance from the Jews. Open doors were a good place to start the ministry. The first seven chapters of Acts show how the apostles reached Jerusalem. In chapter 2, Peter stood up at Pentecost and addressed the audience who wondered about the ability of the Galileans to speak so many languages fluently. In his sermon, he stated it as the fulfillment of prophecy (2:16–21, 25–28, 34–36) and called them to the truth in repentance and belief in Jesus (2:36–39). In the latter part of the chapter, they teach, have communion, and have prayer (2:42–47). This is a description of early church life: building of the body combined with evangelism.

In chapter 3, Peter and John heal a man as they are going to the temple. This man was lame from birth and could not walk. The apostles had no gold to give him but instead gave him the healing of Jesus. They had a request, and they responded to this opportunity. The commotion caused a crowd to gather. Peter's response again was to preach to them and explain Who had really healed this man. He did not take the credit but pointed to Christ. Again, he gave a call to repentance and belief in Jesus Christ. This caused a stir among the religious leadership, and they became upset by content of the sermon (4:1–7). They questioned the apostles' authority to do this and again received a sermon. They gave the apostles a warning and let them go. The believer's response was to pray for more strength and boldness in witness (4:31). Again, the power of God came upon them, and they testified all the more. The fellowship of the believers assured all of having their needs met. Peter was able to answer all of the questions of the curious who wanted to know what was going on and why. Every time he was questioned (or perceived that there was one in the minds of his hearers), he gave answer. He even includes this in his epistle: always be ready to give an answer for the hope that lies within you (1 Pet. 3:15).

This sharing community was ideal until early in chapter 5. Two believers named Ananias and Sapphira devised a plan to raise their respect in the eyes of the other believers in the fellowship. They sold their land as the others had done but kept back part of the price (5:1, 2). When they brought it to the apostles, they declared that as the full price. Peter rebuked them for lying to the Holy Spirit, and they died in judgement (5:5–10). The power of the Holy Spirit filled Peter, and he was able to detect the lie. Lying to God was a severe offence, and the guilty died as a result. The people became fearful, and the apostles performed many miracles and wonders. More were added to the church. The sick were healed, and demons were cast out (5:11–16). Again, the religious Jewish leadership were aroused with jealousy and put the apostles in jail. An angel of the Lord opened the doors during the night, and morning found them teaching in the temple courts again. Meanwhile the jailers and religious leaders could not find them until a report was brought from outside. Warned not to teach in Jesus's name, the apostles replied in 5:29, "We must obey God rather than men…we are witnesses of these things and so is the Holy Spirit." The apostles boldly declared the truth about who Jesus was and why He had died. The Sanhedrin did not want to admit their guilt in His death. The Holy Spirit also was called a witness. This is His role in the life of the church. He is frequently mentioned in the book of Acts because it is His work being done in the spreading of the church. The apostles were close to receiving a death sentence when a Pharisee named Gamaliel stood up and intervened. Gamaliel had strong insight; the church did flourish because it was the work of God. The apostles were flogged and released after another warning. Their response was to rejoice because they were counted worthy to suffer for Jesus (5:41). The growth of the church was because it was God's work. Jesus had said to Peter in the gospels, "I will build my church and the gates of hell will not stand against it." The opposition may be great, but it is God who makes the church grow as it says in 1 Corinthians 3. The disciples counted the suffering as a sign they were counted worthy of the cause of Christ.

A crisis occurred in chapter 6—the widows were being overlooked. So deacons were set up to administer to their needs; these men were particularly chosen because they were full of the Holy Spirit and wisdom (6:3–6). The ministry of the Holy Spirit is not limited to that of preaching the gospel but also extends to caring for physical needs. The number of disciples in Jerusalem increased greatly. In chapter 7, the tension between the Jews and their new opponents, the believers, comes to a head in a significant way. Stephen's preaching and work attracts great attention and the wrath of those in the synagogue. Being unable to put him in his place (he answered them with the wisdom of the Holy Spirit), they stirred up the people and brought him before the synagogue. The truth will always have an effect, whether in conversions or opposition. Stephen's defence was so powerful that the anger of the Sanhedrin broke out against him, and they stoned him for his words. They could not stand the truth, so they killed him to silence it. The church had its first martyr for Christ.

The persecution that started in Acts 8 scattered the Christians from Jerusalem. The intent was, of course, to stamp out the new heresy, for so the Jews thought it was. Instead it only grew. This is the record of history, where God's truth outshines the evil that attempts to smash it. Jesus said to Peter, "Upon this rock I will build my church and the gates of hell will not prevail against it" (Matt.16:18). So it has proved true over the centuries, in many countries and places where Christ has been named Lord by the faithful few. The enemy has attacked the church persistently, but the church, despite the odds, has flourished. Saul's hatred of the church of Jesus had grown from Stephen's martyrdom in chapter 7 where he was a witness. In chapter 9, he is continuing a full-scale vendetta against the church taking in prisoners to Jerusalem. But God stops him in his tracks on the way to Damascus. Now a blind man, he is led to the city where he awaits God's leading. God sends Ananias, a reluctant but obedient believer, and he prays for Saul's healing. He does, and Saul not only receives his sight again but is baptized too. Saul becomes a great evangelist for God. He began preaching in Damascus; when the Jews tried to kill him, he was sent away to Tarsus. After this, the wave of persecution stops, and the church enjoys peace in Judea, Galilee, and Samaria (9:31).

Jerusalem/Judea, Samaria/ends of the earth

Judea and Samaria: The persecution spreads, and many of the believers are scattered throughout Judea. Those who had been scattered began to preach throughout Judea. The apostles break cultural barriers and long-term prejudices by going to Samaria (8:5–25). Samaria had been a place most Jews avoided because they were a branch off true Judaism. The Samaritans were descendants of Jews who had intermarried foreigners. They did not believe all of the Old Testament books as the Jews did, only the first five. There was historical and racial dislike between the two cultures. There, the people who believed received the Holy Spirit. Philip continues on with his ministry in southern Judea by the directive of the Holy Spirit and ends up talking to an Ethiopian (8:27ff). It seemed that here the breakthrough to the other nations would begin in full force at last.

Peter also was busy, performing miracles of healing and even a resurrection (9:36–42). In chapter 10, God tells him to do something new: to go with a Gentile God-fearer. God had called the Gentiles into His kingdom too (10:15, 19, 20). Peter got the message through a vision of clean and unclean animals. That vision shook Peter. He was used to thinking he was one of God's chosen people. But God came to him while he was praying, and Peter believed what God told him. The God-fearer was Cornelius, and Peter began a new thing when he evangelized the Gentiles of Cornelius's household. He spoke to them, and the Holy Spirit came upon them with the gift of tongues (10:44–45). Called to account for his behaviour in chapter 11, Peter explained the whole story to the circumcised Jews and received their blessing for further ministry (11:19). He confirmed that the Gentiles can repent and receive eternal life. To us Gentiles, this is not news. We are enjoying the fruit of God's goodness to us in salvation. But to the Jews, this was an earthshaking idea; even the apostles who sat under Jesus hadn't quite got the idea of who can be saved. The Christians who had been scattered by the persecution were busy preaching, but only to the Jews (Acts 11:19). Finally, some started speaking to the Greeks, and they heard God's word of salvation.

Barriers: God broke some old spiritual and cultural barriers between the Jews and the Gentiles. God had called the Jews out of the world to make a special example of them for Himself. Now He was calling them to go back among them to spread the gospel. This involved actually accepting them into the church and talking and eating with them. The three closest apostles to Jesus appeared to accept this idea along with Saul (now called Paul) in Galatians 2:6–9. The Gentiles could have their own churches and not have to convert to Judaism to be saved. They were a part of the family of God and the earthly fellowship too. This must have been very difficult for Peter. He was used to being apart from the Gentiles. (In fact, he did slip into his old ways according to Paul's account in Galatians 2:11–14. He was afraid of what the other Jews would say about him, and so he ate with the Jews instead.) Paul called him to account, and Peter realized his error.

And to the ends of the earth: Those who had been scattered abroad by the persecution also shared the gospel with the Gentiles in Antioch. Barnabas came to check this out, sent by the church in Jerusalem. After he encouraged the believers, he went and brought Saul from Tarsus. Together they taught the church for one year. This was where the disciples were first called Christians. In chapter 12, the persecution begins again, with James dying at the hands of Herod. Peter was arrested too and imprisoned until the Passover. The church prayed for his release, and much to their surprise, he was! An angel appeared to him in his cell and told Peter to follow him. Peter walked out free and told the church he was safe (12:11, 17). Herod received judgement and died.

The first official international workers were sent out by the Antioch church: Barnabas and Saul. During worship and prayer, God had told them to set aside these men for their work. In Cyprus, they met their first opposition through a sorcerer named Elymas. Paul, according to the knowledge of the Holy Spirit, confronted his deceiving ways and rebuked him with blindness. At the next stop, Paul begins in the synagogue and explains to them the way of God (13:16ff). But the Jews became jealous, and they expelled the apostles from the city.

Worship: It was during a time of worship that the Holy Spirit made known that Paul and Barnabas were to evangelize elsewhere. They were commissioned and sent off with prayer. Evangelizing—whether E1, E2, or E3—needs to be done through and with prayer for guidance, wisdom, and strength. This was why Paul was able to spot the deception of Elymas and confront him right away. He was filled with the Spirit and called Elymas to account for his lies. The best way to stop a lie is to oppose it with the truth.

In chapter 14, the apostles begin their ministry the same way, starting in the synagogue. Jealous Jews again stirred up the people, both Jews and Gentiles, and forced the apostles to flee. In Lystra, a lame man was healed and caused much commotion among the pagans. The apostles were called gods (Zeus and Hermes), and Paul had to set them straight with a sermon. Troublemaking Jews from elsewhere persuaded the crowd to riot, and they stoned Paul. He left the next day and went to other places, strengthening the churches, appointing elders for leadership with prayer and fasting. On their return to Antioch, they reported all that God had done.

Pre-evangelism is the educating of the hearers to understand the gospel correctly. The people in Lystra interpreted what they saw in light of what they knew from their own religion: that of the Roman gods. In order for them to believe the truth, Paul had to tell them foundational truths of Christianity. God had revealed Himself in creation, and this they knew. He attributed the correct source of their life and directed them to God for worship, not Zeus and Hermes. They had to look to Jesus Christ.

Leadership: The leadership of these new churches founded by the believers was not left to chance. They were appointed, as Paul and Barnabas had been, through a time of prayer and fasting. They strengthened the disciples and encouraged them to remain true. The new elders were to care for the church. Making sure there is appropriate leadership is very important in the setting up of local churches.

Chapter 15 contains a major theological crisis for the church. The Jewish believers insisted that the Gentiles had to obey certain laws and rules of the Jewish faith. Paul and Barnabas sharply disagreed, and in the ensuing debate, Peter (who finally came round to the truth) addressed the crowd and declared that they should not burden the new believers with all kinds of laws that the Jews themselves found difficult to keep. Salvation was by grace, not works. Paul and Barnabas also testified to their experiences with the Gentiles being converted. They made some suggestions for the keeping of the law and left it at that. The delegation agreed and sent a letter out to inform others of this decision. The apostles stayed in Jerusalem for some twenty years, and then Paul was called to the Gentiles because he could easily bridge the gap between the two cultures; he was a Roman citizen and a Jew, having studied under Gamaliel, a Pharisee by training. But he also spoke Latin and Greek in addition to Aramaic. He was well-equipped for the task to which God had called him.

Many of the themes in Paul's work refer to his background indirectly and the divisions between the Gentiles and the Jews. Paul declared in his book to the Corinthians that Christ was the foundation (1 Cor. 3:11). As the human race originated in Adam (Rom. 5:12–21), so when Adam fell, so did mankind. Thus, they were all guilty before God (Rom. 1:18–21). Christ represented man substitutionally and justified him by faith (Rom. 3:21–25). When a believing person called upon God, faith came by revelation (Rom. 10:8–17 cf. 16:25–26). Paul's personal call by Christ was an apostleship (Rom. 1:1, 5, 14; 11:13, 25; 15:15–16, 18–23; 16:25–27). According to Paul, all were equal sinners before God (Eph. 2:1–3) and needed salvation from His wrath (Rom. 1:18–3:20). Both Jews and Gentiles were justified on equal terms (Eph. 2:11–3:12) with equal status and privileges (Eph. 3:6, Rom. 8:17). Paul believed in no divisions according to Jews and Gentiles (Eph. 1:23). They were all of the body of Christ, and His family (Eph. 2:19, 3:15) as well as His temple (Eph. 2:21–22). Paul loved the Jews, even although they rejected him. He argued eloquently for the universality of salvation, not only in the first three chapters in Romans but also later on in chapters 9–11. Although the people of Israel had rejected Jesus, they were only temporarily put aside (Rom. 11:25). God had the right and authority to do so. Abraham was a Gentile but was justified by God because of his faith. Paul declares that the people of Israel had hard hearts so that the Gentiles could be invited (Rom. 11:25). Paul is a representative to the nations (Acts 26:15–18; Rom. 1:14, 11:13, 15:16; 1 Cor. 9:22; Gal. 1:16, 2:8–9; Eph. 3:1, 4–8; 1 Tim. 2:7; 2 Tim. 1:11). Paul affirms that the Gentiles have a right to salvation because of God's grace to them (Rom. 9:6–8). It is in the discourse about the Jews' rejection of the gospel that Paul records the great verses of Scripture:

> That if you confess with your mouth "Jesus is Lord" and you believe in your heart that God raised him from the dead you will be saved… How then can they call on the one they have not believed in? And how can they believe in the one of whom they have not heard? And how can they hear without someone preaching to them? And how can they preach unless they are sent?… How beautiful are the feet of those who bring good news. (Rom. 10:9–15 NIV)

These verses sum up Paul's theology of missions: to preach to those who have not heard. He wanted to go where no one had gone to preach the gospel (Rom. 15:20).

Richardson in *Eternity in Their Hearts* goes into great detail about the Abrahamic covenant. This covenant was God binding

Himself to bless Abraham so that he in turn would bless all the peoples of the earth. Paul refers to this blessing in Galatians 3:8, 9, 14, 16, 19, and 29. Peter too referred to this promise via Moses (Acts 3:22–26). The mystery of the gospel of the Gentiles being co-heirs with Israel was revealed at last through Paul (Eph. 3:3–6). Paul in particular was to carry out his part in preaching to the Gentiles (Eph. 3:7–11) with his unique background (Roman citizen, with languages of Aramaic, Greek, and Latin). God's special purpose in history will be consummated in heaven when all the nations are praising Him around the throne (Rev. 7:9, 10:11, 14:6).

Cultural adaptation: The major points of Christian life and witness are included in this area: eating of forbidden items (blood, meat of strangled animals, and meat offered to idols) and that of sexual immorality. This was so that the Jewish believers wouldn't be offended by the new liberalism of the Gentile Christians, especially when they ate. The low moral customs were very common among the unbelievers and often were a part of their worship. The concept of cultural adaptation and contextualization was a part of the ministry of the early church. They needed discernment to decide what was important enough to keep and what they could discard in the church.

A disagreement on who to bring along arises in this part of the narrative. Barnabas wanted Mark, but Paul would have none of it because he had deserted them on the previous trip. Paul left with Silas instead, and it was Barnabas who took John Mark under his wing. They both left with the grace of God. As they travel, Paul spreads the word about the decision in Jerusalem. The Holy Spirit directs them to travel, not into Asia, where they want to go, but to Europe. A vision calls Paul to Macedonia (16:9), and they go in obedience. In Philippi, they get into trouble for freeing a demonized girl and end up in jail. As they sing praise to God, an earthquake frees them. The jailer and his household are saved in response to this emergency. In chapter 17, they come to a city full of idols, Athens, and Paul preaches his sermon on Areopagus. He does it in philosophical style: the style of the Greeks. Paul adapted to meet the cultural situation. In chapter 18, he gets frustrated with the Jews' obstinacy and goes to the Gentiles who are more willing and ready to listen (18:6). Paul continued to do God's work even when others tried to imitate him out of spite.

Obedience to the Holy Spirit is important even when it doesn't make sense. Paul entered Europe instead of Asia because of the leading of the Holy Spirit. The Holy Spirit knew there was a need in Macedonia, and Paul was in the right frame of mind and heart to accept his vision and call to help those who were spiritually hungry. He established a strong church in Philippi as a result. It was to the Philippian church that Paul writes his letter of joy. The other letters contain some rebuke or correction, but the letter to the Philippians does not. Paul also established churches in Thessalonica and Berea, although not without some difficulty.

Power encounter: There are two accounts of demonic activity with very different results:

1. The spirit in the Philippian girl was telling the truth, but she was not doing it of her own free will. The truth sets us free. This girl was not free even though she spoke the truth because she was doing it with the wrong purpose. And so Paul spoke the words of Jesus and set her free. When we encounter truth from a demonic source, we had better be careful, because the devil lies, and he likes to mix the truth with the lie. We have the authority to tell Satan to get lost when he starts interfering with our ministries. Satan has no business dealing with us. He has been defeated at the cross.
2. In 19:13–16, some Jews (the sons of Sceva) try to cast spirits out by Jesus's name without personal belief in Him. The spirit in one man recognized their lack of connection with God's power and beat them. They had no protection by Jesus's blood and suffered as a result. Don't fool around with evil spirits; they will try to harm you. (This will be dealt with in more detail in the chapter on spiritual warfare.)

Open doors: Paul saw that the Jewish hearts on the whole were very closed to the gospel. So he went to where the people were more receptive—to the Gentiles. Today there are more Gentile believers than there are Jews. It is important to minister in all places, both open and closed. Sometimes a closed door is evidence that God is opening another one elsewhere. Paul saw this, and God blessed his ministry greatly. Be sensitive to what a closed door means. This includes Paul's witness to the jailer who had imprisoned him. Paul was willing to minister even to his enemies.

Wherever Paul went, things seemed to happen, from citywide riots in Ephesus to raising of the dead (19:23–20:7–11). He was determined to go to Jerusalem, for God had laid that on his heart despite the dangerous consequences (20:22–23). In Jerusalem, the trouble came as was prophesied from the Jews (20:11). Paul was captured and was able to make several defence speeches on his own behalf, giving his testimony to the Sanhedrin (23:1ff), the Romans (24:1ff, 25:1ff, 26:1ff) including the King Agrippa who was the ruler under Rome over Palestine. He was sent to Rome for Caesar's judgement but was shipwrecked before he arrived.

Obedience: Paul went to Rome as he desired but as a prisoner. He obeyed God's leading even though it meant imprisonment and death for him. His prison stay led to his writing of letters to the churches.

Some further observations that we can apply today from the Scriptures.

Cities: This is the method that Paul used, going to the centres of trade and influence and reaching out from there to the regions beyond. He knew that the cities were important centres where the people gathered for commerce and worship. Many of the Western international workers went to the countryside to do ministry in isolated areas in the past. This limited their reach to the people of that area because only a few could be reached at any one time. Paul started out with cities, and this enabled him to reach more people at once. This is a focus that has been revived again recently in modern missions. Urban missions is fast becoming the focus in today's world. The Christian and Missionary Alliance moved to this focus in the late '80s. There are IWs stationed in Bangkok, Hong Kong, Abidjan, Yamoussoukro, and Lima, for example. These are large centres that are growing very quickly every day. Large numbers flock to the city looking for employment, security, and better opportunities. There are at least twenty-six different languages represented in Los Angeles. Eighty thousand people move into Mexico City every month—over half of these are by birth; the rest is migration (Bakke 1984, p. 73). This then is a key concept in reaching the lost, starting in the cities.

One aspect of the people flocking to the cities is that there will always be some connections elsewhere. The people in the cities often send money back home and will return there for visits. This means that someone reached with the gospel in the city can also bring the gospel back home with them. The kinship network is something that helped spread the gospel to the outer edges of the Roman Empire as people travelled. The same principle applies today. An organization called Global Mapping International has a map of the 10/40 Window that emphasizes prayer for the major towns and cities (Gateway Cities and Strategic Towns). This was following the practise of Paul (1 Thess. 1:8). Once a household was reached, it often meant reaching out to others through that network such as what happened to the Philippian jailer (Acts 16:23ff). The New Testament idea of household carried with it far more than just the nuclear family. It often meant all those attached to the house as well as the dwelling itself (1 Cor. 16:15; Gal. 6:10; Eph. 2:19; 1 Tim. 3:4, 5, 12; 2 Tim. 1:16, 4:19; Titus 1:11; 1 Pet. 2:5, 4:17). Thus, it included the extended family and the servants as well. Once the father came to Christ, then the whole family was involved in believing in Jesus. When cross-cultural missions work is involved, there are some groups more receptive to the gospel, as a group mentality is more prevalent. In working with Japanese, evangelism aimed at the group is very effective. This is a similar idea to people movements (Jones, p. 10–11). The key thing when reaching a people through kinship networks in a city whether through a household situation or house church is the support of the group and community.

The apostles had a firsthand knowledge of the history of the city of Jerusalem. It was a part of who they were. Getting to know the history, cultural and political background is important for reaching the lost. Cities contain ghettos of ethnic groups. The history of a place can be a clue as to how to best reach the city. If it is religious, then that is the place to begin, with links to the other religions. Paul did this in Acts 17; he called them religious even though they worshipped gods made of wood and stone. Athens had a long history of worshipping many gods, and Paul knew this. He deliberately made a connection to this kind of history.

Opposition never kills the truth. It just seems to be like oil poured on fire—it burns all the harder. In the first century, many were martyred for Christ in the arenas such as Polycarp and Perpetua. Those watching were so impressed by the way the early Christians died that they too became Christians against all odds. In 1956, five international workers went to an unevangelized tribe of Indians in the jungles of South America. They were martyred, and as a result, many in North America made decisions to go overseas and spread the gospel. In the early nineteenth century, so many IWs died in Africa of disease that it was called "the white man's grave." And finally, in China, the church has undergone great persecution under Communist rule. But the church has prospered, and today there are over thirty to fifty million churches (estimated) in China.

Our *Samaritans*: What are our Samaritans? The people that we don't care to reach. In Canada we have two main groups: the Indians (First Nations) and the French (Quebecois). There is no love lost between these groups and Anglo-Canadians. There is a history of disagreement, cultural indifference, and injustice. It is difficult to plant a church among these groups. (Part of this is because the idea of the people movement and kinship community connection has been ignored. This meant that those who did come to Christ were left alone and without the support they so badly needed. It did not make for many longsuffering disciples.) In America, the Samaritans would be the blacks (African Americans), the descendants of former slaves. It is hard to break down the cultural and historical barriers between the white and the black because racism is still such a prevalent attitude, especially in the South where the history of slavery on plantations presided. There are many other groups, many of them in what are now called the "unreached segments" of population that many missions don't think about reaching. They are not merely cultural tribes tucked away in the Indonesian valleys. The differences were defined by language barriers, even those people groups living in the same area but speaking different languages. Similar groups living in different cultures are also defined as different. For example, the Jews living in America have a different language as well as culture than the Jews of Russia. Only fifty people groups make up 50 percent of the world's population (Joshua Project), so it stands to reason some of these groupings might be different than the norm. These also include ethnographical groups that have been traditionally ignored. (A former name for them was "hidden peoples.") Parks and Tada in the Lausanne Occasional Paper also separate the different castes in India, even those in the same area, for they are forbidden by their culture from mingling. Included in the unreached are those who have less than 2 percent evangelical witness and are unable to evangelize their own people without any cross-cultural assistance. The hidden groups are often in cities and overshadowed by a group with a larger population. Most of them are not known outside their region.

What cultural *barriers* will you have to cross in order to be a good IW? When I was in Thailand, one of the hardest things to learn was the foot rule. In Thai culture, the head is the holy part of the body while the feet are unclean. This means you cannot even step over someone lying down. You must always go around them. It also means that you cannot sit with your legs crossed because your foot will point at someone and offend them. One time at English camp, someone lost their thongs (also known as flip-flops). So another one of the English volunteers held up the thongs and said, "Who lost their shoe?" The children really started to freak out. The volunteer didn't know why until a Thai teacher reminded her. She was holding the shoe in the air over the heads of the children! To us it was no big deal. But to them it is very important. It's important to try and break the barriers across the cultures, whether it means to follow their rules or to do something new. Sitting on the floor all the time can be hard for a Westerner who is used to sitting on chairs. But being flexible means following the cultural norms as much as possible.

Pre-evangelism: This is a common difficulty for IWs working in non-Christian cultures. There is no basic understanding of the words

God, *salvation*, *righteousness*, *sin*, and *truth* in some cultures, and thus no way to correctly interpret what is seen and heard. Cannibals need to be taught it is wrong to eat people. A sense of sin must be brought to cultures with different morals. One of the problems in India is that of castes. Society is divided up into different levels, and if you are born into a low caste, there you stay. You deserve to be there; you cannot move higher up in society. There was no help for the poor; many die in poverty. There is also the concept of reincarnation—belief that you are born many times, because you were not good enough—as an animal or a human. Finally, the idea of *karma* is also very prevalent. This means that your old sin comes back to you because you are not good enough and you must suffer as a result. Getting rid of suffering meant getting rid of desires. The true cause of suffering is sin, whether personal or from the Fall. We are born only once. And it is only Jesus's blood that saves us. Teaching the truth to a culture steeped in these ideas is difficult. It takes a long time to let the word of God change the hearts and thus the customs of societies with traditions that did not honour God.

Teachings in the Epistles

The epistles fill in the gaps of the account of Acts. They tell the story of behind the scenes of the church: what Paul thought, taught, and dealt with in each church in more detail. They dealt with different problems in the churches that they were experiencing. Paul had, in effect, written the first how-to manual in cross-cultural ministry in his letters to the churches. The epistles deal with Paul's theology as was relevant to each different church situation. Some were to churches, some to individuals like Timothy, Titus, and Philemon. There are also several epistles written by other apostles—Peter, James, the author of the book of Hebrews (possibly Barnabas), Jude, Jesus's brother, and the epistles of John. Revelation is Apostle John's record of what God revealed to him about the end times.

Early Church

The *church* is the body of believers called together in the name of Christ to worship God, to minister to each other in fellowship and to the world in service. The church is God's chosen instrument to do His work in the world. God chooses to work in individuals in mighty ways to accomplish much for His purpose of redemption. But He has also chosen to put individuals together in a group called the church to also do His mighty work in a way that they could not accomplish alone. In Israel's history, God used people like Samson and Moses to do His will in setting His people free. But God also chose Israel to do His work and witness among the nations. This principle of corporate witness and influence is carried on in the New Testament.

There are several ways in which the term *called out* is defined in the terms of the church. The nature of the church is unique; it is called out by God to show what God has done in us. The church consists of those who are "called out." The Greek term is *ekklesia*, which has its roots in the Hebrew idea of assembly. The people of God are called out to worship Him, much as the Israelites were called out of Egypt to worship God. Worship in Scripture is a spontaneous expression of praise. Part of this praise was in songs meant for the edification of the whole gathering. This praise is properly meant in response to the living God who had redeemed His people. Another part of worship is expressed in giving in response to God's love, even in spite of difficult economic situations (2 Cor. 9:1–8). The early church was known for this.

The church is also to comprehend that being called out as a means to obey God, not so much as to be called away from the world. This interpretation has caused some to pull away from the world and to cease being salt and light. In the setting of the church are the virtues of Christ expressed (Eph. 5:25–27). Christ loved the church and gave Himself for her. By dying, He bought and cleansed it. Christ's purpose of reconciliation was expressed through the church (Eph. 3:10–11). The church is God's holy people, His priesthood that were called out as belonging to God (1 Pet. 2:9, 10). This brings to mind the expression of living sacrifice as Paul mentions in Romans 12.

EXPLORING THE ROOTS OF MISSIONS: PERSONAL, BIBLICAL, AND SPIRITUAL

Along the same lines, Watson notes that the church is called to a new community, that of love, fellowship, and forgiveness (Watson 1978, p. 71). The church lives out its unity in equality and brotherhood (Jas. 2:1–13). No one person is to be favoured over another. We are all equal before God (Gal. 3:26–29, Col. 3:11). The rich and poor are all alike before God. His love is available to all those who call on Him, not their status or wealth. The Jew and Gentile are both forgiven of sin against a holy God. The old world with its values has been left behind, and now there are new standards and morals. These are the ideals that God has ordained as godly. We are to put off the old life—the flesh with its tendency to sin in anger, slander, lies, and filthy language (Col. 3:7–10). We are also called to live godly lives by putting to death things like greed, impurity, and immorality (Col. 3:5–6). Paul encourages his readers to live godly lives as children of the light (Eph. 4:17–32). These new ideals meant that honesty and edification were the new standards as well as purity. The body of Christ is called to love each other. The lordship of Christ must also be shown in working together with our brothers and sisters. The concept of interdependence is an important issue; a church must be dependent on God as its head and interdependent on other churches. We are all working together toward the goal of evangelisation of the world. The petty bickering of churches over minor issues is not a sign of our love for God or each other. Various mission groups and agencies should be working in harmony to bring the gospel to the needy. The ability to work with colleagues in ministry in a partner style that reflects our unity in the body of Christ is a witness as much as the words used.

The idea of being called also has that of a godly inheritance (being heirs of God and joint heirs with Christ; Heb. 2:12). It is born of His Spirit and bought at the death of His Son. The church in Scripture is usually the local body of believers (although universal references occur in Matt. 16:18 and Paul's writings). There are many metaphors for the church—the new man (Eph. 2:14, 15), the body of Christ (Eph. 1:22–23, 5:30; 1 Cor. 12:27), the temple of God (Eph. 2:21–22; 1 Cor. 3:9, 16; 1 Tim. 3:15; 1 Pet. 2:5), the bride of Christ (2 Cor. 11:2, Matt. 25:6), household of God (Eph. 2:19), royal priesthood (1 Pet. 2:5; Rev. 1:6, 5:10), and flock of God (John 10:1–6, 16, 27; 1 Pet. 5:3; Heb. 13:20; Acts. 20:28).

The idea of a journey toward fullness in Christ is important in discipleship process. Our change comes from growth, not instantaneous transformation. The process of discipleship is costly and demands all that we are and have. The early disciples suffered much for the gospel as we have seen book of Acts. The offering of grace to us cost God His Son; it may cost us no less in our lives. God may be easy to please, but He is hard to satisfy (Lewis 1952, p. 172). One step of obedience will lead to the next step. The demands of growth for a baby are always a process of difficulty. First comes standing, then walking, and then running. The same is to be said for the growth of disciples in Christ. The author of the book of Hebrews as well as Paul (Heb. 5:11–6:1 cf. 1 Cor. 3:1–3) allude to the process of growth. We must move from milk to meat to be called mature. All Christians, no matter what their age and level of sanctification, are called disciples. The learning process never ends as God continues to move us up to greater and greater tasks for Him. The Great Commission was at the end of Matthew's book, but that was just a beginning for the disciples in the process of their learning and growth as well as their ministry.

So we see that the church is a united body (Gal. 3:28) being a fellowship where service, gifts (1 Cor. 12, Rom. 12), and witness (Acts 2:14–41) occur in the context of worship (Acts 13:1). Although the church has sadly not lived up to its ideals, that is because the human leadership is imperfect and not a fault of the design and purpose. The failures of leaders have been a poor reflection of God's perfection and turned some from the church. The case of the Crusades is a sad and glaring example of this. But on the opposite side of the fence, there have been many cases of unselfish service, sacrifice, and humane institutions and mission endeavours. Where would we be without the work of biblical people like Paul and Apollos who planted and watered the church? The historical examples of Gregory the Illuminator, Columba, Francis Xavier, Ziegenbalg, Moffat, Bingham, and Judson are legendary in mission history. The gifts of the church have been a blessing to many nations and peoples—in education (Duff in India), leadership (Taylor in China), and health care (Brandt in India), to name a few.

The church has many kinds of local expressions. These vary from one denomination to the next and even within the denominations themselves. There is also great variation in the cultures it works in. The presence of Christ is demonstrated among the believers who are sharing the gifts in ministry. This is where the love of Christ can be shown properly. When Paul talked about the gifts in his first epistle to the Corinthians, he did it in the context of love; for without love, the gifts of service and ministry, whether in or out of the church, mean nothing.

> The word has to become flesh before people can see the truth and reality of God…the church as a new society should be a constant challenge to the ambitions and standards of the rest of the world. (Watson 1978, pp. 300, 306)

And so, as we live the reality of Christ, then the gospel will also begin to affect the world around us rather than the world affecting the church. This is a creeping error that ever threatens to encroach on the sanctification of the church. When we put the world's values into the church, then we lose our distinctiveness. When we forget to lean on the Holy Spirit, then we lose our power and motivation. It is the challenge of every generation. The periodic revivals of the church, as was the Reformation, are to remind the church of its origin and focus. It is born of God and must do God's work.

Gifts

The means by which God brings missions to the world is people. Paul mentions the gifts of the Holy Spirit often in his writings (Eph. 4:11, 1 Cor. 12:8–29, Rom. 12:3–8, 1 Cor. 12:8–11). There are ministries to the local church and some to the universal church. The Holy Spirit gives the gifts out as He sees fit. The gifts of apostles, prophets, evangelists, teachers, and pastors—all these are of the body of Christ. Teachers can belong to either the local or universal church (Acts 13:1, 1 Cor. 12:28–29, 1 Tim. 2:7, 2 Tim. 1:11, Jas. 3:1), but the bishops and presbyters are local in nature. The gifts of the Holy Spirit are given to each church as He sees fit (1 Cor. 12:11, Eph. 4:11). Peters maintains that the list in Scripture is neither exhaustive nor final (1 Cor. 12:8–11, Eph. 4:11). It is the Holy Spirit that meets the complete need of the church at any one time or place. Missions comes under the universal gifts and ministry of the local church.

The traditional divisions have been apostles-prophets (functioning only in the New Testament times) and evangelists, pastors, and teachers which are still functioning today. Peters challenges the traditional distinctions changing them into two pairs: (1) apostles-evangelist and (2) prophets and pastor-teacher (Peters 1972, p. 246). The New Testament evangelists were also apostles and responsible for the apostolic function. The evangelist was one sent out but without the original apostolic office, authority, and rank of the apostle. The pastor-teacher is the functional successor to the prophet but does not have the gift of speaking under the immediate influence of the Holy Spirit (Peters 1972, p. 247). The apostles had the Holy Spirit as their authority, and they had combined in their persons the inspirational and original authority as well as the evangelist and pastoral and teaching ministry. This was an incredible gift-cluster and much needed in the early days of establishing the church. Today we place our authority in the Word of God and not the office itself.

Three Greek terms define for us what the work of the early Christian leaders was. The job of the evangelist *euaggelizo* thus brings "good news." Another Greek term used is *martureo*, which is to witness and testify also. A final Greek term used often is *kerusso*—preach, proclaim, and herald what Christ has done. The first two are general terms apply to all believers, while the latter is used of certain individuals. A missionary (or international worker) is sent forth (as the Great Commission defined) to evangelize and establish churches of disciples.

The New Testament focuses on the foundational emphasis on the work and calling of missionary. A believer who is "sent forth" (*mitto* is Latin for "I send"), which is where we get our English word *missionary* from. The Greek term *apostello* also means to send. This term is used one hundred thirty-five times in the New Testament. Another term *pempo* with the same meaning is used eighty times. The authority behind the sending is that of Christ Himself. As the Father sent Him, so He sends us onward. Luke 6:13 says that the disciples were sent out nine times in the gospels. Christ sends *and* works with those whom he sends. Christ is not leaving us alone to the work; He is enabling His people to bear the difficulties and strain of being a light, particularly in a foreign culture, by His indwelling presence and power.

A question that would be appropriate to ask at this time is Who is sent: the called individual or the church? As Christ our great example was sent (Heb. 3:1), so the apostles or disciples were also sent out. The idea here is like a delegation, such as the original eleven (minus Judas who betrayed Jesus and committed suicide), and Paul. These were men instructed by the Lord (Acts 15:2, 4, 23; Matt. 10:1–2). There were also those sent by the churches (1 Cor. 4:6, 9; Phil. 2:25; 2 Cor. 8:23). These were witnesses of Christ's life and work (Acts 1:22, 25–26; 2:43; 3:15; 5:32; 10:39). Paul was appointed to join this elite group (Rom. 1:5, 1 Cor. 9:1–2, 2 Cor. 12:12, Gal. 2:8) as were a few others (these terms seemed to imply a wider usage: Barnabas—Acts 14:4, 14; Epaphroditus—Phil. 2:25; some unnamed in 2 Cor. 8:23; Silvanus and Timothy—1 Thess. 1:1, 2–6; and Apollos—1 Cor. 4:6, 9). The apostolic function seems to have been for the benefit of the local churches as evangelists and the pastor-teacher in ministry.

The term *evangelizing* was used fifty-five times of the travelling IWs who went to the pagans around them. The evangelist also went into the unevangelized territories to gather the believers together and establish them in the faith (Acts 21:8, Eph. 4:11, 2 Tim. 4:5). The present-day IW may be equivalent to the biblical evangelists in that they are sent forth, through the church by divine authority, bearing the good news of the gospel.

The office of pastor-teacher is closely related to that of evangelist (Mark 16:15, Matt. 28:18). The local church work is enhanced by the pastor-teacher (Heb. 5:12; Jas. 3:1; 2 Tim. 2:2; 1 Tim. 3:2, 5:17). Apollos watered what Paul had planted (Acts 18:24, 19:1;

1 Cor. 1:4). Titus established the believers Paul left (Tit. 1:5). The principles of the travelling minister, pastor-teacher fit into what the pioneers did. Schools were established to train young believers in the work of the ministry. There were many schools in Alexandria for this purpose, as well as for apologists. Based on the above examples, it seems that there are two kinds of IWs needed. One kind is the evangelist who engages in pioneer work in a non-churched region and the pastor-teacher who connects with the believers and builds them up into a local functioning body of Christ.

The work of missions is to be ongoing—for Jesus said that He was with His disciples until the end of the age (Matt. 28:20). There is no ending of the discipling of the nations as there are many more to reach with the gospel message. The Great Commission is in effect until all have heard the gospel. Paul argues eloquently that someone must be sent (Rom. 10:12–15). The prayer of Jesus was that God would sanctify others who would come to believe (John 17:20, 20:29).

The task of missions is the nature of the ultimate. Peters remarks that it is truly

> something that neither centuries, circumstances nor cultures change. (Peters 1972, p. 159)

It is certainly spiritual, for only the Holy Spirit can move in the hearts of people to believe and repent, putting their faith in Jesus Christ, who is unseen today except in His followers themselves. The Father designed it, the Son implemented it, and the Holy Spirit does the work in preparing the hearts of the hearers and of the speakers who testify of the grace of Christ. It is biblical, for the Scriptures are full of examples of those who walked in faith proclaiming, preaching, and witnessing the mighty acts of God in salvation. The Great Commission gives faith the framework of missions. The third task Peters notes is that it is a religion of faith, for who else can see God but in this way? The spiritual man sees the same evidence that the natural man sees but knows the source to whom it is attributed. Without faith, it is impossible to please God, and so we walk in the footsteps of those who are listed in the great hall of faith in Hebrews 11. Unless we walk by faith as they did, we will not be able to do the work of missions at all, for in many ways, it looks impossible. God will enable us to be the people equipped to do the tasks He asks of us. Finally, this task is certainly human in nature. It is done by living in culture and society. The difficulties of contextualization, identification, and language learning lie before the international worker who must keep a balanced life. It is difficult to live as a bicultural person, yet a successful international worker must manage this.

Call of God

There are several kinds of calls God gives to mankind delineated in Scripture. The call to salvation is that to all of mankind for all who repent and believe. All believers are called to discipleship, but only a few are called to the ministry of the Word. It is selective, personal, and specific (Peters 1972, p. 171). The call to this kind of ministry is that exercised by the Holy Spirit (Mark 3:13–14, John 15:16). It was He who chose Paul and Barnabas (Acts 13:2). Paul felt his calling was by grace (Eph. 3:2, 7–8; Rom. 15:15; 2 Tim. 1:12). It was both a joy and a burden (Rom. 15:15–19). Moses, Joshua, Samuel, Isaiah, and many others in the Old Testament were likewise called to serve God. The ministry of the Word entails shepherding the flock, evangelism, and teaching. Obviously, this ministry can be done either overseas or at home.

Being sure of God's call does not come with a sense of adequacy necessarily. In fact, it is our utter dependence upon God knowing we can't do it on our own that makes the difference (John 15:4–7). God calls us to meet the need and equips us to do as He has called us (Phil. 1:6), but to assume it in our own strength would be fatal and a failure (Phil. 3:13, 19). There is a peace and sense of deep conviction that accompanies God's call (and the following obedience). Testing God's call does not mean putting out a fleece, for a fleece does not signify faith. Gideon's fleece did not mean faith in God's directions to him. Testing the call is making sure of God's will in this matter. This comes through an ultimate sense of faith in God and

His Word in spite of a call that may not make sense to us. A call to missions applies to any area of geography, not just the exciting ones or ones that are sure to get encouraging responses as opposed to an area known for its hard soil. If the Holy Spirit is still speaking, even if the way is difficult, then the call is still valid.

A call such as this often entails sacrifice (2 Cor. 8:9) such as what Christ did in leaving His Heavenly Father's side (John 17:5, 24) and emptying Himself (Phil. 2:5–8). He died voluntarily so that He could call others to Himself (John 10:17–18) and reconcile them to God. Paul too gave up his rights (Phil. 2:7; 4:11, 12). The call of God to the ministry is to the deepest need mankind has. It is the kind of service which has the greatest dividends, for it reaps eternal souls. Accepting God's call to ministry is paramount to taking on the deepest experiences of God in life. For God will challenge you to the utmost in the process of making you His disciple. In the ministry itself, you will be challenged, driven to your knees amid the need that you cannot meet but God can. For some in this position, they did not feel it was a sacrifice. David Livingstone, in his missionary work and travels, felt it was a part of the debt he owed to God. David Brainerd, missionary to the American Indians, worked so hard for the gospel that he died young.

The Holy Spirit will equip us to do the specific task He has called us to do, but a true servant heart is a part of the spiritual qualification needed. Jesus commended those who wanted to serve Him in humility (Luke 22:25–27) as well as those who would follow wherever He led (John 12:25–26). Paul was willing to say that he would be all things to all men so that he might by all means win some (1 Cor. 9:19–23). The servant's ability to have flexibility (which this passage certainly says) is a part of service in the name of the Master. Flexibility in service is very necessary, as often situations come up that have needs on the spot. The saying "Preach, pray, or die at a moment's notice" is apt here. All this is done with the conviction of the call that the good news must be brought to every creature. Christ died to save sinners; this message is essential to our ministry.

EXPLORING THE ROOTS OF MISSIONS: PERSONAL, BIBLICAL, AND SPIRITUAL

Uniqueness of Message

Along with the missionary call, the uniqueness of the message must not be underestimated. Other religions teach us how to save ourselves. We must be good enough to get to the place of ultimate peace and enlightenment. There is no other world religion that points to atonement and triumph over death as the gospel of Christ does. There is no other name under heaven whereby we must be saved (Acts 4:12). Christ's death purchased our salvation. It was Christ who predicted the necessity of the Holy Spirit coming in power (Acts 1:8, John 15–17). Pentecost is a historical event that has eternal existential consequences (Peters 1972, p. 299). God had called Abraham, Moses, and many in the Old Testament to come to Him and do His will. Jesus had called out the twelve also to come to God. But at Pentecost, the waiting was over; they were now told to go into all the world and preach the gospel of salvation. The Holy Spirit came upon the disciples in power and completed the process of sending (the Father sent the Son and the Son sent the disciples—John 14:16, 26; 15:26). The ministry of the Holy Spirit was to instruct, inspire, and witness to the work of God in the world (John 16:7). The Holy Spirit was active in the production of the Scriptures; the New Testament bore the teaching of the apostles written to the churches (1 Tim. 3:15). He also edified the believers and was their advocate. In the believer individually and the church corporately, He fills as His temple (1 Cor. 3:16, 2 Cor. 6:16, Eph. 2:21–22).

The Holy Spirit persuaded the Jewish apostles to move beyond their traditional boundaries to reach the Gentiles too. Philip went to Samaria (Acts 8:4ff), Peter to Cornelius (Acts 10), and Paul and Barnabas to wider missions (Acts 13:1–3). They spoke of Christ with boldness and power in spite of persecution and followed His leading (Acts 13:50). Paul was led to Macedonia (Acts 16:9) but was forbidden to enter Bithynia (Acts 16:7). God encourages us to enter new frontiers because He has prepared the way and has great concern for the people in that place. God had entrusted to Paul the gospel of Christ (1 Tim. 1:11; 2 Thess. 2:4; Tit. 1:3 cf. Rom. 1:1–7; Gal. 1:11–12, 2:7). Paul was a steward of the mystery of God that included the Gentiles (1 Cor. 4:1, 9:17; Eph. 3:3–6; Col. 1:27, 2:2, 4:3). This gospel is the foundational proclamation—that Christ died to save sinners (1 Tim. 1:15).

The other religions all have their way of salvation: Hinduism has the way of devotion; Shintoism has the way of the gods; Buddhism has the eightfold path; Islam teaches the five pillars; but Christianity has Christ, a living Person. He lived, taught, died, and *rose again*. Christ is still reaching the hearts of those who seek Him today. Peters declares that the "I Ams" in John's gospel are unparalleled in any religion (e.g., "I am the light, I am the bread of life, I am the way, the truth and the life, I am the good shepherd, I am the door, I am the gate of the sheep, and I am the resurrection"). The apostles stated that salvation was found in no one else. Paul wrote in 1 Corinthians 1:30 that Jesus was more than the philosophy of the Greeks and the righteousness of the Jews. Christ was wiser and more righteous than what was known to the Greeks and Jews. Christ was the true God-Man who overcame the power of sin and died for the sins of the world. By this He obtained our redemption and forgiveness (Luke 24:47, Eph. 1:7, Col. 1:14). His resurrection proved His power over death and sin. The forgiveness of sin is related to repentance and faith. We need to hold both the subjective and objective aspects of the gospel. Most of the ethnic religions hold to the subjective aspects of their religions, while Judaism and Islam focus on the objective aspects. The gospel of Christ has both: divine sovereign grace and human moral responsibility. We preach both Christ as Lord and the God-Man crucified. Anyone can have sins forgiven if they repent and put faith in Christ.

The gospel is divine, not man-made in origin and content. It anchors us in God who is love (1 John 4:8, 16). God's holiness separated us from Him when we sinned, but it was His love that also bridged the gap. In Eden, man fell into sin. But even there, God pointed a way past the sin to salvation. His love would not let us die in sin. The perfection of His love is seen in His capacity for sacrifice. Not only did He give His Son, but the degree of love expressed was in that His Son died for us. There is no salvation apart from Christ.

None of the other religious ways of man can reach heaven. Only God reaches down to us in love.

Gospel and Culture

The gospel has had far-reaching effects in culture; in Western culture, many institutions have sprung up as a result of its influence. But let us not forget there is a distinction between the gospel and Christendom with all of these institutions. The gospel is based on historical circumstances, and it was those circumstances that defined it. Man was lost in sin, and Christ died for mankind. When Constantine gave his edict in 313 AD, it became an establishment that was, for the first time, supported by the government. But Christianity is not just an ecclesiastical establishment; it is beyond that. The gospel may have been institutionalized in certain forms, but it is more than these institutions. It is divine in origin and must not be limited by our limitations. Neither is the gospel an ethnic product alone. It may have come from the Jewish culture—God working through the Jewish nation—but it became more than that in Acts 2. Everyone heard the gospel in their own tongue. It operates in and above culture. As the gospel has entered each culture, it has changed that culture. Cultures are transformed by Christ, and all things are made new—but not all is necessarily destroyed. There are some things worth keeping in each culture. At the same time, the gospel must not be limited to a particular culture either.

It is unfortunate that the gospel has become linked with the Western mentality. It is a false joining as the origins of Christianity are in the Middle East. But as the Middle East did not embrace it, the gospel moved west. Now it is identified with the Western culture and remains fixed in the minds of those who look on the West as a "Christian" culture. This fixation is the mark of the colonial and imperialistic age gone by, as well as great misperception and understanding of secularization which is now very Western. Missions of this age and day should be long past the erroneous thinking that promoted the two together in exploration and exploitation. If the gospel is more than an institution (good as many of these may be), the emphasis must be on the fact that the gospel is relational—a living active faith between God and His people. This aspect was forgotten by many of those who brought the sword and the cross together in exploration. They emphasized the institution aspect: a Christian education and the "civilizing" of non-Western cultures. When people were taught about God, it was inadequately communicated to them the personal nature of God. God's love was not just a historical act on the cross. It is a living love that continues to work in and through people by the power of the Holy Spirit. Today this error can still be made. The people who receive Christ become the children of God (John 1:12). They are not just the spiritual children of the Western IWs who may have brought them the gospel. (Contextualization continues to be an aspect of missions that challenges everyone.) In Hebrews 11 are given many examples of those who had faith in God that carried them beyond their present circumstances. Faith such as this is not cultural or based on sight or understanding (Heb. 11:1). Faith is the means by which we please God (Heb. 11:6) no matter what our cultural heritage.

The gospel of a true living love is not found in any other religion, although many have tried to give themselves (or their religion) an equality with the claims of Christianity. Out of these ethnic understandings grew new creations, many of them syncretistic in nature. Brahmo Samaj was the creation of Ram Mohun Roy who liked the teaching of the gospels but not the miracles or teaching of the Trinity. Likewise, the Hindu apologist Sarvepelli Radhakrishnan rejected the idea of a personal God and merged Western and Eastern thought instead.

Religious Fulfillment

Another theory fast gaining ground in the Christian world today is that of religious fulfillment. This takes up the idea that Christianity can in some way be attached to them and thus fulfill both in salvation. These religions are non-biblical in origin and are based on philosophy not God. The non-biblical forces in history are generally against the God of the Bible. The indirect worship of God through idols is not acceptable—only the God of the Bible is entitled to worship (Exod. 20:3–5). The Bible has always condemned spiritual adultery and syncretism as is shown on the episode with Elijah on Mt. Carmel. Other religions are non-revelational and a degeneration of God's intention for worship. Certainly, the worship of nature was never intended by God (Rom. 1:18–25) for He condemns it. The author claims this is not the same as Richardson's concept-fulfillment since the cultural aspects he refers to always point to the gospel of Christ. The Sawi had a peace child, the Hawaiians had a place of refuge, and the Chinese ideographs had Christian concepts embedded in them. But the clearest revelation of all is found in Judaism. Judaism was the forerunner of God's revelation that Christ was His Word of salvation. The Messiah of the Jews had come to save not just the Jews but the world. However, God did place in mankind basic instincts to put something above oneself. When this is not focussed on God, it becomes an error and the beginning of degeneration. The Bible begins in Genesis with monotheism and ends with Revelation where God is worshipped as the Alpha and Omega. This is universal—all the nations who have put their faith in God's sacrifice and salvation (Hab. 2:4; Ps. 2:8; Zech. 14:9, 16; Isa. 60:1–9; Rev. 21:1–22:6).

The gospel is a safe guide for all of life. By it we can become all that God has intended us to be as God's children. We can truly become made in His image. The Bible contains all that is needed for man to escape hell and judgement and come as a whole regenerated man into God's kingdom. In order for this to happen, they must hear what Christ has done for them (Rom. 10:12–15). Contrary to what many anthropologists may think, people are not happy in their delusion of sin. Actually, they are very unhappy; many people live in fear of what may happen to them tomorrow. Animists are always looking to appease the spirits, and people in the West are no different. The search for peace, power, and happiness are a part of life the world over. Only the gospel of Christ can save us from sin and hell. Indeed, bringing the gospel to many nations has improved the health care, education, and many other aspects of society in these places. It was the Christians and international workers who sought to improve the present state of man as well as the future. In Christ we find our true meaning and purpose.

The alternative to the gospel message is that of eternal hell. God reigns and lives in heaven where He will completely give us all blessings (Matt. 25:31–36; Rev. 20:11–15, 21:1–22:6). But hell is God's judgement (Matt. 25:41, 8:12, 25:46; Rom. 2:5; John 3:36; Rev. 14:10–11, 21:8). The state of death is eternal—eternal separation from God. There is no future restoration or annihilation (Luke 16:31). The lostness of man is the centre of the atonement (1 Tim. 2:4–7). The idea of neouniversalism (total redemption of the cosmos) is neither biblical nor possible. The comprehensive truth of God states that the devil and his angels will be cast into hell and judged. So also will be those that do not bow the knee to Christ. God cannot redeem those who reject Him and His truth. The moral responsibility of man is negated if there is such a thing as universal redemption. Salvation lies in repentance—turning away from sin and putting faith in Christ. The whole idea of missions and its urgency to save the lost becomes ludicrous if universal redemption is the case. The energy of the church is thus diverted into other channels.

Prayer: Necessity

There are 657 requests for prayer in Scripture (aside from the Psalms) with over 450 answers. Now 2 Chronicles 7:14 recalls God's response to Solomon's prayer in the dedication of the temple. God promised that if the people prayed in humility and repentance, then He would hear and answer. Psalm 2:8 tells believers to ask for the nations as our inheritance. When Queen Esther prayed for her people about to be annihilated, God answered. In Isaiah 64:1–12, it talks of the fact of no one seeking God—and God answers in Isaiah 65:1—that God reveals Himself to those who did not seek Him. As Isaiah interceded for his people, so God answered on their behalf. Intercession is necessary and indispensable. Jeremiah 33:3 says that God will answer prayer with great and mighty things. James 5:16 says that the prayer of a righteous man has great effect. In the situation in James, this was for the praying of the sick, but certainly this can be applied elsewhere. God's intervention on behalf of His people to save them has been in response to prayer. As God's desire is to save all (2 Pet. 3:9), then there needs to be a movement toward God of great repentance and faith. Movements of people toward God have had a history of prayer behind them.

The teaching of Jesus on prayer emphasized its significance for those who are working for salvation through faith. There needs to be persistence and faith (Luke 18:1–8, Matt. 21:1–22), both for the workers in spite of opposition and for those who are interested in coming to Christ. Our prayer needs to be in the name of Jesus, with sincerity (John 14:14, 16:23; Matt. 15:21–28), with fasting (Mark 9:29; Acts 13:2–3, 14–23), and with specific needs in mind (Matt. 20:32–33, 1 John 5:14) according to the will of God. If God's will be that all might be saved, then the gospel needs to move to those who have not yet heard. There are of course requests for labourers for God's work; there has always seemed to be more work and needs than workers.

The work of missions was commissioned by prayer in Acts 2 as the apostles were praying. Jesus Himself had encouraged the disciples to pray for labourers for the harvest, for the need was great for workers. So as the disciples prayed and waited on God, the Holy Spirit came upon them in great power (Acts 2:1–4). From there on, the early church prayed and continued to pray for wisdom and strength in the face of fierce opposition (Acts 4:31, 6:1–4). They prayed before they chose leaders (Acts. 1:24, 6:6) too. They also prayed for signs and wonders (Acts 28:8). They prayed when the gospel went out to the Gentiles (Acts 10:11) as well as to whom to send (Acts 13:1–3). Peter was released from prison in response to their prayers (Acts 12:12). New believers were commissioned to lead (Acts 14:23). In prison, prayer was essential (Acts 16:25). It was used for receiving guidance (Acts. 22:17) as well as in commending Paul to go forward into danger (Acts 21:5).

Paul's prayer for the churches and the believers he fostered was a part of the quality of the believers in that day and age (Eph. 3:14). He prayed for love (1 Thess. 3:12–13); sanctification (1 Thess. 5:23); God's good pleasure (2 Thess. 1:11–12), consolation (2 Thess. 2:16), love, and patience (2 Thess. 3:5); corporate perfection (1 Cor. 13:7–

9), unity (Rom. 15:5–6), hope (Rom. 15:13), knowledge of God's will (Col. 1:9–14), full assurance of knowledge (Col. 2:1–3), and for the indwelling of the Trinity in His people (Eph. 3:14–21). Paul asked for prayers on his behalf (Rom. 15:30–32, 2 Cor. 1:10–11, Eph. 6:18–20, Phil. 1:19, Col. 4:24, 1 Thess. 5:25, 2 Thess. 3:1–3, and Philem. 22). Paul struggled in prayer even for those whom he had not met in order that they might come to Christ (Col. 2:13).

Prayer and modern missions: The Reformation gave birth to Protestant faith, but they did not have the emphasis for missions for quite some time. When the Protestant churches finally got their footing, it was high time for the mission emphasis to be reaffirmed. The Roman Catholic Church had had IWs going out for quite some time, usually through the Jesuits and various orders. A revival in prayer occurred that gave the missionary dynamic in Protestantism. The Moravian Brethren at Herrnhut were pioneers in missions. They began by praying in response to the need out there. More and more members of churches, not just higher officials, began to get involved. In 1723, Robert Millar, who was a Presbyterian minister of Scotland, published a pamphlet encouraging prayer for mission effectiveness. The conversion of the lost was the goal of prayer for mission work. The Moravians started their one-hundred-year-long prayer meeting for mission. Revival swept through the churches, and many IWs went out. By 1746, this movement had grown so that all Christians were invited to prayer in a concert of prayer for missions that lasted for seven years. Jonathan Edwards was a part of the call for intercessory prayer. In 1782, the Nottingham Baptist Association in England began monthly concerts of prayer. One of the responses to that was the Particular Baptist Missionary Society for Propagating the Gospel among the Heathen was founded in in 1792 in Kettering, England. William Carey began praying before a world map. Monthly concerts of prayer began in America in South Carolina too in 1802. Judson and the other IWs in his group were sent out in 1812. The famous haystack meeting at Williams College in Massachusetts happened in 1806 with Samuel J. Mills and his fellow students.

The work of prayer is not only for labourers (Luke 10:2), but it is for the work they do. In listening to God as well as talking to Him in prayer we find out where His heart is in a particular situation. It is prayer that opens hearts (1 Cor. 16:9) as well as removing obstacles (Matt. 9:37–38) and releasing God's resources for the work. Prayer is a part of the armour of the believer (Eph. 6:18–20). It is taking back what belongs to the Creator and proclaiming Jesus's kingship (Matt. 28:19–20).

Knowing the needs of the people to be prayed for is helpful in the kind of intercession. General prayers are good, but specific prayers allow the heart of the praying person to be involved more deeply. Prayer walking may become a part of this—it is not possible for everyone to do this on site, but one can always pray while walking somewhere. This is effective in releasing captives bound in spiritual darkness (2 Cor. 4:4), for Jesus does what we ask Him in prayer. In prayer we can penetrate the darkness and unleash God's power. God is able through prayer to establish believers in areas where His name was not previously known.

Summary

The definition of missions must needs lead to the biblical theology of missions, the scriptural basis for what we do in other cultures to bring others to Christ. The Old Testament has Israel as a light to the nations, but that sadly fails until the exile wakens them to follow God. In the New Testament, we see Christ the Messiah come and live and die as the light of the world. After His death and resurrection, the disciples take it in turn to lead others to Christ. This calls for persistence and prayer as there is often resistance. From the Bible we go to the author's personal story as she follows God's leading into missions work.

3

Forward to Missions

Background

Growing up in a good evangelical church, there was always a good focus on missions. I learned where places were in the world because international workers would come and speak about where they worked. Various maps of the world would dot the walls of our church gym where we held many missions conferences. I learned about cultures and languages that were quite different from my own. Sometimes a missionary would even teach us a short chorus in the language they worked in. In short, missions was a normal aspect of my growing-up years, and I knew that there were many people in many places who needed to hear that Christ died for them.

My mother told me once that as a young person, she had wanted to go to Bible school and be a missionary. But with six siblings in the family, it was impossible for Grandpa to send her. So she stayed home, married my father, and instead raised four children. Although my parents never pressured us in any way to go to the missions field, it was God's providence that all three daughters became involved in missions. My oldest sister went to work with First Nations (formerly known as Canadian Indians) for several years, travelling all over the country and working with the Cree, Mi'kmaq, and Dene people. My younger sister, with whom I went to Thailand to teach English, also ended up working as a missionary with her husband in northern Thailand.

I grew up near a small prairie town of five thousand people in Manitoba, Canada. I actually lived on a small farm outside the town, along with my parents, two sisters, and a brother. We worked hard, but that was farm life. I totally loved growing up there; my friends were the animals, the creek, and the trees. At a young age, I asked Jesus to forgive my sins and come into my heart. My parents were also believers, involved in the church, and played music (piano and violin) in a couple music groups. I attended the youth group and was baptized at age fifteen at family camp. I joined a Bible quizzing team, and this gave me a great knowledge of the Word as a teen. It also really embedded missions in my heart as that was the focus of many of the books in the New Testament I studied as a quizzer (e.g., Acts, Corinthians, Romans, Philippians, Ephesians, Galatians, and Colossians). I became involved in the leadership of Alliance Youth Fellowship as a teen.

One of my favourite verses (I have many) came out of quizzing. Philippians 1:6 (NIV), "'Being confident of this, that he who began a good work in you will carry it on to completion until the day of Christ Jesus." That verse and many others I learned continued to give me comfort and encouragement in my life. God is still working in me. His faithfulness has been such a wonderful blessing.

My first intense contact experience was tutoring a refugee girl from Laos in English when I was a teenager. This refugee was one of the boat people so common in Canada in the '70s. She was my first Asian contact. I taught her English and learned a bit of Lao in return. The alphabet was so beautiful.

It wasn't long after that I was at a youth conference with a mission focus when I realized God was speaking to me about missions. That was when my commitment to Christ began to include full-time missions work. Before that I had toyed with becoming a veterinarian (because of my love for animals) or a medical illustrator (I loved to draw).

I attended Bible college for four years majoring in Christian education. I enjoyed studying and made new friends. My goal was to become a missionary with the Christian and Missionary Alliance denomination. With this in mind, I went on Alliance Youth Corps, seven weeks in another culture in the summer of 1983. The mission chose to send me to Hawaii, which was not what I was expecting, but I trusted in their decision and went for a good experience. Polynesian culture was very interesting. The alphabet was easy to learn, but the pronunciation took a bit more practise. I managed to say King "Kamehameha" (ka-may ha may ha). There were many Asians there too—Chinese, Filipino, and Japanese. It was a microcosm experience of the world with all these cultures and foods. It was probably my first experience using chopsticks. I learned puppetry with the teenagers and was involved in Bible studies (teens and adults) and some children's ministry. It was good training in things (semi) tropical as well. The people were delightful, and I really learned to love Hawaiian songs and hymns.

The next summer I went to Ottawa, Ontario, on an internship at the church. It was a requirement in my studies to have an internship in church ministry. I plunged into Bible studies, teaching, and learning the things of the church. The experience in eastern Canada was quite new, having lived all my life in the Midwest. Each place and experience added to my world of knowledge, interacting with all kinds of people.

After graduation, I felt a strange prompting to go back to Hawaii. I followed the leading and ended up working in two churches in Oahu on an internship basis in 1986. It was a year that showed me much about Asian/Polynesian cultures as well as myself. I learned a bit of Greek and Hebrew from my pastor. I taught Bible quizzing to both of my churches (one from the first part of my time there and the other of the second). I also trained new coaches to carry on the quizzing after I was gone. I was able to do some puppetry (with the same pastor I worked with in AYC in 1983). I did a lot of work with the children and the youth as well as the college and career age group. I loved doing the Bible studies or lessons, whether in vacation Bible school (for children) or in the adult level. I took a Child Evangelism Fellowship class as a participant too. A few touring trips with youth or college level were included.

EXPLORING THE ROOTS OF MISSIONS: PERSONAL, BIBLICAL, AND SPIRITUAL

To Stay or Not to Stay

After my return from Hawaii, I was in limbo for several reasons. I had applied for a job in Los Angeles working in a church and was waiting for the visa and paperwork to be completed before I could go. Also, at this time, I began dating someone from my hometown area. There were a lot of positive things for me in this relationship—including finances. I wouldn't have to worry about that if I stayed. But to this person, missions was a side show—it wasn't something you did your whole life. Missions was something you did after you retired, he said. I couldn't reconcile that with what I believed. So I struggled, and finally, I looked in the mirror and said to myself, *If I stayed here with this man, could I really look at myself the rest of my life, knowing I had given up missions (at least until retirement)*? That just didn't sit right with me, and so after much thought and prayer, I decided it was time to go on with my missions quest and went on to work at the Chinese church in the next-door province.

The cross-cultural experience continued when I was hired by a Chinese church in Saskatoon a few years later. Leading the youth and children in English ministry was a challenge. I had to work with the Chinese parent culture as well as the English-speaking offspring. This church was largely Cantonese-speaking. I picked up a few words in Cantonese here and there. I was also preaching in the English services. (This was something new to me, and while I enjoyed the speaking, it also made me tremble to feel that I was being the instrument of God's Word.) Occasionally I preached with an interpreter, one of the elders on the board. That was a little harder as I had to stop and wait for the translation. I also led worship with the teens. I taught puppetry to the youth and coached a Bible quizzing team to join in the district quiz meets. It wasn't until I left this job and went back to Seminary that I gave up on that earlier relationship for good, knowing I couldn't leave God's call for my life.

In 1990, I went to seminary and enrolled in an MA of Missiology. The soaking of the Bible in such a godly place with spiritual people encouraged me all the more to follow my passion for missions. But I still had a home service prerequisite to complete if I was to work for the Christian and Missionary Alliance.

Esl Overseas

1. *Christum Suksa,* Thailand

After I graduated in 1993, I went to Thailand with my younger sister and two other girls to teach English. We were a team that worked in a K–12 school in Bangkok. It was an amazing year. Thailand was so different than anywhere else I had been. There were a lot of new cultural things to learn. We English teachers each taught classes with a Thai teacher. The Thai teacher taught the lesson first in Thai with some English. Then we taught the lesson, and the Thai teacher translated. It was a great way for learning to communicate. Sometimes the conversations with our fellow Thai teachers were as confusing as with the students! There were pronunciation issues (for them speaking English), and so getting the correct message could take a long time and be a lot of fun.

I also was living with my younger sister for the first time in several years. It was great to be together but again, the lack of English fellowship off-campus was difficult for us. We sisters were working together all day, sharing a room to sleep, and we socialized with each other too. We found a great encouragement in the Alliance guest house in the city. We connected with international workers there and attended meals there occasionally. It was a fair distance from our school, and in Bangkok, distance means a lot as the traffic was incredibly bad. One time while going somewhere with our teaching colleague, she got off the bus to eat a meal, and then got on the SAME bus with us to continue the trip! That just goes to show you the rush hour traffic could be REALLY slow.

We also had an issue with one of our English-speaking co-workers. The team leader had gone home after four months, having introduced us to the school and Thai culture. The other English teacher had a room to herself after our team leader left. It seemed she had difficulty dealing with working with children for one thing and kept trying to give us her classes. At other times she seemed antagonistic to us and we didn't understand her behaviour. Perhaps she was suffering culture shock but she didn't share her struggles with us. We were at a loss as to how to deal with her.

Thailand was a place where so many people were lost in the national religion of Buddhism (mixed with animism.) We went to Thai temples occasionally and asked questions of our Thai colleagues. We observed the spirit house at the gate of our school and asked why it had a Coke bottle with a straw in it (for the spirits to drink from). My sister and I had a chance to spend New Year's with a colleague who was going to her hometown. That was a very interesting experience—the scenery up north was so different than Bangkok; we saw silk weaving, visited a local school (and taught songs and English games on the spot). We also had a chance to celebrate New Year with the parents of our teaching colleague. The Thai ritual and customs for that time was very interesting. I even had a relatively in-depth discussion of Buddhism with my Thai teacher translating for her mother. When I completed my ten-month contract, I felt I wanted to come back to Thailand to work someday. In the meantime, I had things to work on, both personally and spiritually. I also needed to save up money for any future trips.

In between my cross-cultural trips, I worked odd jobs in Regina, Saskatchewan. This was where I had gone to Bible college and seminary, and so I knew the city and had some friends there. I worked in a doughnut shop (night shift) for several months before one trip. Other times I cleaned houses. It was not exciting, but I told myself it was a good way to practice humility. I also was involved in the youth group at my college church as well as on the worship team at various times. Being on the worship team was a wonderful ministry for me. It really helped me to appreciate the words in songs.

2. Seoul, S. Korea

Months later, after having sent out letters for work in Asia, God opened the door for me to go to South Korea. My heart was still in Thailand, but God had clearly showed me South Korea was the place for me to be. I was back to being a cultural and linguistic learner. I worked in Seoul for a head office of a church denomination. One odd thing was being a woman in the office, but not a secretary. My title there was missions co-ordinator—I was the go-between the Korean denomination I worked for and the missions connections in English elsewhere. Another challenge was not having a life in any social sense outside of the office. The pastors I worked with there were fantastic, and I really appreciated my supervisor. In the beginning of my stay there, I was busy many Sundays touring the churches of the denomination with my boss. But he couldn't translate the services there for me (his English wasn't quite good enough), and so I was just the "white wallflower missionary," introduced to the churches but unable to participate much in conversations or understand sermons unless someone knew English enough to speak to me. It became very stifling after some time, and I approached my supervisor for some help in getting more English connections. He understood the issues (his English was fantastic, and he was a very sympathetic person) but was unable to facilitate much change due to my boss's interpretation of things. I eventually connected with a guest house place that provided some fellowship which I needed.

One very interesting experience was a visit with my boss and his family to their son in the DMZ. Military service was required of all South Korean males, and so we visited the son one weekend. Just getting into the Demilitarized Zone was a big effort, and I came away with a new understanding of the soldiers who kept South Korea safe. I was also able to visit a Buddhist temple or two and go to Prayer Mountain where Dr. Yonggi Cho had prayer closets set up for believers to pray. We were also able to visit the denominational Christian university. The campus was amazing. The visit there would prove to be fruitful in the future.

I taught English classes with the aid of a *katusa* (South Korean soldier) and also taught a missions course there. Having very few English books for resources, I started to write the material (this was at the beginning of the internet age in 1995) for me to use. I was able to borrow some from the university library we had visited earlier. I ended up with a book of one hundred pages on missions that I had written to use in my classes.

Unfortunately, in spite of my job teaching, things were not easy; in fact, there were so many difficulties I felt compelled to leave. (Some of the issues were culturally related; others were connected to the leadership style that was used by the leader of the denomination.) The night before I left, I was engaged in major spiritual warfare in my little house next to the offices. If the enemy didn't want me to leave, then leaving was definitely what God wanted. I prayed and sang and won the battle. I was so stressed by my experience that the plane flight home itself reduced the amount of tension in my body. (Usually plane flights *don't* reduce stress, but this one did.) Another confirmation that it was the right thing for me to do was leave when I did.

I came home to Canada discouraged and disheartened with such a negative cultural and spiritual experience. I settled back into Regina, Saskatchewan, where I had been working before I left. After a few months of feeling oppressed in church, I realized I was still dealing with the aftereffects. I brought the matter to some spiritual friends, and as we prayed, I felt that it was time to let the negatives go and forgive the one who had wronged me.

3. Pohang, S. Korea

After that I felt free to pursue my desire for Thailand. I sent out letters requesting work in both Thailand and Korea. But as God would have it, I ended up in South Korea again. Different school, different city, and different living conditions—and the teaching contract was one year. I was wondering why God wanted me back in Korea when I wanted to go to Thailand. This job was teaching English in a Korean *hogwan* (after-school academy). This school ran from 2 p.m. to 9 p.m. going from the youngest students (age four/five) to the oldest (age sixteen). It also ran six days a week, which was not quite what I'd been told beforehand. Teaching the classes was fun. We had teachers that helped us, but we were on our own in the classrooms to teach English. The students were mostly used to single-sex schools, so it caused some excitement having the other sex in class. Occasionally I had to call in Korean colleagues to break up a fight/argument. We taught games and songs in English too as a part of classes.

I learned to do a lot of things on my own in Pohang which was on the east coast of the country. I hopped the bus to go downtown and visited the markets, quite the experience in themselves. I even went to another city for a holiday weekend and learned to survive on what little Korean I had. Seoul became a popular spot to visit as it was not far (by plane), and I still had some friends there in the guest house. I didn't live alone; my roommates were other English-speaking teachers from my school. We lived only a few blocks from school, which was convenient for a quick walk to work, but not so much if the students wanted to follow us home. I found working six days a week quite tiring.

I started going to church, but the services were in Korean only. The people were very kind, and someone gave me a bilingual English-Korean Bible with hymnal in the back. That in itself was of great encouragement. My knowledge of Korean was only good enough to find the scripture passages and follow along in the hymns. That wasn't quite fellowship in the deep way I needed. So I stayed home, read my Bible, sang hymns, and journaled on Sundays. It was lonely and challenging. For a long time, I didn't go to church as I couldn't find one that held an English service. I really learned to depend on God for strength in many situations. Being in South Korea was a challenge in many ways. It was hard to find fellowship in English, and at one point, I connected with some paramilitary people in the city. Hanging out with them was also challenge to my faith at times. We had fun chatting and bowling together, but I made sure I left once they got too diligent with their drinking. God kept me safe at that time while saving my sanity. Eventually God opened the way for a Christian friendship with an American ESL teacher from another school and then an English church service in another church.

4. Bangkok Christian College, Thailand

After six months, I began praying for Thailand and looking for a job there. I felt a burden to go back in a very strong way. I would pray over a map of Bangkok until I was lost for words, weeping. God was moving in a way I didn't understand. Three different contacts informed me of a particular school in Thailand that needed a teacher. By the third time, I got the point that God wanted me in THAT school and applied. The school was a large private one (four thousand boys K–12!). The word 'college' was used in the British style which didn't necessarily mean adult students.) I worked with the young boys in grades 1 and 2 as a teacher's assistant. This was a great time of learning and adventure, both as an expat and as a believer. I took a weekend trip with some other tourists to Kanchanaburi on a jungle raft adventure. We hiked down a muddy trail (which totally killed my white runners), waded across a river, and stayed overnight in a village. Then, as it was the rainy season, we took elephants back across the river (which had flooded overnight) to continue our journey.

There was a large number of expats working at that school. They were great to work with—Brits and Australians in the bunch besides the majority of Americans. We even had a couple of Canadians. The majority of them worked in the English Immersion Program (EIP) department as I did. A few worked in the general English program, and I became friends with two expat American believers from that department. We mutually encouraged each other. I was discipling one of them for a while. I got connected with the guest house for my denomination as well as their church for my spiritual life. There were many ESL teachers in that church. It was there I met and married my husband a few months later in 1998. (In itself a long and amazing story.) Together we were searching for a way to serve God in some capacity. Due to some unfortunate events, we ended up leaving Thailand and moved to the UK where my husband was from.

Europe Experience

Living in the UK was a big challenge for me. It was English-speaking, but everything was quite different. It was harder living there than in Asia, as in Asia I had had no prior expectations. My husband found work, and we settled in. For both of us, it was difficult but in different ways, so much that we ended up moving to France less than a year later where my husband taught business English. Being fluent in French, this was not a problem for him; it was his third trip to that country. I was thrown into the deep end linguistically as I had never studied French in high school, although that had been an option. So I used a French dictionary and Bible and studied on my own while my husband was away working. I loved the architecture and history in France. We even found an evangelical church (not a common thing in atheistic secular France). My husband translated the sermons for me. I picked up enough French after a few months to get 50 percent of the sermons (listening only). But it was not to be. Once again circumstances forced us to leave and return to the UK. Even then, God provided amazingly for us to return.

Back in the UK, there were struggles to find work and a place to live, as our home had been rented out. We settled in my husband's college city in public housing. We had the advantage of a few friends nearby. My husband had taken work in another city, so he commuted home on weekends but stayed there during the week. I worked on painting the house and doing other housewifely activities. I had sent out a request to work in South Korea, at the university of the denomination I had worked at before. (The request had actually gone out when we were in France, but by the time the answer arrived, it was November, and we were in Britain.) We had to wait a few months, as classes didn't start till March. The contract term was for two whole years (a year longer than usual ESL terms).

5. Sungkyul University, S. Korea

Little did we know that God had paved the way for us. Although this was a different city than my last two trips, Anyang was relatively close to Seoul by train. By the time we arrived in February, we found there was another couple on campus that we could connect with—culturally and linguistically. An American-Korean couple (he was American, and she was Korean) who were great to work and chat with. He was teaching English with us, and she took care of their daughters, who were nine and eleven. They helped us navigate the maze of Korean bureaucracy when we needed help and were also good friends. They were a great help to us when we needed a translation of something or just some company. Some of the Korean professors could speak English, and the president of the university welcomed us warmly. Also, we'd discovered I was pregnant just before we left Britain. We planned to teach, and then I would take a semester out after the baby was born.

First, teaching ESL was very different than what I had anticipated in some ways. The classes were large—too large for language classes (about 15 students maximum is good for speaking practise). The ability of the students was generally poor. Practise in English speaking had not been encouraged so much as the grammar aspect. Our textbooks also varied greatly in usefulness. We adapted and managed in class as well as in dealing with the administration. The administration style also took some adjustment, due to some cultural differences. Some things were not as direct as we were used to. It took some creative maneuvering to find a way that would work efficiently for us English speakers. We found great people to work with and encouraged those who really wanted to practise English.

In addition to English as a second language, I was offered several opportunities to teach other subjects. As I had an MA in Missiology and this was a Christian university, I was able to give a lecture on contextualization, with the missions professor interpreting for me. I also taught a class to senior students in tentmaking using much of the material I had prepared the last time I was in Korea. I was able to add to it as the internet was now much more common in 2002 than way back in 1995. The material mostly developed at this time was tentmaking.

In fall, our daughter was born—and grew up with a lot of attention as the "white" baby on campus. We tried to take Korean lessons so as to communicate better, but it was hard to study with a baby around. What little we did take was helpful. Interestingly enough, although I did not go out formally as a missionary with any North American denomination, the South Koreans considered the time I worked there as missionary work. I did, however, always go out on my overseas trips with the church's blessing and prayers behind me. That made a big difference to know that I had people praying for me wherever I went. As a couple this was even more important especially as we had expanded to a family of three.

To Canada 2003

In 2003, our contracts were up, and we went to Canada as my husband felt the desire to study at seminary. We ended up in Calgary where he entered his first year. After that, funds were low, and finding jobs was hard as we had to consider child care with both of us working. Eventually he ended up driving for buses in the city. My jobs were mostly teaching English as a second language, although I did work in retail for a short time.

We attended a couple of churches in the city, the first one having been quite far from our house. The second one was found through two friends who moved into the city from out of province. There we received much encouragement to follow God, even though the way might be difficult. In-between jobs at one point, I began researching and working on an expansion to my original missions course notes, including the tentmaking and contextualization sections I had added in 2002. After two years, I felt I had finished what was required but ran into a roadblock—the cost of editing. I left the project for the time being. In the meantime, I was able to use some of my material in my missions segments that I gave in the church.

We received encouragement from our pastor to apply with some missions as that was our ultimate desire. I started researching one mission, moved to another, and we started the application process. We talked to the mission recruiters and began to see God opening doors for us. We attended two retreats with the mission we chose, learning much about God's grace and power. The final meeting was a preparation with other pending IWs, and it included a psychological evaluation. The result was that we were not allowed to go forward with the mission. They decided we had been through too much too fast as a married couple and needed time to deal with it. I was crushed, and it took me a long time to come to grips with this. In addition, our beloved little church closed. We felt adrift, without a purpose, and a place to call our spiritual home.

We dropped into a few churches seeking a place to belong, and one church welcomed us and provided for some of our needs as we were also struggling financially at the time. I went to a counsellor to work on some things, and God began opening doors for healing, not only for the loss of missions but many other issues in life as well. I got my CELTA certificate so I could refine my ESL skills. There was a lot to unlearn, especially as more grammar was a part of the job. Conversation English overseas was quite different than the focus on grammar in ESL schools in Canada. Since then I worked in several ESL schools in this city.

The most recent ESL job came to me in an unusual way. I met a former colleague from a school I'd worked in at a coffee shop. I'd been looking for ESL work, and if I didn't get something soon, I'd have to do something else. This former colleague said hi to me and said his school needed subs. I'd sent emails to that school, but no one had answered. I went in person and got the job. Two weeks later I was hired on full time. I eventually became lead teacher and later in charge of curriculum development.

Summary

This has been my journey through the various stages of missionary work. Of all the things I did, I was most sorry I did not get deeply into language learning. I dabbled in a few areas—French, Korean, and Thai—but nothing approaching fluency. I was at the bare beginnings of being understood and understanding what others said. I had also studied a bit in Greek and Hebrew while in Hawaii and really enjoyed digging into those aspects of biblical languages.

All of my learning and growth has come to make me the person God wants me to be. I can say it is a process which has not always been enjoyable but fruitful in hindsight. My story is not without its failures and disasters, but these are not the focus of the book. (Perhaps another time, should God lead that way.) My journey, in many ways, has been unique, but it echoes much of what this book is about: seeking God's face in all things and looking for His grace in life as I have explored missions and ministry.

Now that we have gone over my personal story and the roots of what missions is, covering ground from home to abroad in various cultural situations, we'll look at some of the aspects of the preparation and call of the individuals who are moving to the geographical place of obedience in ministry.

4

Discerning Call and Preparation

Becoming a missionary/international worker is one of the most difficult callings, for in order to do it, you must leave everything that is familiar and go somewhere where things are very different and sometimes very difficult. Being a international worker does not mean that you must be perfect, spiritually or otherwise. But it does mean that you must be spiritually aware and in tune with what God wants and what is happening in your life. A look at the types of calls as seen in Scripture will be helpful.

Calls in Scripture

There are many examples in Scripture of those who were called to do God's work.

Many of the people called in Scripture were surprised and doubted the call and argued it. The Old Testament records several who did this. In the time of the judges, Barak was afraid to answer unless Deborah accompanied him to battle. Barak's reluctance and doubt meant that Jael, Heber's wife, got the glory of defeating Sisera (Jud. 4:8–10). Jonah was famous for not arguing but running from the call. God told him that Nineveh was going to be destroyed for its wickedness. Jonah didn't like the Ninevites who were known for their cruelty. So he ran from God and got swallowed by a big fish. In the belly of the fish, Jonah repented and was coughed up. He did preach repentance, and the Ninevites did repent, but Jonah was still not happy (in a very unspiritual fashion).

In Exodus 3–4, we find an example of a reluctant servant at the beginning of his ministry. Moses was born a Hebrew and saved from death by a faithful mother and sister. He killed an Egyptian for beating a Hebrew slave. He fled the country and ended up being a shepherd in the wilderness of Sinai. In Exodus 3:1–3 (NIV), God got Moses's attention: he saw a burning bush that was not destroyed by the fire. When God called him in verse 4, he responded by saying, "Here I am." When God identified Himself as the God of the patriarchs Abraham, Isaac, and Jacob (v. 6), Moses hid his face. Moses knew the stories of the patriarchs and knew that this was the God of his ancestors who was speaking. God identified His purpose: the problem with Israel in captivity in Egypt. God's solution was that Moses was to go (vv. 7–10). Moses's response was, "Who am I to go to Pharaoh?" (v. 11). God promised that He would be with Moses and even gave him a sign, that of worship on Sinai when they were done (v. 12). Moses wondered if the people would know who God was, what name he would use (v. 13). God's response was the unarguable "I Am."

> God said to Moses, "I AM WHO I AM. This is what you are to say to the Israelites: 'I AM has sent me to you.'"[15] God also said to Moses, "Say to the Israelites, 'The LORD, the God of your fathers—the God of Abraham, the God of Isaac and the God of Jacob—has sent me to you.' This is my name forever, the name you shall call me from generation to generation." (NIV)

God goes on to tell Moses in more detail of what he would tell the elders (vv. 16–22) and the difficulties they would face in leaving Egypt. Mighty wonders would be required for Pharaoh to be convinced.

In Exodus 4, Moses brings up his doubts (v. 1). First, he lists his doubt about the Israelites believing him being God's messenger.

God's response shows him that he has his staff (4:2). Here God gives the first of the signs Moses can use for the elders. In Exodus 4:3, He has Moses throw his staff on the ground. The staff turns into a snake which turns back into a staff when picked up by the tail (Exod. 4:4). Moses obeys and also receives a second sign, that of the leprous hand (Exod. 4:6). An instruction to place his hand into the cloak turns it leprous. The leprosy disappears when the hand is placed into the cloak again (Exod. 4:7). The third sign is that water taken from the Nile and poured onto the ground turns into blood (Exod. 4: 8, 9). Moses's final objection is that he cannot speak well (Exod. 4:10). At this point, God loses patience with him and replies that He made people, and He would help Moses (4:11, 12). Moses still wants him to send someone else, and so God uses Moses's brother, Aaron (4:14–17). Moses's obedience enables him to lead the Israelites out of Egypt and to the promised land. He continues to serve God well (with a few exceptions) throughout the forty years the Israelites wandered in the wilderness.

Usually God's call is to those of upright character and heart like David. But God uses anyone who listens to Him—Jacob, for instance, was not known for his honesty. (In fact, a dishonest streak ran right through his family tree.) Certainly, God demands obedience (1 Sam. 15:22) and a willing heart. Unlike Jonah, we need to humble ourselves to His plan, not ours, regardless of our feelings and impressions. The person best used by God is one who has a clear conscience (Eph. 1:18, Col.1:9) who lives as a living sacrifice (Rom. 12:1, 2). Following God takes patience, for He often tries us out in little tasks first (Ps. 25:3, Luke 19:17). A mind saturated with His Word will also be able to sort out the difficult issues in life (Ps. 119:11) as well as in prayer (Matt. 9:37–8).

A biblical example of obedience is found in Samuel. Samuel was an obedient servant of God from the time he was a child in the temple (1 Sam. 3:1–9). His response to God's call was "Speak, Lord. I am listening." Speak and I will obey, speak and I will do it. When Samuel was called to anoint the new king after Saul, he had to obey God's instructions. It wasn't appearance God wanted; it was the heart (1 Sam. 16:7, 13). King David was called the man after God's own heart in 1 Samuel 13:14. He was a man who obeyed God. There were many others who also were called to serve God; among them were Jonah, Jacob, Peter, and Matthew. Each one responded differently to the call of God. Some ran away, like Jonah. Some openly confronted God like Paul. Some made mistakes like Peter. Others disobeyed God as King Saul did by sparing the animals and the enemy king from death. God calls many kinds of people with different gifts and abilities. He wants your obedience above all else.

The important thing about being called is *obedience in availability, not ability*. God wants available people more than able ones. That is why He could use Jacob, in spite of Jacob's disreputable character. God chooses the weak vessels to do His work (2 Cor. 4:7). If we could do everything ourselves, then we wouldn't trust God or need Him. God chooses the vessel to do His work. An international worker named Julie Fehr had a very hard time studying other languages. She couldn't pass Greek in Bible college although she did her best. But God called her to be a missionary, and she was able to learn the language of the Tsogo people in Gabon well enough to translate material into TEE (theological education by extension). Julie obeyed God even though it was difficult. God does give us gifts to do His work, but sometimes He just wants us to trust Him (1 Cor. 1:25–27).

Being Called to Missions

There are many more biblical examples we could list as to those receiving a call from God. Now let us proceed to what the call means for us personally, as those looking at missions and what we need to do about it. What does it mean to be called to mission work? A call to missions is a strong definite assurance from God and from the church that you are to be involved in ministry in another culture.

> It means that you are willing to let God use your life to this end. It does not mean that you have necessarily received a supernatural vision/explanation of exactly what God wants you to do. (Willits, website)

EXPLORING THE ROOTS OF MISSIONS: PERSONAL, BIBLICAL, AND SPIRITUAL

God may not, however, give you specifics right away as to how to go about this task of answering His call. There are various options to consider in this process, but the first thing to consider is the aspect of being called.

1. Acknowledging the claims of Christ on your life (1 Cor. 6:19, 20). You are not your own; you are bought with a price. It says in 2 Corinthians 5:14–15 we are to live for Him who died for us. The call of God comes first before any personal ambition or desires you may have. God has to be first in your life. He may call you to do something scary, or it may be something you love and cannot imagine doing anything else. Know this, that God's call and His equipping always come together. If He has called you, then you will be able to accomplish the task. Personally, for me as a teenager at a youth conference with a mission focus was when I realized God was speaking to me. That was when my commitment to Christ began to include full-time missions work. I have been in the process of pursuing that path and call ever since.

2. Understanding God's will—the Great Commission in Matthew 28:19–20. God's will is that everyone should hear the gospel of Jesus. Not only should we understand God's will for the salvation of the world but also our own role in the will of God. This demands an open heart and study of the Scriptures along with an awareness of what God is doing in the world. People in William Carey's day did not recognize the fact that they too were to spread the good news of the gospel to those far and wide. They were convinced in their selfishness that God could and would do it Himself. God chooses to use us so that we may be involved in it—as a blessing and part of our obedience. J.I. Packer says this of our role regarding evangelism:

> We must realize therefore that when God sends us to evangelize, He sends us to act as vital links in the chain of His purpose. (Packer 1961, p. 98)

The call to missions is a general commitment to follow Christ wherever He may lead with a specific openness to going overseas or cross-culturally in local situations. Being led to a specific area can be a part of a step-by-step process. It is much more than a subjective sense of God's call alone. The development of God's will for a person can be a very gradual thing, each step building on the step or process before it. Awareness of the spiritual need is the beginning of the call. Many early international workers or leaders were consumed with the spiritual need they saw. William Carey saw that the Lord's command was still in effect in his day, no matter what the other ministers said. While they were convinced that God didn't need their help, Carey saw that the Scriptures said to go, and he did. We are in partnership with God, because He has chosen us. He could easily do the job without us, that is true. But He chooses to use the weak and foolish things of this world (1 Cor. 1:18–31), His own people, to spread the message. He started out with His disciples who exhibited much of that weakness—and also has entrusted this to us too.

3. Openness to the leading of the Holy Spirit (Acts 13:2–4). Be willing to follow wherever He may lead you, near or far. This is more difficult for some than for others. God's leading may not always be easy, but it will always be the best place to be. Being in the centre of His will is the safest place. The Holy Spirit has a role in confronting the individual with a specific need to go. If He is convicting you, it will be unmistakable. It may also be a conviction about a group or people. Hudson Taylor and Albert Simpson saw the incredible need of millions of the lost, particularly the Chinese. The hymn writer talks about *the hundred thousand souls which are passing away every day*. There was a real concern for the well-being of this group. Amy Carmichael had a dream in which she saw many going over a cliff unheeding of the danger. For my oldest sister, this meant working in the northern parts of Canada. She went to a camp that was a ministry to the First Nations and from there on felt a call to work with them. She enjoyed her work, despite difficult working conditions. My oldest sister was willing to go where the First Nations were living and work with them.

4. Confirmation by the local church: The recognition of the local body of believers is important in providing both affirmation and spiritual support as you go. You do not go out into the mission field alone; this is the joint work of the sending and the sent ones. This includes getting input from your pastor as well as the elders. Paul and Barnabas were set aside by the elders to go to Antioch. They were recognized as having God's call on them by others in the church (Acts. 13:2–4). The counsel of spiritual friends and leaders on this matter is valuable. They can see your strengths and weakness better than you can. An ability to work within the body of Christ in ministry is a crucial part of this. If it seems that the best thing for you to do is go, then likely it is—listen to your common sense. Some early IWs went against the common sense of their friends and neighbours, but they obeyed what was common sense to them. The spiritual aspect of confirmation, God's peace about the decision, the affirmation of the group's counsel—be it the church, the friends, or godly leaders (Olson 1994, p. 79ff). God's confirmation will be a solid part of your call once you have reached the place or people you are going. You will go back to it many times when things get rough. Sometimes these things develop and become clearer as you go through the process of testing out God's will. For instance, a short-term mission experience would be a good opportunity to try out your ability to handle living in another culture. This can be a good indicator of how it would be working overseas. A "no" answer is as clear a direction as a "yes." Various skills and talents may be useful overseas as well; medical or health skills coupled with a desire to serve may well lead one overseas in a ministry for God.

5. Inner peace and assurance. You need to know that this is God's ultimate will for your life. You should not go for your own reasons but because you have been called and set apart for God's work in this area. There are a lot of good reasons to go to the mission field: the need is great, the workers are few, and there are needs to fill. The most important is knowing that you are doing what God wants you to do. It is a confidence of this is where one ought to be. This confidence will keep you going in the trials of culture shock and the rigors of life on the mission field. It is from God, not of yourself; if

the decision is made in your own strength, you will find it out pretty quickly on the mission field. For my youngest sister, this meant going to Thailand and working among the Thai in Bangkok. My oldest sister might not have felt comfortable in Thailand or my younger sister comfortable with the First Nations up north, but both went where they felt they were called to go.

Practical Steps I

Culbertson advocates the following practical steps:

1. Read about IWs and missions. IWs can be a very unconventional people, and they can accomplish amazing and incredible tasks in their roles. Robert Jaffray left a lucrative job in Canada to go overseas and laboured in Asia, translating vast amounts of scripture in brief periods of time. He died in a Japanese prison camp at the end of World War II. Reading their biographies will give you some idea of the trials they faced and and overcame. They were victorious in God's strength. It will be a source of great inspiration and encouragement. It may let you know what you have desire to do or not. If you cannot do pioneer work, then translation with Wycliffe is not a good idea. But if you love figuring out grammar and syntax, then it is an option to further explore. Biographies of various IWs working for various missions will be a great help.
2. Get involved in the mission education and mobilization program of your church. There is a lot of good material designed both for children and adults. It is informative and fun to get involved, as well as meeting international workers when they do come. In addition to the above, exposure to mission work can make the will of God known to you as you see the need. William Carey had a map on his wall and added notes to it from various sources. He included material from Captain Cook's expeditions, the East India Trading Company as well as travel reports.

EXPLORING THE ROOTS OF MISSIONS: PERSONAL, BIBLICAL, AND SPIRITUAL

3. Listen to IWs speakers when you can. Listening to them speak about their experiences, the tremendous need, and what God is doing firsthand is a great indicator of what could be in store for you in the future. It was by hearing an IW speaker at a youth conference that I was convicted about working full-time in missions work.

4. If possible, go on a short-term mission trip and get your "feet wet." You may learn a few words of language; get an idea of culture shock and different lifestyles. You will likely stay with IWs and learn firsthand from them. This experience will confirm that overseas work may be for you or not. If you enjoy the experience despite difficulties and challenges, this may help you. If you don't at all, then it's possible that God may not be calling you. While in Bible college, I signed up to go on an overseas trip for the summer. I was assigned to go to Hawaii, and it turned out to be quite the immersion experience. I enjoyed my work a great deal and learned a lot about the Hawaiian culture in the process. A lot of people may not think that Hawaii would be a difficult place to work as a Christian leader, but in addition to the Asian influence on the islands, there are a lot of local cultural things one must be aware of to be effective. The average American takes two years to adjust to the island/Asian cultural mix properly. If you do not adjust properly, then you cannot minister there. Some would assume that just because Hawaii is a part of America, then going from the American mainland to Hawaii would be easy. This assumption is not the case culturally. Island attitudes are different than those of the mainland in many areas. Listening to their comments about life and about the attitudes of the many tourists (from the mainland US) taught me many things. Assuming something is one way, the way that is familiar to you, may be a serious error when you travel overseas.

Often God uses a crisis experience too, in order to call one of His servants to this special kind of work. Paul was on the Damascus Road when Jesus stopped him in his persecution mode and touched him with true call for God. St. Patrick was kidnapped by pirates, which years later resulted in his returning to Ireland to evangelize. Ignatius of Loyola was laid up with a crushed leg from battle when he began reading the lives of the saints. It was he who began the Jesuit order. Nommensen, who worked with the Batak of Indonesia, committed himself to missions while on a sickbed as a boy. Luther was hit by a bolt of lightning and then committed himself to God's work.

The deaths of many IWs too were a breeze that fanned the flame of mission zeal. It was the death of Dr. William Cassidy, an IW en route to his field, that spurred others on to spend themselves for the gospel in 1887. In 1957, it was Jim Elliot's martyrdom in Ecuador that led to many others committing themselves to mission work. The list goes on and on.

For some it is just a matter of reasoning out that a call and opportunity together made a responsibility (Spener quote: Peters 1972, p. 283). James Gilmour felt that the work was abundant and the workers few. Liddell, the Olympic sprinter (of *Chariots of Fire* fame), could not refuse the call to China. Keith Falconer of Arabia felt the onus of proof rested on those who felt they couldn't go (this was echoed by the late musician Keith Green).

Prayer and Missions

The whole avenue of prayer and missions cannot be underestimated. God works mightily when the power of prayer is applied. God wants us to come to Him first so we can see how mighty He Himself is and what mighty works He does (Jer. 33:1–3). Indeed, the author of the book of Hebrews reminds us to approach the throne of grace boldly so that we can ask God, confident that He will answer our prayers (Heb. 4:16). Duewel here also makes the comment that while we cannot approach earthly royalty with any confidence, (indeed, one is not allowed to speak unless spoken to), but it is that when we talk to God, we can call Him "Father," as we are His children. We can, through prayer, move mountains (Matt. 17:20), and that is the kind of confidence we are to have.

Jesus said all power was given to Him (Matt. 28:18), and all power was also given from on high to the waiting apostles (Acts 1:8). They were told to wait in prayer, and they did—then was started the mighty work of evangelizing from Jerusalem, Judea, Samaria, and to the uttermost parts of the earth. As the early apostles started in the cities, so they are a great starting point for evangelism today. Cities are where people come looking for a new livelihood and a new chance at life. Duewel says that God has a wonderful plan for us "to join others around the world in prayer." He refers to, of course, the amazing modern technology that enables us to receive prayer requests immediately: phone, fax, or email or simply by text messaging.

> It is not the only thing you must do, but it is the greatest thing you can do. (Duewel 1986, p. 14)

Since Christ is returning soon, we can, through prayer, pray for reception of the message to those who have not heard and be a part of what God is doing in bringing in the harvest all over the world. Duewel assets that the population has grown so fast in recent years that we can hardly reach everyone, except through prayer and using urbanization, which is rapidly sweeping through the world, to reach others for the gospel. At the time Duewel wrote his book *Touch the World through Prayer*, there were 276 class cities in the world (cities with a population of one million or more). In 2015, the top ten cities have shifted somewhat to include Egypt and the US.

The chart below illustrates just where these bulging metropolises are located:

Top Ten Cities in the World

1. Tokyo
   Country: Japan
   2015 Population: 37.26 million

2. Delhi
   Country: India
   2015 Population: 25.87 million
3. Shanghai
   Country: China
   2015 Population: 23.48 million
4. Mexico City
   Country: Mexico
   2015 Population: 21.34 million
5. São Paulo
   Country: Brazil
   2015 Population: 20.88 million
6. Mumbai
   Country: India
   2015 Population: 19.32 million
7. Kinki major metropolitan area (Osaka and Kyoto)
   Country: Japan
   2015 Population: 19.3 million
8. Cairo
   Country: Egypt
   2015 Population: 18.82 million
9. New York, Newark
   Country: United States
   2015 Population: 18.65 million
10. Beijing
    Country: China
    2015 Population: 18.42 million
    (U.S. News & World Report)

Asia takes the lion's share including India, Japan, and China. The rest are in Egypt, South America, and the US. One of the most effective times of evangelism can be for newcomers to the cities. They are looking for a new life and are away from family and other social influences in their communities. In the cities, they are lonely and looking for some meaning and open to new ideas.

EXPLORING THE ROOTS OF MISSIONS: PERSONAL, BIBLICAL, AND SPIRITUAL

Duewel points out the role of Jesus as prophet, priest, and king (Rev. 3:14) and urges us to pray in the mighty name of Jesus to accomplish all the things that He desires to accomplish in the world today. We are partners with Christ in the gospel (1 Pet. 3:22) and are to give Him all honor (Phil. 2:9). Although Christ's kingdom is not here yet, Duewel claims that He reigns now by prayer (Duewel 1986, p. 40). Even as Christ reigns on the throne in His priestly-kingly role, He intercedes for us (Rom. 8:34) so that we also are being prayed for. The book of Hebrews makes much of Christ in this role (Heb. 4:14–16, Heb. 7:25, Heb. 8:1–3). We too are of the royal priesthood (1 Pet. 2:9, Rev. 1:5–6) and work with Christ in this area of prayer.

> God has ordained work through the prayers of His people. He is waiting for your intercession. You were not only created to pray; you were redeemed, justified, and sanctified to pray. (Duewel 1986, p. 41)

When we approach God in humility, agreeing with Him who we are and what we can do, then God is able to answer what we ask (Stanley 1982, p. 22). Satan neither likes prayer nor its effects. If we doubt God, we can't pray, so we need to rebuke Satan's doubts and bind him. Not every prayer will be answered with a yes, but if we go with a pure heart, pure motives, and with persistence, we can be sure that God will answer according to His faithfulness (Stanley 1982, p. 27).

Hartley reminds us we are to be as faithful as the early Moravians were during the time of the Reformation. At Herrnhut (the Lord's Watch), the leader Count Zinzendorf preached a sermon to the community. The Holy Spirit descended, and they felt God's mighty presence. The response to this was to set up a prayer meeting for the evangelization of many—the Moravians ultimately sent out six hundred teams in the next one hundred years. During those one hundred years, they had prayer going around the clock for the whole time, 365 days a year. This prayer was fuel for the mighty mission work that the Moravians began at that time (Hartley 1996, p. 99).

Jesus, the author and perfector of our faith, started out His ministry with forty days of fasting and prayer (Matt. 4:1–13).

Praying for IWs and their work is an incredibly powerful partnership in the ministry of God overseas. Once at a prayer conference, many international workers were gathering from restricted access countries. An IW from Myanmar, Ouan Lei, tried to attend for one year, but the government would not allow it. The first night of the conference another IW stood and prayed for Ouan Lei to attend. After twenty minutes of binding Satan in prayer, the IW from the United States sat down. Within two hours the phone rang, and Ouan Lei passed a message along to say he was free to attend. God had answered prayer!

Alliance Women, which is a part of the Christian and Missionary Alliance work in the local church, has a wonderful program for supporting IWs in many ways. They pray for and financially support the outfit for the IWs when they leave to go overseas. They also support in prayer the children of the IW parents. Susan Gailer reports the following story that illustrates how God answers prayer for the international worker families in their personal lives. In 1977, a missionary mom was concerned for her nine-year-old daughter who had been very sick for weeks. The only thing she could eat was Jell-O as three serious illnesses had left her very sick. No medical care was available, so they prayed and fed her the Jell-O. As the last packet was used up, the mom truly prayed for help. That afternoon, her husband came home with a package sent from the United States. It was full of Jell-O packets sent by a group of Alliance Women seven months earlier. Many women sent notes and asked about this family's needs. They had also been burdened in prayer.

Sometimes we get burdens to pray on another's behalf while not knowing why. One woman did so, praying for her pastor for half an hour instead of preparing supper. Later she found out that he'd been flying low on fuel and needed a place to land. He'd landed at the same time her burden to pray for him lifted (Stanley 1982, p. 43). Strange as it may sound, God often burdens us and then He meets the need—in effect making us active partners in His work. This happened to me while I was working at a school in South Korea.

EXPLORING THE ROOTS OF MISSIONS: PERSONAL, BIBLICAL, AND SPIRITUAL

I had a burden to go for Thailand for some time—approximately two years. Finally, I wrote letters and sent them overseas, and Korea was the answer to my prayers for work overseas. While in South Korea, I continued to have a burden for Thailand and actively pursued ways and means of getting a job there. I specifically felt Bangkok, the capital city, was where I was to go. I took out my slides from my first trip there and prayed for months over Thailand. Not only so I could go but for the lost there. One day I travailed mightily in prayer over a map of Bangkok. I felt moved beyond words that day, with great tears and groanings. From time to time I got job offers sent to me by friends who knew of my desire to return. One was sent from a couple in Canada. Another job was sent to me by a couple in the same town where I worked in South Korea. After that time of prayer, I soon got a letter from my contact in Bangkok; it was a job offer for the same position as I had previously received twice. Originally, I had not been interested in working in a school of four thousand boys. It seemed a bit much to me. But when I got the final letter with the job opening, I laughed. It was God hinting for the third time that He wanted me to take this job. The date on the letter was the same day the burden of prayer had been so heavy on me. God had moved and finally answered my prayer.

Prayer begins with God and ends with God. Lewis explains it:

> An ordinary Christian kneels down to say his prayers. He is trying to get in touch with God. But…he knows what is prompting him to pray is also God… But he also knows that all his real knowledge of God comes through Christ… standing beside him. God…is the goal… God is…the motive power. God is also the road… along which he is being pushed to that goal. (Lewis 1952, p. 142)

God knows your need, burdens someone on your behalf, then sets out to meet it. He is involving the community of Christ in answered prayer.

Stanley goes on to say that worries and burdens are not the same. A worry is something that primarily concerns you. A burden is for other people. They may vary in length between minutes, hours, and months until a change happens that says the burden is no longer there because the need has been met. This comes as a release. Nehemiah felt a burden for a long time for the walls of Jerusalem, and the king somehow must have been prepared to help meet his cupbearer's concern, for he sent armies with him when he granted Nehemiah's request to rebuild the walls of his home city.

When praying for others, we need to be aware of our leaders (1 Tim. 2:1–8), those called to the harvest (Matt. 9:38) and also the lost (1 Tim. 2:4–6).

> Our prayers are the link between God's inexhaustible resources and people's needs. Through prayer we direct God's hand of infinite resources to the hand of the person in need. (Stanley 1982, p.95)

We need to practise standing in the gap on behalf of others in the forefront of warfare.

Part of prayer is identifying with the needs/feelings of those whom we are praying for (Matt. 20:34, 9:36, 14:14; Mark 1:41; Luke 7:13). Suffering also enables us to identify with people so we can pray more effectively. We are especially to pray for their highest good, not ours. Being willing to be a part of the answer is also praying with honesty and vulnerability.

Part of being faithful in prayer is being like Aaron and Hur on Moses's behalf in Exodus 17:8–13. They held up Moses's arms while Israel prevailed in battle. If Moses got tired and put his arms down to rest, Israel began to lose ground. Jesus pointed out that we are to prevail in prayer and not faint (Luke 18:1). We need Aarons and Hurs to support us, especially as God's emissaries overseas. Good prayer supporters (Stanley 1982, p. 106) are to be spiritually minded, do warfare on our behalf, and to be compassionate and faithful.

EXPLORING THE ROOTS OF MISSIONS: PERSONAL, BIBLICAL, AND SPIRITUAL

Prayer for IWs as workers and also the lost in their strongholds (as in the 10/40 Window) are a very important part of the ministry of the work of God (John 16:13). Wycliffe reports that as they hand out Scripture tapes and New Testaments, that the prayers made a big difference. One of the volunteers prayed over the lack of interest in the materials one day. Suddenly she was surrounded, and the materials were all taken.

Being adequately informed for the unreached people groups is also a part of support for missions and the IWs who work among them. A stress is laid on adopting the people group and finding out as much as possible about them in order to pray more effectively. The idea is to pray until a church is planted among that people group. The prayer for these peoples can be held in different settings with continuously updated information. Specific prayer for protection of the international workers as they work and travel is something needed as we often take safety for granted. Another is compatibility with other workers and sensitivity to the culture as well as wisdom and vision for their ministry. It is important to share about people in sensitive areas so that they and their work are not jeopardized. Pray that God will bless the peoples in hearing of His Word (Isa. 12:4–5, 34:1, 49:6, 52:15; Matt. 24:14; Rev. 5:9–10). Prayer for the lost that they would have prepared hearts and be able to hear a culturally appropriate message. Prayer for perseverance for new believers in persecution and hard times.

News events tell of the intervention of God after prayer. The communist governments fell, and churches now are in the countries of Albania and Mongolia because many Christians prayed. Over thirty people groups are in the Turkic cluster (from west China to Turkey). There was no existing church among them and almost no Christians. Now there is at least one church among each people. There are churches among the Kazakhs, Kyrgyz, and Uzbek peoples. The prayers of Christians for the unreached groups is in effect to speak up for those who cannot (Prov. 31:8–9). In this way, the passage in Isaiah 55:5 will come true—peoples who had not heard previously will come to God.

Desired Qualities of International Workers

There are several *qualities* that must be in an effective IW. Reapsome and Lane mention the following qualities as being very important:

1. *Spiritual maturity*—the fruit of the Spirit shown in love, faithfulness, patience, and hope. This is an essential aspect to surviving overseas away from many of the conveniences and comforts of home. A strong daily walk with Christ must be developed before you go anywhere else or you will fall apart. Dependence on God alone is what will give you strength and perseverance. You cannot pretend this overseas; it will come out in one way or another, and others will see it even if you don't. One who is spiritually mature can be of great encouragement to others on the field.
2. *Sacrificial spirit*—John 12:24 speaks of dying as a kernel of wheat in order to serve and grow. The sacrifice may involve giving up family and friends, a good career, and many possessions. Sometimes it is hard to give these things up. This is one of the great difficulties that students have during their times of study—to leave it all behind and give it up. This is another example where the great biographies of IWs who gave up lucrative careers may be useful in inspiration.
3. *Servant's heart*—the attitude of helpfulness to others, teachability, "backbone," and self-starters. Serving means being willing to do more than one job: the small things as well as the big, important things.

Learning to trust in the sovereignty of God is a challenging task. The following poem illustrates the three qualities already mentioned:

> When God wants to drill a man,
> And thrill a man,
> And skill a man

EXPLORING THE ROOTS OF MISSIONS: PERSONAL, BIBLICAL, AND SPIRITUAL

When God wants to mold a man
To play the noblest part;

When He yearns with all His heart
To create so great and bold a man
That all the world shall be amazed,
Watch His methods, watch His ways!

How He ruthlessly perfects
Whom He royally elects!
How He hammers him and hurts him,
And with mighty blows converts him

Into trial shapes of clay which
Only God understands;
While his tortured heart is crying
And he lifts beseeching hands!

How He bends but never breaks
When his good He undertakes;
How He uses whom He chooses,
And which every purpose fuses him;
By every act induces him
To try His splendor out—
God knows what He's about.
(Author Unknown)

4. Able to *serve under authority* of the mission board or the national church. Some people do not work under others very well. The kind of mission board you work with is important because it may determine how well you work with them. Finding these details out is a part of the sifting out process we will deal with in more detail later.
5. *Flexible*—not just confined to one job or role but willing to do many things, even beyond one's sphere of experience or training. In my role of ESL teacher, I have had to do

things like catch geckos (lizards) in a classroom of boys, teach art and music to elementary children, draw pictures on the board to illustrate things, and lead in singing time. I was also involved in English camp and the Christmas concert in a singing group. While teaching ESL in Canada, I did some lessons on Canadian geography and developed a game to help them remember the difficult Canadian names of provinces and cities. All of these things were not necessarily ESL-related, but they came under the broad umbrella of whatever-it-takes to get the message across. A missionary friend in Africa has led medical teams to help with vision issues and built a brick oven to help conserve wood in a drought-ridden area in addition to regular duties of teaching Bible studies and praying for the sick in her work. Sometimes the umbrella of what you do to achieve your goals must be a wide one; lots of things come under the influence of that umbrella.

6. *Personal integrity and honesty*—healthy interpersonal relationships. Successful IWs are always learning culture, language, and education skills. They build a support base at home for prayer and encouragement. They are good examples at home. Olson adds to the list: humility (not a know-it-all attitude). Not only in language learning but also in how to function in the local culture. Learning from the people you are working among also creates mutual respect. International workers must earn the right to be heard before they can speak with authority. Coming in with "*all the answers*" can be seen as being very arrogant. The target people won't accept your new ideas if you can't learn from them either. The give-and-take applies in many ways and many areas.

A strong sense of self-discipline is also important. If you are the only one on your station or in your area, you must be able to do things yourself. You cannot expect others to always help you out or to give you spiritual food. A personal walk with God will be a part of your own growth overseas (Olson 1994, p. 285). I survived for six months on my own during my second trip to South Korea. There was no Christian fellowship available to me, and so it was me and God, my Bible, my journal, and my hymnbook. That was a great growing experience for me, difficult though it was at the time.

A second type of qualification is that of *psychological.* Spiritual health is related to emotional or psychological health. *Adaptability and a sense of humour* are important for IWs. Being able to adjust to new situations and laugh at oneself is a healthy trait. It releases tension and helps to focus on the job at hand. The first several months of being in a new place there are many new things to adjust to culturally. Learning a new language means that you will make a lot of mistakes. A certain amount of *emotional stability* is also important. Missionary work is very stressful, and if one is not stable at home, they will never survive overseas in another culture. It will not work. The pressures of being new in a culture and having to learn a new language can be very trying at times. An IW who is comfortable with themselves and at ease with who they are can adapt more readily than one who is tense all the time. A *spirit of co-operation* is as important as being able to work alone. Teamwork is a strength in certain field situations. Learning to work well with others can be a very profitable asset. Being able to *endure hardship* is another part of missionary life. Granted the early IWs had it rougher than international workers do now, but the changes required for many pioneer efforts are difficult. Patience and perseverance are very necessary ingredients for the successful IW. It takes both to learn a language and a culture. And it takes all you have to be able to win souls for Christ in the midst of difficult surroundings both physically and spiritually. *Humility* is not only a spiritual quality; it is not feeling superior to others. International workers are put into a constant learning mode for the first two to four years on the field where they learn the language and the culture. This can be very intimidating unless they have a humble heart to begin with and can accept their new status as learners, not just teachers. It is difficult to come from home where one is respected and well-learned to a place where little (of local culture) is known. This includes *racial complexes.* You cannot minister properly if you are feeling you are better than the people you are working with. This is an integral part of humility on the part of the IW.

It is important to remember that as important as biblical qualifications are, in addition to training, that it is as Peters says:

> Not more or mere academics but also upon the character, resourcefulness and personality of the Christian workers. (Peters 1972, p. 292)

Not only are the qualifications spiritual and doctrinal (as already discussed), but there are also personality and social aspects to be considered as well. Where would Carey have been if he had allowed the dissension in his mission team to grow? He was the personality able to overlook the faults and encourage his fellow labourers. Those whose personality and social aspects are the most helpful may vary depending on what the sending church or missionary society desires. They are determined by several factors: the government of the country the IW is working in, for example. Certainly, if it is in a country with antagonistic attitude to the gospel, then professional qualifications are as valuable as good people skills. The needs of the church in the given country may have certain requirements as well. Are there technological needs or basic biblical teaching and education of leadership? The type of ministries dictates to a large degree the general needs to be filled. Usually there are many tasks an IW does that are not on the professional resume, but necessary, nonetheless.

Practical Steps II

Discovering Details: Willits has several ways of weeding out options and discovering what prospective workers want to do. Praying about every step of the process is vital for ultimately a peace is necessary for the work or field chosen. He lists them in several distinct categories.

Support services: these include tasks like teaching missionary children, bookkeeping for the mission itself, or becoming involved in manual labour such as carpentry or mechanics. One of my fellow students from seminary is now working in an administrative capacity in Spain. This is one way of being involved. Many short-term missions also do building projects like this as you do not need a second language to get the job done, with other evangelistic tasks (using an interpreter on the side). This really helps in countries that don't have the regular manpower to get building jobs done and encourages missions on a personal level for churches.

Community development: these are services for the general welfare of the people—medical work or medical teaching, relief work, agricultural projects, business enterprise development (like home crafts, etc.), building projects, literacy, orphanages, and education work. I have a friend who is doing literacy work in Niger, teaching the women how to read. I know of others in my home denomination who are doing other kinds of community development. The needs are many for this work.

Evangelism/Church planting: this is the traditional kind of missionary work. The international workers get to know the people and relate to them from a spiritual perspective. Translation of the scriptures was a valuable part of the early IW work and is also included here. Many of those in Wycliffe Translators do more than just translate.

Discipleship: this is leadership training, on individual or church group basis, teaching in schools for leaders and pastors, Bible translation, and counselling.

There are *partnering options* in the field, whether you want to work in a new area, with an individual IW, or on a team. This allows for diversity and support in the new area. Another possibility is to work with an established organization with a proven record overseas. There are many mission groups with informational literature in their area of specialty.

The third area which Willits details as a part of his criteria for narrowing down the possibilities is that of *ministry preparation*. Be sure to contact the church or mission you are interested in and get their particular requirements. Spiritual preparation requires personal maturity and the ability to do what God asks. A spiritual mentor is very helpful in learning how to walk with God day by day. Formal training is required by many denominations and missions. Some Bible colleges have a lot of mentoring built in with their programs. Team preparation can help foster unity as the individuals prepare together. The final aspect of ministry preparation is building a support base. This is for spiritual and financial support. It is also important for people who are supporting IWs to write them and let them know they are praying for them. Prayer for IWs has long-reaching effects.

Willits mentions missionary work and *location* as a factor. Sometimes this happens at the same time the person received their sense of calling. I myself have always been interested in people from Asia. My first intense contact experience was tutoring a refugee girl from Laos in English in high school. Later I went to Hawaii, which has many folk from various parts of Asia. I also worked in a Chinese church for a time. Finally, I went overseas to teach English in Thailand and, later, South Korea. All of these seemed to point the way for me to work in Asia with Asians. God's pattern for me has been clear. For others it may not be so simple and direct. Willits has some other practical suggestions—thinking about what they'd like to do and how to do it which will help them decide where to go. Interest in working with Muslim people will then narrow the focus onto where these people are concentrated. Prayer and research both will help you decide this. Willits says thinking about the *where* in blocks will be helpful. Consider the religious blocks (Muslim, animist, Hindu, Buddhist), the socio-economic background (developed, underdeveloped, and rural), or the general culture and race for ways of looking at the possibilities.

The final aspect is that of *personal profile*. Where you are *from* can be as valuable as where you are *at* or *going to*. This is general information such as married or single, absence or expected presence of children. Single people can be fairly flexible as to where they go. They can be limited to *whom* they minister to in certain situations. Some cultures do not understand the whole idea of singleness, and it comes across to them in a very negative fashion. In this situation, married people can minister more effectively. The presence of children will often open up many opportunities with neighbours. Children will draw people out and become a common ground for meeting neighbours. There are advantages to each role in the adopted culture.

There are certain circumstances that may affect these kinds of life decisions. *Special needs* are one of these considerations. *Health* needs can limit where you can go and how long you stay. Many a Western IW has come back because the health care is better at home for their situation. There are also considerations of education for children—home schooling or boarding school or even local schools in some places. Finally, last but not least are outstanding financial *debts* which can make ministry very difficult indeed. Training is one thing, but paying off debt can take a long time and hinder those otherwise ready for ministry elsewhere. Abilities and talents can be easily plugged in to the needs available. Many missions start by listing the needs they have, and people looking at websites or brochures can then respond as they see fit. Foreign languages are good, and a diverse academic background may help in many developmental situations overseas. Finally, there are *personality traits* that may affect how the work is done. Would urban or rural situation suit you best? Is there a team to work with or will you be alone? Do you need more adventure or security? Not all the mission groups consider all of these factors. Some international workers are just assigned to wherever there is the greatest need, regardless of background and experience. It is a good idea to know which mission or agency does that, so if it is an issue for you, then you can then decide who you won't be going with.

And, finally, if you cannot go, as K.P. Yohannan says from Gospel for Asia, you can always finance native IWs for much less of the cost it would be for someone from the West. This is a valid way of looking at missions, especially as the third world (now known as the developing world) is becoming a growing force in sending out IWs. However, as Guthrie cautions, one must again do some research and find out which agencies are able to send out (and keep on the field) their IWs. Sending out IWs is a vital part of church health and growth, but native IWs cannot reach the world alone. There would be a shortage of four thousand people groups unreached if there were no Western international workers out there, says Guthrie (Guthrie 2000, p. 15). One way of resolving this problem is to work in partnerships with mission agencies; many of them are international in origin as well as personnel. The Christian Literature Crusade (now the CLC International) has a seven-hundred-person missionary force in fifty nations with six hundred locals and one hundred foreign IWs.

Summary

Having covered the spiritual foundations as well as the preparation of the individual for the work, we now go to another kind of preparation—that of spiritual warfare. This is so fundamental to the believer's life and work that it cannot be overlooked. It is as important as knowing your scriptures for salvation. It is an integral part of the spiritual armour of the Christian worker.

5

Spiritual Warfare

Spiritual warfare, whether it is for personal protection as a Christian believer or on the forefront of what God wants doing, is a valuable part of missions work today. Being prepared in terms of spiritual armour is just as important as having the academic or practical training. In fact, without knowing the basics of the Christian walk, you cannot be effective no matter how well prepared you are in other areas. God will teach you along the way, as discipleship is always a learning curve. However, it is good to be aware of the religious atmosphere one is walking into as well as the daily practise of walking in the Spirit.

Part 1: Understanding the Basics

Old Testament Patterns

The history of the Old Testament is a pattern of our walk with God. Even more, the Old Testament is a manual for spiritual warfare. The battles then (often but not only) were in flesh and blood, but the results were the spiritual purity of His people. God showed Himself to be the Father and Creator of His people, Israel. Israel struggled with obeying God, and even in taking the land God had given them, they did not obey the instructions of destroying the people of the nations around them. They were told not to fraternize with their new neighbours. These neighbours worshipped pagan gods with detestable practises. Worship of those gods (especially Baal) included sexual prostitution. That was one reason why they were told to wipe out their Canaanite neighbours.

Combined with the worship of false gods also was the concept of high places. They were the places where the Canaanites worshipped their gods. Destroying the high places was a command that God gave to the Israelites as they battled the Canaanite nations around them. When they failed to tear down the high places, the worship of the false gods persisted, and the Israelites polluted worship of the One True God. Sadly, even Solomon, the king who built the temple, was also one who worshipped the high places (Couturier 2017), favouring his pagan wives (1 Kings 11:4). Thus, the pattern began that was to follow throughout the reigns of the kings of Israel and Judah; the good and godly kings worshipped God and took a stand against the false gods. The bad kings followed the Baals and went against God. The prophets of Israel loudly denounced the sins of Israel and Judah with Asherah worship (Isa. 17:8, 27:9; Jer. 17:1–2; Micah 5:13–15). Even the children would remember them, which showed the extent to which they had become common. It was the worship of false gods which led to Israel's captivity, as well as Judah. There, forced away from the God who had claimed them, they learned how to devote themselves to God alone.

Spiritual Grounding for International Workers

The first half of this chapter will deal with basic foundational material for the personal use of the IW, then to ministry time principles as well as some specifics for the IW to consider in dealing with spiritual issues internally. Then the material goes on to the practical missionary applications overseas. More and more often these days IWs are becoming aware of the necessity for spiritual warfare on many levels. Certainly, if one is not prepared in North America, then the difficulties overseas will quickly overtake the newcomer. Often the practise in facing the enemy at home will help in the task ahead. God always makes the challenges of the Christian life a little harder so that the growth goes on par with the difficulties. He grows His people into the task—sooner rather than later is usually better than a plunge into the deep end. Walking by faith always takes courage and a spiritual deep breath. Being prepared to defend against the attack of the enemy on his home territory is certainly a part of the missionary task in taking people from one kingdom into another. Satan's grip is stronger (and less subtle) in areas where his political and spiritual control is obvious. It may be more difficult to see where Satan is working at home until one has been overseas and become sensitised to these areas of spiritual influence.

It is as basic as putting the armour of Ephesians 6 in place. Spiritual warfare is not simply a matter of being prepared to defend yourself when you are going into ministry. It is a lifestyle because we Christians are all under attack from the enemy of our souls, Satan. He is always prowling around, looking for someone to devour (1 Pet. 5:8). We need to have a lifestyle that enables us to defeat Satan here, where we are at home, preferably, before going to where so much is new. In fact, John White declares that becoming a Christian totally changes your relationship with Satan. Instead of being his puppet and servant, you are now his enemy. You have gone out from under his control; you have moved from the kingdom of darkness to the kingdom of light. Being properly grounded in Christ is a part of being an effective Christian. Dr Timothy Warner makes this statement in his workbook for cross-cultural ministry:

> Most counselling problems in Christians are the result of failure to deal with basic issues in the discipleship process. (Warner 1993, p. 26)

Today in the new century, we are facing more and more problems in society than ever before. Christians and Christian families are not immune to these problems either. They are facing major spiritual battles and are helpless because they do not know how to defend themselves. Green makes a list of the influences that Satan has in this world (Green 1981, p. 100).

1. Sickness—Luke 13:16, Matthew 9:32
    Distinguish between the healing and casting out—Luke 13:32, CR Luke 4:40

Demons are expelled, diseases healed.
2. Historical situations—Revelation 2:10, 13
3. In nature—chaos vs. Leviathan in OT
    Jesus speaks to the wind and waves: "Peace be still," as if the elements are alive.
4. Jewish law—Romans 7:10–14, Revelation 2:9 under Satan's power
5. False apostles—1 John 4:1, 2 Corinthians 11:13–15, 1 Timothy 4:1
6. Human sin—sin does it (Rom. 7).
7. State, government—CIA, Mafia, etc.
8. Death—Hebrews 2:14

The above are situations which may be taken at face value, but there may also be a spiritual element which all too often is ignored by Western Christians. We take for granted that Satan isn't involved, whereas we should be asking if indeed there is more to any situation than meets the eye. From simple things like sickness, is the cause disease or a germ, should be asked. Also take into account events in history—are they the result of man's disobedience, or is there something demonic as well? Agencies as well as individuals can be coerced to do something which is not of God's will, especially if led by the right kind of leader who can talk them into it. One must be cautious, however, not to take everything as an attack from the enemy. That can make anyone paranoid and focussing more on the enemy or what might be the case than on God's revelation and will for that moment in time. Trusting God for guidance and listening to His Spirit at all times are keys to discerning what is going on and who is behind it. The key here is in balance; God has the power to change anything that is wrong, and we need to learn to listen to what He says is going on in the world.

In addition to these are the lies of secularism, humanism, relativism, materialism, and pluralism. These lies put man in the centre of the world (humanism), take God out of the universe which is a closed place (humanism, secularism), and place the focus on the here and now, not eternity (secularism, materialism) (Weerstra 1997, pp.

5–6). Furthermore, knowledge itself is deemed to be relative (relativism: not absolute or absolute truth), that there is more than one spiritual reality in the world and that these are all okay (pluralism). Thus, there are many ways of getting to heaven. Finally, there is naturalism, which has no purpose to life because there is nothing beyond the scientific laws. It is quite amazing how these contradictory currents can be swirling about us in Western culture. These have permeated Western culture and crept into our Christianity as well. It is very difficult to preach a unique Christ if you have in mind that all religions are equal. The backpedalling that the Western world is doing (and the Christian church as well) in order not to offend others of other faiths is not helpful to the truth of Christ being the only answer.

The walls in the days of the Old Testament were for protection. Nehemiah built a wall before he built his home or the temple. They were a basis for defence. Today they are a symbol for protection of authority in society. When these walls are broken, Satan can rule quite easily. When there is no authority or submission, Satan can infiltrate. In chaos or rebellion, Satan rules. This means that marriages, families, churches, and schools are under attack to promote this chaos.

Certain kinds of actions and people can destroy these walls of authority. Sherman lists the kinds of things that destroy these walls (Sherman 1990, p. 89). (1) Godless leadership—when leaders don't live according to biblical principles, their leadership is abdicated to the unseen rulers. That is why we need to pray for leaders and intercede for them (1 Tim. 2:1–2). The leaders we have need to be strong and lead with integrity. If we undermine authority, we are helping Satan. (2) Neglect can also destroy the walls. If we neglect our responsibilities as leaders, parents, and teachers, then Satan takes over influence. (3) Rebellion—this is a large issue because everyone does it. If we exercise our rebellion by being stubborn and defiant, we can hand the power over to the enemy. Rebellion is the rejection of authority, that is why it is like witchcraft (1 Sam. 15:23). It lets Satan in to rule over us. Romans 13:1–3 says that all are subject to authorities. A modern example of this could be residents of the US rebelling against the COVID rules of wearing masks and self-isolating. This rebellion is endangering their very lives, and the people do not see it. The authority of the leaders can be protection and slow down evil, says Sherman.

Dealing with these issues at home is just the beginning. It is easier to do so in one's own culture than dealing with them in a foreign country with different kinds of social pressures. Being aware of the gaps in our Christianity will be helpful in warning us not to pass these things along to new believers. Rediscovering a biblical worldview is a part of the process of finding out who God really is, not what our Western culture has determined Him to be. In fact, if you don't deal with these many issues before you leave, they will cause a lot of trouble. In addition to rediscovering our biblical worldview, knowing and affirming one's position in Christ is one of the best preventatives to serious problems. People are becoming Christians from all types of dysfunctional backgrounds. A dysfunctional background is one which gives you an unhealthy view of life and unhealthy coping methods. For example, if you come from an alcoholic household, you could develop several attitudes. Anderson gives this example of three brothers in this situation. One is afraid of his father and hides from him. The second one tries to please his father as much as possible. The third is big enough to fight back, so he stands up to his father. So as these boys grow up, they learn to see authority in the same way. One hides, one pleases, and one fights back. This is also the way they see God. This leads to several questions that these three will face as a result of this lifestyle: How can you serve God if you are afraid of Him? How can you love someone you are afraid of? How can you please someone who is irrational? How can you come to God if you are angry with Him? That is why we need to deal with these problems. These issues are why we need to deal with basics in grounding of oneself in Christ, in your Christian identity before going into ministry.

So not only do we have a troubled society, we also have this view that has permeated our views as believers, that is of the Enlightenment, working in our increasingly secularized society. This shall be referred to several times in this chapter as it is something many believers do not notice.

EXPLORING THE ROOTS OF MISSIONS: PERSONAL, BIBLICAL, AND SPIRITUAL

Worldviews

Worldviews are how we see the world. It is like a pair of coloured glasses that tints everything we see. It is our presuppositions about how the world functions. People will not always live the way they say they do, but they will live what they believe deep down inside. It is unconscious for most people. This affects all their actions and behaviour because we build our lives on what we believe. For example, the person who goes to a doctor is told that they must take the medicine to get well. But if they don't take the medicine, they won't get well. What do they really believe? They believe that taking the medicine will not help them. In the same way a person who says they believe in God but does not live that way does not really believe in Him. People who pray in church but then go to read the horoscope do not really believe that God makes a difference, that He is in control of their lives. If you say you believe that the plane is safe, but you are too afraid to fly in it, you do not believe the plane is safe.

Warner gives several examples of worldviews. One example of a worldview that is that of animism. Many people believe in animism all over the world. It is even in New Age thinking. Animism is the belief that the world has spiritual power in the rocks, trees and mountains, etc. Animists always assume that there is a supernatural meaning behind everything. This power is not God's power, but it is impersonal. It is not good or bad but just an impersonal force similar to electricity. It can be controlled by people—the shamans, medicine men, or witch doctors. They are experts in controlling the power. In Thailand, the people believe that making an offering to the spirits in the spirit houses will keep them safe. They believe that Buddha can answer their prayers and give them blessings.

A second example of a worldview is that of the Western mindset or secularism. This view separates science and religion. It says that there are answers to our questions about life apart from God. It says there are natural explainable laws for everything. Weerstra points out that the many "isms" in Western culture (relativism, secularism, humanism, materialism, pluralism, and naturalism) have eroded any kind of spiritual dependence whatsoever (Weerstra 1997, pp. 5–6).

In fact, these unconscious factors are as dangerous as any direct spiritual attack. They are lies about who we are and where we came from. These "isms" have taken any the idea that God is actively at work in the world. Dr. Warner tells of a woman who was diagnosed with over two hundred allergies by her doctor. Once she dealt with her spiritual issues, the allergies were completely gone. There are connections between the spiritual and the physical; we just don't always see it from the Western viewpoint because we have excluded God from our thinking to a very large degree. Our very Western Enlightenment heritage does not allow for it. We don't automatically include Him in our presuppositions. We forget about the realm of the spirit. The spiritual dimension to our lives is largely forgotten and left out. Thus the Westerners are the bringers of materialism and science to the tribal folk, forgetting that God is over all, and it is He that makes the science work as much as He is the one who stops evil spirits from wreaking havoc. It is the mental picture of God that limits the Western Christian mind.

Green comes up against the typical Western mindset with a view that tends to approach the whole issue in a matter-of-fact way, without undermining Scripture. His standpoint of philosophy says that "there is no power without personality."

> Eastern mysticism in its rejection of matter
> is no more convincing than western materialism
> in its rejection of mind. (Green 1981, p. 19)

God cannot be good if we see what happens in nature (disasters like tsunamis and earthquakes) or human wickedness (genocide or ethnic cleansing, wars) as reason alone for what happens. There must be a reasonable explanation for the evil in the world and, at the very least, that points to a presence we call Satan.

A third example of worldviews is that of Jesus as shown in the Bible. The Bible sees three realms: God's realm, the realm of the angels, and the realm of people and things. God is the only one in His realm—He is sovereign. Satan wants to rule in God's realm (2 Thess. 2:4, Luke 4:7). He likes us to think he is the equal in power and might to God. He is not. Angels were created holy (Matt. 25:31) by God. They are also able to come into our realm of people and things. They help believers in protection and guidance (Heb. 1:14, 2 Kings 6:17, Matt. 18:10). Satan was one of the highest angels, and he rebelled against God (Ezek. 28:12–15, Isa.14:12–15).

Sherman talks about three kinds of angels: warriors (Dan. 10, Rev. 12), messenger angels (Gabriel, for example), and worshipping angels (Rev. 5:11–12). Lucifer was a created being (Ezek. 28:13–15) and wise among the angels. He was beautiful but proud (v. 17) and was driven out of the garden. Lucifer was a mighty angel, but God's angels cast him out (Rev. 12:8–9).

> God has never fought with Satan and never will… God is infinitely greater in every respect… which is precisely why we are supposed to carry out the battle in the power of God. (Sherman 1990, p. 83)

Satan is the great adversary; that is in fact the meaning of his name. Satan opposes God, although God is not his equal in any way. Scripture urges us to resist Satan (1 Pet. 5:9, Jas. 4:7). We resist by speaking out our resistance. We need to rebuke and deny them access to our lives. Mark 16:17 says that in His name we would cast out devils.

The story of mankind includes Satan's existence because of the Fall. Mankind had everything, then lost it all due to yielding to temptation in the garden. Eve and Adam were deceived, and we suffer because someone evil has it in for us. People are blind to the evils of this world even in the environment and the way we have treated it so poorly (Green 1981, p. 21). The god of this world is in charge, and mankind is dutifully wrecking things according to his pleasure. We all experience temptation; no one is immune. There is also direct worship of Satan in the occult. This also gives Satan a good deal of power because people are giving in to what he wants. They are letting Satan's plans come to fruition to a certain degree. Finally, Green wraps this up by noting that Jesus said more about Satan than anyone else. The temptation in the wilderness (Matt. 4:1–11) was just the beginning of Satan's opposition to Jesus. Then came the parables with the devil sowing weeds (Mark 4:15, Matt. 13:39), and even in the Lord's Prayer (Matt. 6:13, Mark 3:22–26), Satan is the chief opponent of God's people. In John 14:30, Jesus said the ruler of this world was coming and His end was near. On the cross, Jesus declared His victory would be ultimately complete (John 12:31). Satan attacks us as believers because we are God's children. Satan and his angels are also able to come into our realm. What Satan started in the garden of Eden he continues today.

Many times Christians are confused by what realm their power comes from. They are not aware that there is such a huge disconnect between what they say they believe in their theology and what they actually do in practise. When international workers thinking this way work overseas, they may unconsciously teach the worldview that excludes God even though they are Christians. This is directly the result of our Enlightenment heritage in the West. We tend to give verbal service to God's power but don't see it because we don't really expect God to be present. The perspective of spiritual power being active in life, from both good and bad origins, was very much left out of the picture until recently. This can be seen in the type of converts that were made. In Africa, a Christian man went to the witch doctor to get a charm. He wanted the charm so he could get elected to be bishop in the church! There was something very wrong with his approach and understanding of both the role of the bishop and the power of God in his life. We do not need charms to help us as Christians. We have God's power working in our lives to help us. God is helping us Himself. In the West, we tend to be just like the animists, except we rely on power from science (as opposed to other spirits) to get what we want. Some IWs have told new Christians to depend on science instead of the spirits to get good crops. It is God who makes the crops grow, and it is He who makes the laws of science work. We need to learn to depend on God even in our science and technology, because it is God that makes science work, not us. It is His laws that enable function and activity.

EXPLORING THE ROOTS OF MISSIONS: PERSONAL, BIBLICAL, AND SPIRITUAL

Weerstra proclaims that we need to get back to Scripture in order to correct our worldview. In this way, we deal with the underlying layers of culture of behaviour, values, and beliefs (Weerstra 1997, p. 8). The disciples on Emmaus road did not recognize Jesus (Luke 24:32ff). He challenged their worldview about His death and showed them from the scriptures what God's true plan had been all along. They had been so caught up in their traditional Jewish view of the Messiah they had missed it in His teaching.

Kingdom Authority

Warner uses the term *warfare relationships* to describe what is taking place between the believers, the non-believers, and the spiritual realm. God is at the top; He is the Creator and Ancient of Days (Ps. 33:6, 9; Dan. 7:9–14). Williams and others point out that it is the worship of God that should be first and foremost in our minds, as that sets Him in His rightful place. He is not a Watchmaker who is distantly out there, winding up clocks when needed. God is actively involved in our day-to-day lives, more than that He is our King. As King and Lord of the universe, He deserves our full attention, respect, love, and honour. He is the one in control of the heavenlies—the angels and demons are subject to Him. God has true kingdom authority and graciously shares it with us. Psalm 8 says that we are made a little lower than the angels, but that does not mean we are worth less than they are. In fact, God says that one day we shall judge them, and so we have an important role in God's kingdom. We can use His authority to fight our spiritual battles.

Ancient kings of the East provided prosperity, justice, and security for their people. Like them, God is our King and provides for us but on a much more extensive scale. We need to recapture that kind of vision of God's kingdom extending over all the earth and worship Him, understanding how great and wonderful and holy He is (Isa. 6:1–3, Ezek. 1:1–28). God, in a very real sense, invades this world and our lives to establish His reign (Williams 2002, p. 3). We have forgotten who He is, in this post-Enlightenment world, and have replaced Him with humanism and secularism. He is our judge and judges the nations too (Ps. 99:4, 67:4; Rom. 1:18). Our God is righteous (Ps. 51:4) and has declared Himself our Redeemer (Exod. 6:6 cf. Mark 10:45). He has unconditional love for us (Deut. 7:8). He is the Chosen Servant (Isa. 49:7) who declares our souls are without price (Ps. 49:7–8).

As Christians, we need the guidance of the Holy Spirit every day in our lives to have proper discernment and right living. We often do not seek it as often as we need it; we are so used to being independent and deciding on the most logical or convenient option instead of asking God what He wants. Most of the time following God's written Word will be clear enough, but practise in seeking God's specific guidance cannot be overstated. This doesn't mean we seek out for every little thing but to keep in mind that the thing that seems the most reasonable is not always the approach God wants. Noah building an ark was not a normal thing in his day. Yet this was God's will. Neither was taking only three hundred men into battle against a formidable enemy army of thousands as Gideon was asked to do.

In addition to this, we need to see our world through His eyes and catch all the things we are so used to as being a part of our Western culture but are not explicitly Christian. In fact, many of these things are quite inappropriate for us to think as Christians. We really need to, as Paul says in Romans 12:2, transform our minds. The legacy of the Enlightenment and all the "isms" it has left behind has warped our Western Christianity out of biblical proportions. Getting rid of the idea of God's intimate absence in our lives and welcoming the Holy Spirit in, even if it means He tells us strange things. Many of the prophets of the Old Testament were told to do things in the course of their prophetic lives that were totally against the norm (Massey 2000, p. 5). But God had a point to make through them. Becoming comfortable with the Holy Spirit on a daily basis takes practise garnered through time spent in reading God's written Word as well as in prayer.

Our relationship with God must be based on truth. We must not only say the truth in our lives but also put it to work in our belief system or worldview. We need to practise saying to ourselves what the Holy Spirit has said in Scripture, and this often requires walking by faith. There is a disconnect between the reality of God's truth and the world around us. The world presses in on us and effects the way we feel. This is not an accurate reflection of truth; just because one is having a bad day does not mean one is forsaken by God or that God is not there. A negative experience does not mean abandonment or rejection by God. That is an illusion sent to us by the enemy. Deep in our hearts we tend to have attitudes that are contrary to God's truth. We just say one thing out loud, but inside it's a different story. Sometimes it's a bad day, something is wrong, and people are hurting. If someone says, "How are you?" we say, "Fine." We don't tell the truth that we are hurting. We don't say that we are worried about something or that we are struggling with victory. This is a Christian game we play, particularly in the West. We pretend we are fine, and we are not. This is not being truly honest with ourselves. Some people really have difficulty believing that God loves them. So they pray really hard and hope that God will love them (even though He already does). But they don't believe it and thus are unable to put it into practise in their lives. Learning to connect the theology in our head with what we live in our lives is vital to being victorious as Christians. The "law of the excluded middle" is not only in our worldview "out there," it is in our lives and faith, or lack of it. Understanding this is important in the role of the Holy Spirit in our lives. Depending on Him for understanding who we are in Christ is the key to our growth and spiritual strength. We must believe that the Holy Spirit will guide us in our life, and we must listen to His guidance. He is the One who leads us in spiritual battle and in the understanding of truth. The Holy Spirit is the one whom we need for our guidance and life (John 14:26–17, 16:13). Learning to listen to Him instead of the lies is a part of our growth in spiritual warfare. He is the spirit of wisdom and revelation for us (Eph. 1:17) that we may know God better.

Gordon opens his book *How Much More* with the following illustration. A mission conference was being held, and there seemed to be a good deal of resistance for no particular reason. Finally, the wife of one of the ministers prayed around the pews and other parts of the sanctuary against the forces of darkness that were hindering the work. That night a marked change came over the group, and many were blessed by the work (Gordon 1983, p. 122). The battle is before us as believers, and although old, it is not finished yet. In prayer we can defeat the enemy because of Whom we are praying to. It is by God's mighty power that Satan is defeated, but we have to take a hold of that power by faith and apply it as God's faithful servants.

The battle takes place at three levels: (1) Within ourselves—the struggle of right vs. wrong (Rom. 7:15, 23). We know the power of temptation, and that is the easiest way to spot an attack. Jesus was confronted on this level and did not yield. (2) In the world about us—in the nations (1 John 5:19). There are many policies and governments that are definite tools of evil, and some that are unwittingly so. Some do not seek the good of their peoples, only for themselves. (3) In heavenly places (Dan. 10:13). Scripture talks about Satan being the god of this age (2 Cor. 4:4) who has blinded the minds of the unbelievers so that they cannot see the truth in Jesus Christ. Jesus talked about when the prince of this world (John 12:31, 14:30) would be no more and would be condemned for his usurping of power (John 16:11). Finally, he is called the ruler of the kingdom of the air (Eph. 2:2) who works in those who are disobedient.

Duewel makes a quick survey of the names of the spiritual powers mentioned in the New Testament (Duewel 1986, p. 104). Some of these are just descriptions of human rulers, others are not. Some would add that the principalities are the ruling spirits over the nations/cities (Hammond 2010, p. 14). This can also be considered a rank.

- *Archai/archas/arche*—rulers or principality (1 Cor. 15:24; Eph. 1:21, 3:10, 6:12; Col. 1:16, 2:10, 15)
- *Exousai*—authorities (1 Cor. 15:24; 2 Cor. 10:8; Eph. 1:21, 3:10, 6:12; Col. 1:16, 2:10, 15)
- *dunameis/dunastes*—power or powers (Luke 9:1; Rom. 8:38; 1 Cor. 15:24; Eph. 1:20–22, 3:10, 6:12)
- *Kuriotes*—dominions, lordships (Eph. 1:21, Col. 1:16)

- *Thronoi*—thrones (Col. 1:16)
- *Archontes*—leaders, princes (1 Cor. 2:6)
- *Kosmoskratores*—world rulers (Eph. 6:12, 2 Cor. 4:4)

Satan is seen as the *archon* (the ruler of this age) as the judgement; "It is finished" was announced on the cross. When Christ comes back, then Satan's time will be completed here. Now he rules with limits, to test and try those on earth. In Colossians 2:15, the meaning of disarm is to "to *undress completely and render powerless.*" The victory of Christ on the cross took away any power that he and his minions had in this world. In ancient times, it was the idea of taking off the robes of office of a deposed official. Christ certainly made a public exhibition of them while triumphing over them. In the triumphal victory march of Jesus's day, the defeated leaders of the enemy army were led out in chains, their shame open to the public. This is the idea of what Christ did on the cross. He took the worst that the enemy could throw at Him; He took on Death itself. Jesus endured the pain of separation from His Father and bore our sins for us. This He did as a sinless innocent Lamb, the High Priest who offered Himself as the ultimate Offering. Christ was enthroned (1 Cor. 15:54), and the other spiritual powers were all put under his feet (Eph. 1:21–22). Jesus predicted that Satan would be driven out (John 12:31) when He was lifted up on the cross, and it was so.

Another factor is that of principles or *stoicheia* of the world. Van Rheenen takes the idea of *stoicheia*, the Greek word for the elementary principles that are in control of this day and age. These *stoicheia* are not bad in and of themselves. These have invaded much of human society, including Christianity (Van Rheenen, Worldview and Syncretism, 2003). Much of the ancient history of Israel is the battle of the Jewish people with syncretism. The people of Israel kept buying into the ideas of the nations around them and so lost their distinctiveness (2 Kings 17:33, Zeph. 1:5). It is the principles that hold in bondage (Gal. 4:3, Col. 2:20) and manage to diffuse themselves into cultures. For example, the traditions of the Pharisees had become quite ingrained with the rules of the principalities, that is why no one could ever come to faith through them (Matt. 15:1–20).

The Pharisees were more worried about their traditions than about the truth of God. These kinds of rules could be anywhere—in Jewish law or pagan beliefs—and ultimately replaced Christ. As Paul said to the Colossians (Col. 2:8, 20), "If you have died to the elements, then why are they still in control?" Obeying rules that are not relevant to Christianity is as bad as listening to satanic powers. Paul speaks in more detail of the spiritual principalities more fully in Ephesians 1, declaring that we are above the heavenly realms as believers because we are with Christ. Christ is head over them all, both in authority and power (Eph. 1:22–23, Col. 1:15–20). Some of the names that are listed in Paul's writings (see Duewel's list) are descriptions of human institutions (leaders, princes, dominions, lordships.) These powers were created (Col. 1:15–20) but became independent and left God's rule. Their desire is to estrange us from God (Rom. 8:38). Sherman describes the hierarchical rule as part of Satan's prongs of attack (Sherman 1990, p. 87). Satan's infiltration of human authority structures is so that he could rule through them through the wrong choices made. The authority structures can be local, regional, and national. This can also apply to schools, businesses, churches, trade unions, and other organized groups.

Sherman also refers to principalities (aka territorial spirits) that have broad influences in Satan's kingdom. Many spiritual warfare proponents state that the territorial spirits are deployed according to a map of the world. There are particular forces for each area and group of people. The strategy for India would be different than that of New York City. This means we believers can feel God's progress and peace in one place, whereas in another we experience the conflict and oppression. The ratios of murder, as well as drugs and violence, can differ from city to city.

Sherman goes on to say that those who are serious about spiritual warfare need to become serious about praying for people groups and places. There are few believers in certain places such as Sikkim, Bhutan, Mozambique, and Mauritania because no one is praying for them. We need to become the church triumphant over the powers of darkness in these areas.

Our prayers are to be a part of our relationship to God, as children to a Father. It is not a power tool, declares Van Rheenen, and not to be used as such by any with animistic bent, as Simon found out in Acts 8. Simon wanted to buy the power so that any he laid hands on would receive the Holy Spirit. Paul warned him sternly to leave such ideas behind. Ideas such as this are animistic syncretization of Christianity. Paul urges the Colossians not to follow the powers that have such a deceptive philosophy that can take us captive (Col. 2:8–9). Instead we are to depend on Christ. We are to acknowledge Christ, who is the Head over all the powers and authorities included.

Deception

Satan does not want us to live for God. He tries to deceive us and control us through his lies (Rev. 12:9, John 8:44, 2 Tim. 2:24–26). He deceives unbelievers by telling them that they don't need God in their lives, that they don't need to become Christians to have peace and fulfilment. Penn-Lewis adds that there are deceptions for the carnal Christian as well as the advanced one (Penne-Lewis 1956, p. 8). International workers would generally fall under the latter category and so be subject to many subtle attacks but not exclusively so.

Warner points out four things we must be on the lookout for:

1. We must anticipate temptation (Heb. 4:15).
2. We must expect to be attacked in other ways (1 Pet. 5:8, 9; 1 Thess. 2:18).
3. Deception is his main attack (2 Cor. 11:3).
4. He wants believers to be ineffective in their lives for God. In this way, he attempts to block God's glory, says Warner. God's glory is to be supreme in our lives (Exod. 20:7, 1 Cor. 10:31).

As regards deception, Warner differentiates it in two main areas: that of power and enticement. (1) *Power*—Satan likes to scare us by (a) intimidation. He likes to make us think that he has power, greater than God (1 John 3:4). Satan is the god of this world, but he is not greater than God. If Satan can make us afraid, then he has won the battle. Panic attacks at night on adults and children can be Satan's way of showing his power. If we are afraid of him, then we won't be able to do what God wants us to. Sometimes he will cause an illness or a physical sickness. Warner recounts the story of a sick child in the family. The doctor could not find out what was wrong, so the pastor prays for the child and rebukes Satan's attack. The child recovered in response to the prayer. Warner says, "*We don't have to run from Satan—he runs from us,*" because we are protected by the power of Jesus Christ as a believer. Resist the devil in the name of Jesus and he will flee (Jas. 4:8). You can also teach children to rebuke Satan themselves, and he will leave.

Another area under power is that of (b) enticement, the lure of power for yourself. This is an offer of power to meet your needs. Some people ask for power in various ways. One woman needed money to go to university. So she asked God for money. When God didn't answer her, she prayed to Satan. She got the money and finished her education. Then she was in trouble because Satan wanted her life. She renounced that vow, and she was set free. People want power to tell the future, to be wealthy, and against/for people. Some people ask for spirit guides; this is a part of the New Age movement. Those are not good angels; they are bad ones. Sometimes Satan even counterfeits the spiritual gifts of healing, tongues, and others. Any time you reach out to someone other than God for power you are reaching out to Satan. We will deal more with this in detail later.

The second main area of deception is in the area of (2) *truth*. Any time Satan can tell you a lie about God he will. Many people see God as a judge or policeman. This is a part of the lie. Sometimes their parents were very strict and unloving, and so this is how they see God. If the view of God is wrong, then the whole view of life will be wrong as well. This covers areas such as unconditional love and trustworthiness, for example. (Perhaps we feel that God loves others but not us.) Satan also tells us lies about ourselves. If we think we are not loved by God, then we will have trouble. Our identity in Christ is so important. Satan likes to fool Christians into having less power or control than they think they do. We often forget that Scripture reassures us that God is greater than the evil one (1 John 4:4, Rev. 11:15). We can overcome Satan because God is the ultimate Victor.

One very telling illustration of this happened to an IW in Panama by the name of Jacob Loewen. Like many Westerners, he had not been taught about spiritual battle with real entities, and so his worldview had not prepared him to pray with faith for the sick. Even though he was a Christian, he still had the worldview that God didn't intervene in our daily lives. Consequently, when he was asked to pray for a sick pastor's wife, she got a little better but relapsed. The Christian elders gathered again to pray for her but this time did not ask the IWs to join them, because they sensed that the IWs did not have the faith required (Loewen 2000, p. 60). Indeed, as often was the case in early missionary days, the natives soon went back to their own medicine men, since the new God didn't have the power to answer prayer, but the Western medicine did.

> The degree to which we live by the lie is the degree to which Satan controls us. (Warner, tape #2, 1993)

Some people get used to looking at the negative messages only and miss the positive ones. It goes along with the question, "Is the glass half-full or half-empty?" Whichever way you answer may be the way you view the world or life—in a positive way or negative way. The Western culture is a shame-based culture; we receive seven to ten negative comments for every positive one. Eventually people give up because they decide they can't win no matter what they do. Warner tells the story of a boy who brought home a C report card. His father looked at it and said, "I bet if you really tried hard you could get a B." So the boy studied hard, and he brought home a B. Then the father said, "If you really tried hard, you could bring home an A." And the boy did that: he studied hard, and then he brought home his report card. His father looked at it and said, "I know those teachers. They always give A's."

One of the biggest lies of Satan is within the Western culture itself—the legacy of the "Enlightenment." True, the Enlightenment did shed more understanding on the physical sciences and man's ability to understand medicine. But it stripped the worldview that included God, His interest in us and power to intervene in our lives, and His personal involvement with us. Science superseded theology and spiritual realities as reason took over the whole realm of thinking, including that of faith. People are deluded into thinking that mankind is improving, despite evidence to the contrary: every war, every evil of mankind upon itself; 9/11 will stand forever as the modern Pearl Harbor of terror. Is not the Western worldview so pervaded with the idea of science controlling nature that we neatly avoid God and any other spiritual powers?

Biblically speaking, nature is controlled by God, and any battle Israel had against her enemies included fighting foreign gods as well. Although we are made in God's image, the prince of this world seeks to deceive us and to usurp our dominion on this planet. God made a covenant with Abram to bless all the earth and rescued Israel from Egypt as a part of that promise (Williams 2000, p. 80). Our God is *not* dead, but sometimes we behave as though He is.

> Is he in a continuing battle with forces of darkness even when they are masked behind religious ideologies and political empires? Does he still command healing? Or have you embraced a "lesser god" benevolent…but…defenceless against supernatural evil. (Williams 2000, pp. 8–9)

Biblical History

Throughout biblical history, God showed Himself again and again to His people. To Noah and Abram, he made covenants of His faithfulness. God rescued Israel from Egypt with the great accompaniment of wonders and signs so that His name would be glorified (Exod. 14:18, 31). While they wandered in the wilderness, God provided for them manna, quail, and water. After Moses and Joshua died, the wonders continue into the time of the judges (1 Sam. 8:18). But when they choose a king, the wonders stop as a rule (Williams sees this as quite significant). Since the people want a king to lead them, then it is by the faith of the king that they stand or fall. Israel continues to win battles against incredible odds, but wonders, in the spectacular sense, are not present. The power passes to the prophets, especially Elijah and Elisha (1 Kings 18:38). Many of the kings did not follow God wholeheartedly, and thus the nations of Israel and Judah end in captivity for their disobedience. The wonders revive again in captivity, with Daniel's faith being an example to follow. Against the odds, Jerusalem is rebuilt.

When Christ entered the scene, He ushered in a new era that made possible the power of the Holy Spirit to everyone (Acts 1:8). Angels preceded His entrance, and the wonders began again with Elizabeth and Zechariah having a child in their old age. Satan started the attack right off with the three big temptations to Jesus with no success. Jesus began by declaring that the kingdom of God was at hand (Matt. 4:23, Luke 4:43, and Matt. 10:7). Jesus was the fulfilment of the prophets, and He was God's authority, doing things beyond the limitations of the Pharisees' understanding of Scripture.

Williams records Jesus's plan for His work on earth as being in the vein of Isaiah 61—his anointing (Luke 3:21–22), evangelism of the lost (Luke 5:30), release to the captives or demonised (Mark 1:39), and recovery of sight to the blind (Luke 7:21). Jesus is the king taking back his people from captivity (Williams 2000, pp. 113–114,). In order to do this, Jesus cleanses the temple (Matt. 5:20). His people must be seeking Him first (Matt. 6:33). Although grace and forgiveness are part of the package (Luke 6:36), so is persecution (Matt. 10:29–30). The promise of the kingdom of God in us is Jesus's promise to the disciples as he drives out demons by God's Holy Spirit (Matt. 12:28). The Lord's Prayer calls in all of these themes as a unit. God is holy, and over all, His kingdom is our goal; He provides for us daily and delivers us from evil.

Since Jesus was Jewish, He viewed the world holistically instead of into nice little compartments like we do today (borrowed from the Greek thinking). Kraft pulls the following comments together in reviewing Jesus's worldview. First, Jesus *assumed* the existence of spirits; He didn't question whether or not they were there. He knew it. Jesus often spoke of the two kingdoms—God's kingdom against the god of this world in major power confrontations (Luke 4:32, 36, 39; Luke 6:28, 9:1–2, 10:9; Matt. 10:1, 7–8; Matt. 28:19–20). Everything that Jesus did was because He was full of God's Holy Spirit (Acts 10:38, Luke 3:21–22, Acts 1:8, John 14:12). In fact, Jesus did God's works as He listened to God (John 8:28–29). In the West, we often don't believe something until we see it, but to Jesus, believing is seeing (Luke 8:9–10, Matt. 9:22). The act of stepping forward in faith indicated belief, and therefore they believed. The obedience of the disciples brought them confirmation that Jesus's teaching was right (John 7:16–17). Loving God with all one's heart, soul, and mind (Matt. 22:37–40) and seeking His kingdom first are our priority (Matt. 6:33). We need to learn to risk with God, not presume for God (Matt. 25:14–30). Stewardship is not just saving or hoarding something; it's investment. Jesus also trusted those He was training to become servant-leaders like Himself, not just giving orders behind the lines or getting all the benefits and privileges. Leadership was to be involved personally in serving as well (Matt. 20:25–28).

To Kraft, Jesus's whole viewpoint was that God's way was natural (Kraft 1989, p. 27). He didn't see the world divided into natural and supernatural, since God was the Creator of it all. Our Enlightenment-blinded minds have segmented the world into these sections. We can't even explain how nature works half the time, so how can we hope to explain the supernatural? God asked Job this very question. Jesus echoed that when he talked to Nicodemus in John 3. The natural and the spiritual are both from God, and yet they are beyond us. Certainly, the natural has properties we can see and predict, to a certain extent. Kraft even declares that Jesus didn't pray the way we do; He consulted God and then did a miracle (Luke 8:25, Luke 9:13, Luke 9:19). If we get sick, we think of germs as the cause. Many tribal peoples think, "Who have I offended?" Jesus was thinking positively about the spiritual interference: God actively involved in saving his people.

> Jesus reproduced his kingdom ministry in the apostles so they were authority ministers of that kingdom. (Williams 2000, p. 127)

The giving of the ministry continues (Eph. 4:7–12) through the disciples, through Paul (Rom. 15:18–19), and through the followers of Jesus. We need to remember who God is—Creator, King, Redeemer, and Judge—and also who we are as heirs of the promise made to Abraham. When Jesus gave the Spirit at Pentecost, a door was opened up for the ministry of the disciples in a whole new way. The prayer of Paul in Ephesians 1:17–2:7 illustrates our new position. Our Father has given us the Spirit of wisdom and revelation in order to know Him better. Paul also prays that the eyes of their hearts will be enlightened in order that they would know three things: *(1) the hope to which they were called, (2) the riches of His glorious inheritance in the saints, and (3) His incomparable great power for us who believe.* God's power in Christ has raised us up above all rule and authority, power, and dominion above the demons and servants of Satan. It is in Christ that we have our authority over them. Although we were formerly dead, we are now raised up and seated with Him.

It is safe to tell this loving God everything because we know that we cannot lose our position in Christ. He has raised us up in the heavenlies because of what Christ has done for us. God loves us, and that will not change.

Armour of God

Regarding evil spirits and Christians, Warner states that the issue is not of possession but of *control*. Who is in control over you, you or the demons' lies? Deception is tricky because it is hard to discover. You don't realize you are being deceived. It is hard to undo a lie. To fight a lie, we must learn to say about everything what God says about it. The truth is the only remedy for a lie (John 8:32–36). We need to learn to affirm the truth. In 2 Timothy 2:24–25, it says that we need to come to our senses to escape from the trap of the devil's lies and temptations. We say the truth in a positive sense more than the truth in a negative sense—e.g., we are saints who sometimes sin. We are not sinners in the same way that unbelievers are. We can go instantly to Christ for forgiveness and cleansing for our sin. In Romans 5:1ff, it says we have peace because of what Jesus has done, not because of what we do. It is God's unconditional love that changes us, not His condemnation. It doesn't matter what happens to us or what others say; our position is secure in God. We tend to think that forgiveness is the most important thing for us to have. Warner says,

> Becoming a Christian is more than having your sins forgiven…it's becoming a new person in Christ.

We must become that new person that we have been given. It's like being given a costume and having to wear it and play the part. C.S. Lewis calls it "dressing up like Christ" (Lewis 1952, p. 161). The more we wear His righteousness, the more we will become like Him.

We have a new identity in Christ and thus a new motivation for living. We have gone from victims to victors because we are now seated with Christ in the heavenlies. Because demons are spirits and not flesh, they do not occupy space. Walls are not a problem to them; they are not kept out by walls of a church or any other building. They also cannot be kept out of our minds and lives. The only thing that can truly protect us is the blood of Christ applied to our lives as we put on the armour of God (Eph. 6:10–18). We do not give place to the devil and allow him a foothold in our lives. You do not say the words like a magic formula; it is your relationship with Christ that makes the difference. If we don't know the truth and don't claim the promises, the devil will get through the armour. We need to actively use the weapons God has provided for us. Just because we are Christians doesn't mean God will automatically protect us as His children. We must be active participants in the process. God does not reward carelessness or laziness. The people of Israel lost the battle at Ai because someone disobeyed God's instructions. God does not work on our agenda or plans; we must work on the truth as a part of His plan. Satan cannot drive the Holy Spirit out of your life as long as you put your faith in Christ. As long as you trust and obey, you will be under God's protection.

The book of Ephesians has a lot of material that is crucial to our walk with Christ. Sherman points out that in chapters 1–3, it focuses on our position in Christ and our relationship to God. Who we are is based on what God has done. We are recipients of wonderful benefits of God's riches in Christ Jesus. We are seated with Him in the heavenlies. The seated position means we have finished our work. In chapter 4 of Ephesians, we are walking in obedience to light. Chapter 6 has us standing against the enemy.

Let's look at Ephesians 6:10–18 for an example of how this works. We must put on the armour of God for our daily protection against the attacks of the devil. Putting on God's armour is putting on Christ (Rom. 13:12–14). We put the armour on so that we can stand against the plans of the devil. He plans to overthrow and deceive us. If we put the armour on, we are ready. For our battle is a spiritual one—against the demons under Satan's rule.

1) First, we are to put on the *belt of truth*, using the truth against everything we hear and see. If it doesn't line up with God's truth, then we can dismiss it. The truth in our lives is to line up with God's truth, what He says. Gordon adds that we have the truth, *aletheia*—ability to see into the heart of the matter to help us understand what is going on by God's Spirit. We tend to underestimate ourselves, and then we are afraid of Satan's attacks on us. Satan loves to tell us lies that sound so good. For example, Satan told Adam and Eve in the garden that eating the fruit would make them wise like God. In other words, God was keeping something good from them. But in reality, God had made everything good and perfect. God Himself was good. The only command He gave was not to eat of the fruit of the one tree. The serpent told Eve that God was holding back on her, that He was not giving her something good by saying no. She believed him and ate the fruit. She ate the fruit because she believed she was better off by disobeying God. Some people feel that God is like an angry parent, ready to punish them whenever they do wrong. This is a wrong concept of God. God is not always angry with us. The Bible says that He is slow to anger and full of compassion. He is willing to forgive us our sins, and He loves us

no matter what. For some reason, we tend to go toward the lies. Stanley makes this observation

> Holes in our theology are where Satan builds his strongholds. (Stanley 1982, p. 114)

2) Then comes the *breastplate of righteousness*. We may feel condemned whether we have sinned or not. Satan loves to torture us either way. We are to put on the righteousness of Christ, not our own. For our own righteousness is as filthy rags (Isa. 64:6). We stand justified before a holy God. We cannot be good enough for God no matter what we do (Rom. 3:21). But Christ has already become our righteousness (1 Cor. 1:30). If we sin, all we need to do is to confess our sins (1 John 1:9), and God will forgive us. Revelation 12:10 calls Satan the accuser of the brethren. One of the things that Satan does is to counterfeit God and His goodness. The Holy Spirit convicts but Satan accuses (White 1989, p. 85). Both are telling the main truth—that we have sinned—but the result is quite different. We are to repent when God convicts us, but Satan's goal is to make us feel bad and give up altogether. Satan loves to accuse us when we have been forgiven. He even likes to accuse those who have not sinned: Job, for instance. Job was righteous and yet stood accused under Satan's brash approach to God. However, Romans 8:1 says we are not condemned if we are under Jesus Christ's blood. The provision for our forgiveness has already been made in Christ. Peter may have felt that denying Christ was a terrible thing. but Christ forgave him and told him to feed the sheep: the church. God stands ready to forgive us and to give us the righteousness of Christ to wear as our own. That is His promise to us and why we can stand in God's presence, because Christ has become our righteousness.

3) *Feet ready with the gospel of peace*—we have peace with God (Rom. 5:1) and peace inside ourselves (Col. 3:15–16)

through His word. We are also to have peace with each other (Rom. 14:19). If we don't have peace, then Satan can use that to make problems in the church. Jesus is our peace, and He gives it to us. If we have disagreements with someone else in the church, the unity of Christ is broken. Gordon adds that the peace comes from the Hebrew term *Shalom*, which means wholeness or completeness. Satan wants to divide (steal, kill, and destroy; John 10:10), and so we need to be ready to heal the breaches that Satan makes in this world among peoples, families, and toward God. The peace in our lifestyle is a witness to the world around us that Christ is able to do for us what we cannot in our world of turmoil and anxiety.

4) The *shield of faith* is our protection against Satan's attacks. The more you know God's Word, the better your protection will be. Anderson says that the arrows of Satan are the *lies, temptations, and accusations* that he likes to throw at us (Anderson 1993, p. 83). If Satan tempts you to sin, resist him with scripture. If you do sin, then he will tell you that you are a terrible Christian for sinning. Claim Christ's forgiveness and move on. Don't believe Satan's accusations. If you realize you have been believing a lie, then renounce it and confess it as sin and tell Satan to get lost. The scripture says that we have overcome the world (1 John 5:4–5). The cross is our victory over Satan (Col. 2:15). Defend yourself with scripture just as Jesus did in Matthew 4:1–11. We practise believing what God says versus our feelings of fear or anxiety.

5) The *helmet of salvation* is our confidence in Christ that he will never leave us nor desert us. The battle for the mind is a spiritual battle, and we must remember that nothing can separate us from the love of Christ (Rom. 8:35). Since we have become Christians, we are transferred to the kingdom of God's Son (Col. 1:13) even though we live in the world open to attacks from Satan. Hope is what keeps us (1 Thess. 5:8) that Christ will enable us to live eternally.

Since Christ, we have a new hope, a new covenant (Eph. 2:12, Rom. 15:13).

6) The *Word of God* is our sure defence and offence against Satan's schemes. Speaking out the Word will cause Satan and his demons to flee because we are standing in the truth. When Christ stood against Satan in the wilderness, His answers to Him always were "It is written" (Luke 4:4, 8, 12). Scripture is powerful and sharper than a sword to cut through to the truth (Heb. 4:12). It says in 2 Cor. 10:4–5 we are to come against Satan and his strongholds with the Word. Stanley defines a stronghold here as an area where sin has become a part of our lifestyle (Stanley 1982, p. 188). This can be a habit like drugs or an attitude like rejection or worry. In any case, renounce the lies that support the rationalization for living with this sin. One woman struggled with her eating habits. She felt she studied better or needed to eat because she was hungry. However, when she faced these lies and rejected them with God's word, she was victorious every time (Gal. 5:24, Rom 12:2).

7) *Prayer* is our best and surest defence in our warfare against Satan and his lies. *Prayer is the mightiest weapon*! The early Moravians had prayer around the clock for one hundred years. It was prayer that brought Communism in Eastern Europe to its knees. Prayer against the enemy, his lies, and his tactics is what will win the battle for us. There is the power of praise in prayer, as Jehoshaphat's men discovered (2 Chron. 20:21ff). The army of Judah went out to battle with the singers in the front. As they praised, God moved against the enemy, and the victory was won. Praise is a mighty weapon, as Paul and Silas discovered in the Philippian jail. When they began praising God in spite of the awful situation they were in, the earth shook, and the prisoners were released. Not just Paul and Silas but the other prisoners too. (Talk about a captive audience!) They not only sang but freely told the jailer not to kill himself. God's mercy extended to the jailer as well as the prisoners.

He wasn't just interested in Paul and Silas; he was interested in all of the people in that situation.

The following chart was adapted from Warner (Warner 1993, p. 14) wearing the spiritual armour of God.

Armour pieces	Satan's Lies	God's Truth
Helmet (salvation)	You sin too much; God cannot save you.	God promises to forgive our sins (1 John 1:9). God will save all those who ask him (Acts 2:21).
Breastplate (righteousness)	You can be righteous. You can never be forgiven.	God says no one is righteous (Rom. 3:23). Our righteousness is as filthy rags (Isa. 64:6). Christ is our righteousness (1 Cor. 1:30). God forgives us when we ask (1 John 1:9).
Belt (truth)	God does not love me; I am too bad.	God loves everyone (John 3:16).
Shield (faith)	You must not be a good Christian if you are tempted.	Everyone is tempted (1 Cor. 10:13).
Shoes (readiness for peace)	If my neighbour does not believe as I do, we cannot be friends.	God has made us all brothers (1 Cor. 12:13).
Sword (Word of God)	Don't read your Bible; it is too hard.	Man cannot live by bread alone (Matt. 4:4).

In prayer, we need to realize that we are in a war, although war is not the sum of our life with God (Piper 1993, p. 41). We have broken fellowship with the kingdom of darkness and are now in the kingdom of light (1 Tim. 6:12, 2 Tim 4:7). Naturally the evil one is not amused by this turn of events. Satan's desire to destroy us through defection (1 Thess. 3:5) increases, if anything, in response to our conversion. Paul contends that ministry is war to Timothy, his young protégé in the faith (1 Tim. 1:18). This war is even greater than World War II was because it is in every town and every city. It is just as difficult to fight as a guerrilla war is, for the enemy is everywhere and hiding in unexpected places. For this reason, we need to pray without ceasing (Eph. 6:18). This prayer is not for comfort, asserts Piper, but for more orders from our commanding officer, Christ. This is not an age-related issue, where retirement happens, and you get to rest from the warfare. This is going on when God wants you to go. John Eliot, of Puritan background (1631), started studying the First Nation language of Algonquin at the age of forty. Ultimately, he translated the entire Bible so the Algonquin nation could read it in their own tongue. By the time he was eighty-four years old, many native churches had been planted among the Algonquin people. (This Bible was the first one printed in North America; English copies followed a century later!) John Eliot was known as the apostle to the Indians (former name of First Nations). Certainly, John Eliot understood that Jesus wanted other sheep than just the Jews in His fold (John 10:16).

The scope of prayer is as wide as the world itself (Piper 1993, p. 60). Everything falls under its umbrella. We exalt God's mighty name (Matt. 6:9–10) so that we can extend His kingdom. That is warfare prayer. We pray that the gospel will triumph (2 Thess. 3:1) and that the unbelievers will be saved (Rom. 10:1). We pray with boldness and proclamation (Eph. 6:19), with signs and wonders (Acts 4:30) and healing (Acts 28:8). They even prayed to raise the dead (Acts 9:40) where Peter raised Dorcas, much to the joy of the believers. We need to pray for wisdom and discernment (Phil. 1:9–10) and for encouragement of fellowship (1 Thess. 3:10). Above all, we need to prevail in prayer for God's answers. We need to always be asking God for what He wants of us next, whether in actual warfare situation or not.

> We are to be in constant contact with God and claiming his power in the living of life. (Kraft 1989, p. 102)

EXPLORING THE ROOTS OF MISSIONS: PERSONAL, BIBLICAL, AND SPIRITUAL

Cleaning the House

There are a variety of ministry approaches dealing with spiritual warfare on a personal level. They deal with aspects of truth and power designed to show both who God is and that we can be set free from sin and oppression of the enemy. When we get rid of the old things in our lives, the things that have held us captive, we are cleaning house inside ourselves (Mtt. 12:43-45). Basic principles set out by Gordon in spiritual warfare include the following:

1. Doing it in the name of Jesus since He is the source of truth and power itself (John 14:12, Acts 4:30, Col. 3:17, Phil. 2:10). In Acts19:14–16, the seven sons of Sceva try casting out demons in Jesus's name. This backfired badly on them, and they were beaten by the man oppressed by the demons who turned on them. If these men had been true believers in Christ, they would have been all right, but they were attracted by the dynamic of power, and this didn't work. Spiritual warfare is successful only because of the relationship with God through Jesus Christ. God's power does not work in a vacuum; it operates through the dynamic of His relationship with His children. When they call, He answers.
2. The fellowship of faith is also important; make sure you are covered in prayer with people behind you. The Roman shield used in battle was not one piece but a number of layers. Each layer of protection helped, and as others stand with us, they are a part of that layer. Thus, faith builds faith (Gordon 1983, p. 135).
3. The power of the Word of God—the words of Scripture are powerful as a two-edged sword. These words are God's directions and full of power against Satan.

One ministry that does a lot of biblical teaching is Freedom in Christ Ministries by Neil Anderson. Timothy Warner does an adapted version of this material for overseas work, and it is very useful. Freedom in Christ Ministries does a lot of basic doctrinal teaching and emphasis on correcting one's worldview and Christian understanding as well as lifestyle. The emphasis here is in the true makeup of the struggle of the Christian in spiritual warfare. It is not a war between equals, one side good and one side bad. God has all the power, and therefore Satan is not truly His equal, as Satan is a created being. So are angels and demons. C.S. Lewis remarks that it is really a civil war, because it is the creation, the created beings fighting against God. If we, as believers have the right understanding of who God is (all-powerful, loving, and wise), we will be able to defeat by faith through Christ our enemy Satan and his demons. Satan's chief method of using his power is in deception; Satan wins if you believe the lies he spreads. Putting your faith in God and His work in Christ enables us to believe the truth and defeat the lies. In Christ, we are the victors as we have the heavenly blessings in Christ (Eph. 1).

The nature of the Steps to Freedom is a moral and spiritual inventory in all areas of life. These are common areas of bondage that relate to basic beliefs about life. Anderson's contention is that proper discipleship will prevent many of these problems in the Christian walk. If there are basic problems such as these in Christians in all levels, then likely it will be passed on to new believers in the mission setting as well. Acknowledging the truth as the situation is, believing what God says, confessing the sin, forgiving others who have sinned against us, renouncing the sin and involvement in non-God oriented practises, and forsaking all else to follow God will result in spiritual freedom. Satan must often be confronted verbally, and spiritual ground reclaimed to win back one's proper standing and understanding in Christ.

The steps to freedom in particular deal with four main areas:

1. *Mind: beliefs and thinking*—Step 1 concerns beliefs in counterfeit and true faith in God (false religions, cults, and occult practises). Step 2 handles deception: general lies in our sin-ridden cultures and specific ones that relate to our life and grow out of our negative experiences, leading us to wrong thinking patterns. The mind needs to be reset in

these two areas by professing proper biblical faith in Christ and learning to defeat the lies with the truth of God's word.
2. *Spirit: attitudes and emotions*—Step 3 is bitterness vs. forgiveness: letting go of old hurts. Step 4 is rebellion vs. submission: doing things God's way, not our way. Step 5 is pride vs. humility: developing the true attitude of Christ in us.
3. *Body: behaviour and tendencies*—Step 6 deals with bondage and freedom: physical sins of the flesh, usually having to do with food, mutilation or self-injury, or sex.
4. *Family associations*—The final step deals with family association: ancestral spiritual ties that may hinder our spiritual life. Each step outlines the erroneous thinking and with the scriptural answer.

Kraft speaks of the aspects of spiritual warfare in varying degrees, each one proceeding deeper than the last. He includes physical healing in the process of praying for others. For many people, a spiritual attack may be related to the issue of health. For instance, an issue may start out to be a *physical problem* in need of healing, but God wants to go deeper than that and heals more than what is just visible physically. This seems to be exactly what C.S. Lewis said when he talks about God's thoroughness. We go to him for a sore tooth, for example, and he wants to heal our whole lives and set us straight in following him. Healing is not the whole story, but it is a part of what God wants to do for our lives. Blue mentions that James 5:14–15 tells us to call for the elders to pray if we are sick. God may work in many areas of life, not just the physical. Blue mentions that there may be spirits behind the sickness or pain, and so when they are rebuked, the pain leaves. One woman Blue was dealing with had constant migraines (Blue 1987, p. 85). They prayed for her symptoms with no result. When the spirit causing the pain was discerned, it was rebuked, and the pain left immediately.

Another type of ministry is *inner healing*, which can often follow a physical healing. This deals with any emotional pain or blockage. Forgiveness is a good example of this. A lot of healing cannot happen unless forgiveness comes first. It may be a deep wound in the past has not been dealt with until and needs a special touch of God in order for that person to grow in their personal walk with God.

Third comes *deliverance*, which again may be needed after some deep inner healing has occurred. Honesty is very important in this area, as the counselee needs to be honest with themselves and God in order for this phase to be effective in his/her life. Green also advocates several first-century traditions of renouncing the devil and his works (also mentioned by Warner in *Steps*). Kraft lists several levels of demon holds, ranging from 1 being the lightest to 10 as the strongest. Oppression in the 1, 2 level means that there may be a bit of a struggle, but the hold is relatively slight, and the demons leave fairly easily. Personally, my husband and I have experienced several of these levels in our daily life. One night we could not get our daughter to go to sleep. She was not even two at the time, and we didn't know what the problem was. Every time we put her in her room, she cried. When we brought her into our bedroom, she was okay. Finally, we thought of a spiritual attack happening in her room and told the spirit in her room to leave, and it did at once. At level 3 and 4, there is more of a struggle. We've had a few of those too—usually something has come up at night, and when we started praying, one of us realized something was wrong, and so we started the battle in earnest. At levels 5 and 6, it can be an hour or so before they leave. Again, at this level, we have felt an attack and battled in prayer and scripture reading for some time. My ring finger began hurting one night, and I didn't know what was wrong. Finally, we started praying, and an hour or so later, my finger stopped hurting so badly. It was several days before the pain was entirely gone. Levels 7 and 8 may involve several hours of struggle. Demons like to go undercover, and use of the Word in fighting them is very important. Satan cannot hide from the Word and ultimately must leave.

Kraft includes *blessing*, which is often done before a session. These can be general or specific, depending on the need that is sensed at the time. Healing is not dependent on "enough faith," for Naaman the Syrian was healed, and he was not even a believer. He just obeyed a servant girl's instructions. Taking authority and commanding the condition itself to leave is the approach that Kraft takes. The whole time of working with someone in prayer does not need to be rushed. This is ministry time, and it is important. Opening the ministry time with an invitation to the Holy Spirit to come, reveal, and lead is important. God is in charge, and His will must be done. Warner and Anderson add in their ministry (Steps to Freedom) that the Holy Spirit come and set a hedge around those in prayer so that no one is open to a particular spiritual attack or violent response. Kraft blesses the person, and that helps them relax and sense what God is doing. Then is the interview, with the tentative diagnosis of the situation. During the prayer time, the prayer leader or counsellor asks God for guidance and authority in the situation and command the negative conditions to leave, both physical and emotional, and blocking interference by the spirits who do not want freedom and healing for the counselee. In prayer, taking the situation to God is important and to watch what He will do next. Keeping your eyes open to see what is happening is a good idea. Warner and Anderson also advocate this, as sometimes visual clues are given during the time of prayer. The counselee may start to shake or not be able to talk.

Asking how things are progressing helps in assessing how correct the diagnosis is. Blue says it is very important to be honest for the counselee to say if there is no improvement. It may be that the focus is on the wrong area, as in the case of woman with the migraines. Continued sessions may be possible for progressive healing of particular symptoms or for continued deliverance and encouragement.

Sometimes words of knowledge will come to the counsellor, and he/she may feel led to ask questions about a certain area. If confirmed, then the way is opened for that area to be dealt with. Some will get a pain in a certain area (the same as the counselee); others will get a picture showing them something. The important thing is to bring it under God's authority and test it out. If it is true, then the healing/praying process can continue. Some who are more liturgical in background prefer to use the sign or work of the cross, the Eucharist, holy oil, or water in this process of flushing the demon out.

Teaching the person to take authority over the problem is very important as the condition may return to plague them. Everyone prayed for should be in a small group of caring Christians at their own church so as to receive continued support and caring. Not everyone prayed for is healed in Kraft's ministry, but everyone appeared to get a blessing. Blue states that although not all are healed, some are, and it is a part of regaining dominion in a fallen world. Expanding God's kingdom through the practise of healing is pushing back Satan's control and boundaries.

Teaching the counselee to walk in the Spirit and obey the Word of God is very important as often it is a faulty doctrine or belief that led to some of the problems in the first place. Learning to resist the devil too and putting on the armour of God is very important. Green emphasizes the value of praise in this process so that the individual can resist the devil in more than one way.

At this point in the book, we will go into the steps to freedom (according to Freedom in Christ Ministries) in some detail for the individual. We will summarize these steps in a much more abbreviated form of the FICM material. For further details, you may consult the original material with the prayers included. (See the bibliography for those books and resources.) If these steps are taken before venturing into cross-cultural work, it will be greatly beneficial.

Breaking Chains

"We are not helpless victims caught between the good and bad spiritual powers," says Warner. For some reason, this idea is a common misconception even among believers. There is only one power, and that is God. Satan is a deceiver who likes to make us think that he is God's equal in power. Only God can do anything, be everywhere, and know everything. Sometimes the reality of sin may seem more real than God, but that is a part of the deception. Satan is defeated. Knowing who God really is and who we are in Christ are the greatest factors in our mental health. A false idea of God, the self, and Satan are strong components in mental illness.

Satan's power is mostly in the power of the lie. As soon as you expose the lie, the power is broken. The battle is for the mind. We need to break the chains of bondage that hold us in many areas.

If you believe the lies of Satan, he can control your life. Thoughts like, "This isn't going to work," or "God doesn't love me," can only interfere if you believe those lies. Be aware of what is going on in your mind as you go through the steps with a trusted spiritual leader. Praying authoritatively to stop any interference before beginning this process with someone you trust is important.

The steps to freedom are a thorough spiritual and moral inventory dealing with the key areas in which we give ground to the enemy. These are the areas where there would not be so many difficulties if the person had been properly discipled in the beginning. God has many ways in dealing with human problems, and this is only the starting point. This is not all the counseling that is needed. It is important to commit this whole process to God in prayer before they begin. Realizing your freedom in Christ will be the result of what you choose to believe, confess, forgive, renounce, and forsake. No one can do it for you. You must personally choose truth. Only God has complete knowledge of your mind. Satan cannot read your thoughts. You must confront him verbally and resist him by reading aloud each prayer and declaration.

Preparation

It is important to hear the story of the counsellee. This includes several areas: 1) Family history—the history of the family both spiritually, emotionally, and physically. Any areas of bondage that could be passed down should be included—e.g., spirit worship, alcoholism, etc. Also ask about the home life of the parents and grandparents: did they get along with each other, how did they treat the children, how did the counselee get along with siblings, etc. If there was adoption or guardians, include this also. Home life from childhood through high school—look for any trauma or upsetting events.

2) Personal history—eating habits (any anorexia, bulimia, compulsive eating); addictions (drugs, alcohol); prescription medications; sleeping patterns and nightmares; rape or any sexual or emotional molestation; thought life (obsessive, blasphemous, condemning, distracting thoughts, poor concentration, fantasy); mental

interference in church, prayer, or Bible study; emotional life (anger, anxiety, depression, bitterness, fears); and spiritual journey (salvation when, how assurance). *Remember there are only Christian answers; you cannot resolve your problems outside of Christ. The counsellee must be saved before going through the process.*

After you have heard the story, you can then determine the teaching they need. This varies from person to person. This essentially includes the materials already covered in this course. Reasonably correct views of God, self, and the enemy need to be a part of this process. Find out where the lies are, the deceptions, and the areas of bondage. This seven-step process will deal with areas of bondage and strongholds in the Christian's life. This will free them to deal with many more things that may follow this work. If there are more things to deal with, then this will make it easier.

It is important to get their co-operation in going through this process. They must tell you anything that is going on in their mind. They may get physical (shaking or headaches), mental, or emotional reactions to what is going on. These are clues as to problems and interference by the enemy. They must tell you what is going on and say it out loud. They may hear voices saying, "This isn't going to work, or I don't think it'll work for me," or even, "Kill the counselor." As they say these out loud, the power of these lies is diffused, and you can renounce them for what they are. Stopping to pray may be helpful. After this, you may pray the prayer and declaration.

In the declaration, you claim Jesus's authority to command Satan and evil spirits to release people and leave. There must be a freedom to know and choose to do God's will. Reminding out loud that we are children of God seated in the heavenlies.

Preview: Before we begin with the steps individually, let us take an overall look at the steps as a group. This will give us a preview of what the steps are in relation to our lives. The areas of the mind, spirit, body, and family associations are all involved. As you can see, all of these are a part of our lives. Our spiritual life is not something in a box marked "religion." It is something that reaches into every corner of who we are. It is also something that is affected by the things we think, feel, and our actions. Sin in these areas will affect

EXPLORING THE ROOTS OF MISSIONS: PERSONAL, BIBLICAL, AND SPIRITUAL

our spiritual life greatly. This is why we must deal with these things in relation to our ministry—it is not just our job or occupation; it is our life system that is controlling all of what we do. Whether you are in a position that involved spiritual ministry as your occupation or whether you are a layperson, these things will come out in your daily life. It is important to set these things straight spiritually so that all of life can be one unit working toward one whole, complete life in Jesus Christ, not separate little compartments with labels on them here and there (Col. 2:6–10). Colossians 2:6–10 talks about continuing to live in Christ, being rooted and built up in Him. This means we must take out all of the old sinful roots that are already there. (See diagram: Anderson 199, p. 241).

(Excerpt from *Victory Over the Darkness* by Neil T. Anderson, copyright © 2000, 2013, 2020. Used by permission of Bethany House, a division of Baker Publishing Group)

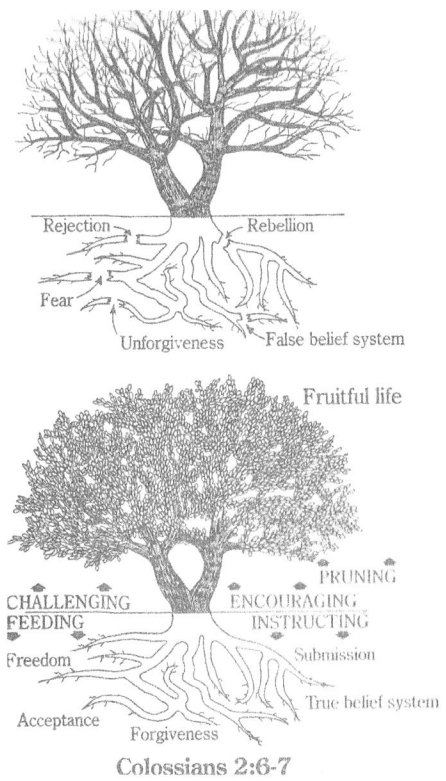

Colossians 2:6-7

This is a particular problem in the West. We tend to artificially divide our lives up into sections, not realizing that you can't do it in reality. What you do is that you end up with a disjointed life on the outside with an underlying belief system that puts things together on an unconscious level, in an attempt to fit it all together. The pieces don't fit, nor is there any harmony in life. Instead, there is a lot of fear and discouragement, frustration, and failure. People don't like to talk about these things; they feel there is something wrong with them, that they aren't good enough Christians, or that they are lacking in their faith. That is why we talk about worldview first, because it may not be something that you are aware of, but it is present, and it is underneath all that you are and think.

The *Steps to Freedom* take a thorough look at one's life in an attempt to find these views, values, and belief systems that we are not even aware of. Once they are brought out into the open, they are dealt with for what they are. This then allows the truth to become active and prevalent in one's life instead of the lies, instead of the worldview that is hiding underneath it all and twisting your life. Setting the captives free is the goal of these steps, free from the thinking bondage and traps set by Satan in this world system and in your personal life.

Steps Preview (adapted from Fehr 1995).

Mind: Beliefs and Thinking
Step 1: Counterfeit vs. Real—false religious systems
Step 2: Deception vs. Truth—wrong thinking patterns
Spirit: Attitudes and Emotions
Step 3: Bitterness vs. Forgiveness—emotional ties
Step 4: Rebellion vs. Submission—attitude of spirit
Step 5: Pride vs. Humility—attitude of spirit
Body: Behaviour and Tendencies
Step 6: Bondage vs. Freedom—physical sins of the flesh
Family Associations
Step 7: Acquiescence vs. Renunciation—ancestral spiritual ties

Step 1: Counterfeit vs. Real

Renunciation of false religions

EXPLORING THE ROOTS OF MISSIONS: PERSONAL, BIBLICAL, AND SPIRITUAL

Renunciation of current or previous associations with satanically inspired occultic practises or false religions. You need to renounce any activity or group which denies Jesus Christ; offers guidance through any other sources other than the word of God; or requires secret initiations, ceremonies, or covenants.

Non-Christian spiritual experience inventory

Check any of the following with which you had any involvement, even if it was participated in out of fun, curiosity, or in earnest (the following tables have been granted permission for use).

Taken from: The Bondage Breaker® by Neil T. Anderson; Copyright © 1990, 1993 by Harvest House Publishers, Eugene, Oregon 97408. www.harvesthousepublishers.com

_____ Card laying   _____ Palm reading   _____ Tea leaves
_____ Crystal ball   _____ Psychic   _____ Other
_____ Read or follow horoscope
_____ Been hypnotized   _____ Practised yoga or self-hypnosis
_____ Attended/participated in a séance   _____ Ouija board   _____ ESP
_____ Attended/participated in   _____ Table lifting   _____ Tarot cards
spiritualist meeting
_____ Telepathy   _____ Levitation   _____ Crystal ball
_____ Cabala   _____ Automatic writing   _____ I Ching
_____ Clairvoyance   _____ Water witching   _____ Sorcery
_____ Dream interpretation   _____ Self-realization   _____ Witchcraft
_____ Magical charming   _____ Astral projection/ travel
_____ Mental suggestion   _____ Mystical meditation
_____ Metaphysics   _____ Had a spirit guide
_____ Read or possessed occultic literature, especially the *Satanic Bible*, *Book of Shadows*, *Secrets of the Psalms*, and *Sixth and Seventh Books of Moses*
_____ Read/studied parapsychology
_____ Possessed occult/pagan religious objects which were made for use in temples; rites; or practise of magic, sorcery, witchcraft, divination, or spiritualism
_____ Seen or been involved in Satan worship
_____ Sought healing through magic conjuration, charming, psychic healing, or New Age

_____ Tried to locate a missing person/object by consulting someone with psychic powers
_____ Encountered ghosts or materializations of people known to be dead
_____ Entered into a blood pact with anyone
_____ Been the object of sexual attacks by demons
_____ Been involved with heavy metal or allied kinds of rock music
_____ Heard voices in your mind or had compulsive thoughts foreign to what you believe
_____ Had periods in childhood or present when you cannot remember what happened

Participated in any of the following:

_____ Worldwide Church of God	_____ The Way International
_____ Hare Krishna	_____ Zen Buddhism
_____ Christian Science	_____ Swedenborgianism
_____ Jehovah's Witness	_____ Rosicrucianism
_____ Unification Church	_____ Unity
_____ Transcendental Meditation	_____ Mormonism
_____ Spiritual Frontiers Fellowship	_____ Baha'i
_____ The Local Church	_____ Masons
_____ Unitarianism	_____ Children of God
_____ Hinduism	_____ Inner Peace Movement
_____ New Age	_____ Eckankar
_____ EST/The Forum	_____ Mind Control

When you are sure your list is complete, confess and renounce each involvement.

Step 2: Deception vs. Truth

Truth is the revelation of God's Word, but we need to acknowledge the truth in the inner self. When David lived a lie, he suffered greatly (Ps. 51:6, 32:2). We are to lay aside falsehood and speak the truth in love (Eph. 4:15, 25). A mentally healthy person is one who is in touch with reality and free from anxiety.

EXPLORING THE ROOTS OF MISSIONS: PERSONAL, BIBLICAL, AND SPIRITUAL

In addition to false teachers, prophets, and deceiving spirits, you can deceive yourself. Now that you are alive in Christ, and forgiven, you never have to lie or defend yourself. Christ is your defense.

Read through these verses on self-deception to see if the descriptions fit you (James 1:22, 4:17; 1 John 1:8; Gal. 6:3; 1 Cor. 6:9; 1 Cor. 15:33). Thinking that you are not vulnerable to getting caught or getting away with sin is a step down that dark path. Self-defense (instead of trusting Christ) is also an area where you may be deceived. Think about areas of denial, fantasy, withdrawal, or regression where you may be hiding yourself from the realities of life. Also think if you have been taking out your frustrations on others, blaming others, or rationalization.

For those things that have been true in your life, pray aloud and renounce it.

Choosing the truth may be difficult if you have been deceived for many years. You may need to seek professional help to weed out the defense mechanisms you have depended upon to survive. The Christian needs only one defence—Jesus. Knowing that you are forgiven and accepted as God's child is what sets you free to face reality and declare your dependence on Him.

Faith is the biblical response to truth, and believing the truth is a choice. If someone says, "I want to believe, but I can't," they are being deceived. Faith is something you decide to do. Believing the truth doesn't make it true. It's true; therefore, we believe it. The New Age movement says we create reality through what we believe. Reality is not created by your mind; you face reality with it. If what you believe isn't true, your life won't be right. The affirmation of our faith is important, as in the Apostles' Creed.

Read this aloud and do it often to renew your mind.

> Because of the unconditional love and acceptance of the Lord Jesus Christ, I am free to accept truth and to face reality. Since God is light and in Him there is no darkness at all (1 Jn. 1:5), I choose to walk in the light in order to have fellowship with Him and with other people. I

understand that this is not perfection on my part, but a willingness to say about everything in my life what God says about it and to be completely honest and in agreement with God concerning my present condition. (Warner 1993, p. 33)

The affirmation is one of being committed to the truth. Emphasize the *I*—you are doing this. It is not just an academic exercise. You *are* believing these affirmations. Some people think freedom comes another way other than facing the truth. But facing the truth is the only way to freedom. Read the following statement of doctrinal affirmation of the truth and do it as often as necessary to renew your mind.

Step 3: Bitterness vs. Forgiveness

This problem of bitterness causes more harm in the Christian community than any other thing. We need to deal with this the way Scripture tells us to—with forgiveness. We need to forgive others so that Satan cannot take advantage of us (2 Cor. 2:10–11).

We are to be merciful just as our Heavenly Father is merciful (Luke 6:36). We are to forgive as we have been forgiven (Eph. 4:29–32). Ask God to bring the names to mind of those you have not forgiven.

Include also yourself and God on this list. Including yourself means that you also accept that God has forgiven you. Sometimes we believe God has forgiven us, but we don't forgive ourselves. Include God because sometimes people blame God for things that happen to them. This makes them feel angry against Him. We need to stop blaming God and blame the real object of our anger—Satan.

Forgiveness is essential to our freedom; we need to forgive as we have been forgiven, and only in this way can we deal with our pain and hurt.

Warner gives a few more points on what forgiveness is and isn't. It is letting go of the person who harmed you and holding them to blame. You can't forget on purpose, but that may happen as a result of this choice of the will. God forgives us by not using our sin against us (Ps. 103:12). Bringing up the past means you have not forgiven that person. Let God take any revenge instead of you doing it (Rom. 12:9). Forgiving someone frees you from that person and the pain. Bitterness will destroy you if you don't forgive. Jesus took the consequences of sin on Himself—the cost of forgiveness. We may have to bear the consequences of another's sin in ourselves. Recognizing the hurt and anger in you will help you deal with it—your feelings are involved in forgiving. Don't use the incident as proof against them in future dealings. Finally, Warner says, "Don't wait until you feel like forgiving—you won't do it. Freedom is your goal, not a feeling" (Warner 1993, 35–36).

As you pray, remember that you are doing this for your sake. God wants you to be free. Don't rationalize or explain the offender's behaviour. Deal with your pain and leave the other person to God. Freeing yourself from the past is the present issue. This needs to be done out loud because then you can truly release yourself from this victim relationship. Stay with each individual until you are sure you have dealt with all the remembered pain: *what they did, how they hurt you, and how they made you feel.* For each person on your list, pray aloud the prayer.

Step 4: Rebellion vs. Submission

Many people believe they have a right to judge those in authority over them. Rebelling against God and His authority gives Satan an opportunity to attack. God promises if we obey Him, he will not lead us into temptation (Matt. 6:13). God sees rebellion so seriously because rebellion made Lucifer into Satan. It is a part of his character. Don't rebel against legitimate authority like he did. When you rebel against authority, you are the one that gets hurt. If you disobey the law of gravity, you will get hurt. If you disobey God's authority, you will suffer.

Biblically our response to authority figures is that of prayer and submission. Morally wrong commands are the exception. You need to obey God, not man, in those cases. Being under authority is an act of faith. You are trusting God to work through his established lines of authority. Pray the prayer.

Don't put yourself at the centre and put yourself above the law. There are several lines of authority in Scripture:

- Civil government (Rom. 13:1–7, 1 Tim. 2:1–4, 1 Pet. 2:13–17)
- Parents (Eph. 6:1–3)
- Husband (1 Pet. 3:1–4)
- Employer (1 Pet. 2:18–23)
- Church leaders (Heb. 13:17)
- God (Dan. 9:5, 9)

For each area you have not been submissive, pray for forgiveness.

Step 5: Pride vs. Humility

Pride is a killer. Pride says, "I can do this myself without anybody's help." We can't! We need God and each other. Humility is "confidence properly placed" (Warner 1993, p. 39). We are to be strong in the Lord and in the strength of his might (Eph. 6:10). The opposite of pride is not debasing yourself or having a low self-esteem. Inferiority is Satan's counterfeit to humility. Inferiority is looking at yourself. Confidence comes from looking at God. My pastor in Canada is a perfect example of this. He had such a humble spirit. When he ran into a situation where he didn't know what to do, he would pray and commit himself to God for an answer. He didn't mind admitting he didn't know everything. He would pray and trust that God would show him what to do next. This was very true in counseling situations. If he met someone with a problem he didn't know how to handle, he would pray about it. He had a humble attitude about his abilities. Commit yourself to God in the prayer.

Certain areas that may include this kind of pride would be having a stronger desire to do your will than God's will, more dependency on your strength and resources than God's, etc. Admitting that you have needs is also important because it humbles us to have to go to others for help. Admitting you are wrong is also a way of giving up pride. Consider whether you tend to please people more than God. Don't be overly concerned about getting credit either. If you think that you are humbler than other people, be careful—that too can be a form of pride.

Step 6: Bondage vs. Freedom

These are habitual sins of the flesh. Don't take any of this for granted in who will have trouble with which area. Seek out a righteous person who will uphold you in prayer (Jas. 5:16). Scripture assures us that when we ask forgiveness, God does forgive us (1 John 1:9). Confession is not saying, "I am sorry"; it is saying, "I did it."

Galatians 5:19–21 gives a list of some of the deeds of the flesh. It is our responsibility not to allow sin to reign in our bodies (Rom. 6:12–13). If you are struggling with habitual sexual sins (masturbation, pornography, sexual promiscuity) or experiencing sexual difficulty and intimacy in your marriage, pray and renounce every occasion, whether it was done to you (rape, incest, or sexual molestation) or whether you did it willingly. Then commit your body to the Lord. Sexual sins are in a category by themselves because they link you to the other person. We need to claim the power of Christ in the breaking of that link so that you can be free.

Step 7: Acquiescence vs. Renunciation

Acquiescence is passively giving in or agreeing without consent. The last step to freedom is renouncing the sins of your ancestors and any curses which have been placed on you. Exodus 20:4–5 says that the sins of the fathers are visited upon the children.

Familiar spirits can be passed on from one generation to the next if not renounced and if your new spiritual heritage in Christ is not declared. Because of your ancestor's sin, Satan may have gained access to your family. Problems can be transmitted genetically, from an immoral atmosphere or spiritually. These three conditions can predispose you to a particular sin. Deceived people may try to curse you, or satanic groups may target you. You have all the authority in Christ you need to stand against such curses. Even things like church splits can be the result of sin, and the hurt can be passed on to the new church congregation that results. There needs to be a public and corporate repentance of this. All the areas of ancestors' sin need to be given to Christ. This is especially true in cases of adoption. A claim of the godly inheritance is made so that evil influences taking advantage of feelings of rejection can be dismissed. Declare these things verbally before God.

After these steps, you may find yourself attacked again. Just renounce the spirits and their lies, and they will leave. Stand firm in the truth (from Freedom in Christ Ministries).

Part 2: On the Field

We will now turn the focus to spiritual warfare as it relates to the mission field. Working overseas with open eyes to the ideas of spirituality to life as a whole will solve certain questions that are sure to crop up in experience.

Wrestling

I will start with a personal reference to an episode that occurred in Korea on my first trip there. I was working for a very authoritative boss in the headquarters of a denominational office. The work was enjoyable, but at the same time, the atmosphere was oppressive because of the dominant attitude of the leader toward all of his staff. Combined with culture shock, this was an oppressive experience. One weekend I was praying about whether to stay longer or to leave as I was beginning to suffer great emotional strain. There didn't seem to be any other option as I had already discussed my situation with my supervisor, a compassionate bilingual pastor. One night I had a dream in which I saw an enemy. As I rose to rebuke it in my dream, I awoke, and behold, something was sitting on me in the bed. I joined in the battle with scripture, prayer, and praise. It took some considerable time before the presence left, and I knew then what I had to do. If the enemy did not want me to leave, then it was certainly time to go, as much as I disliked the option.

This experience totally sums up why the scriptures use the term *wrestling* (Eph. 6:10–12 KJV). A wrestling match means that there is a lot of struggle back and forth. It is a close and personal form of fighting. We fight against an enemy who seeks to have us fail in serving God and His purposes for us. The Greek term for *wrestle* is used in this passage. Soldiers needed to be in close combat, and that included wrestling one-on-one. This is not a kind of wrestling to be taken lightly. This is an important aspect that we need to see; we are wrestling with the enemy for souls, for God's grace to be given to the lost, and for many to come to the cross.

Enemy Forces

Robb's article on Satan's tactics is very insightful and contains a myriad of examples from this whole area of spiritual warfare (Robb 1993). He maintains that the agenda of the demons is to achieve dominion over the planet. This they have been able to do because of man's fall into sin. There is a wide range of spirits in control of various things such as government leaders, educational systems, and religious movements (Robb 1993, p. 173). We have already discussed the role of *stoicheia*. In twisting man's worship of God into idolatry, they subvert man's created purpose. One way in which Satan seeks to dominate the planet is through controlling spirits.

The Bible speaks of many spirits that apparently controlled the land of Canaan—Baal-Peor, Baal-Gad, and Baal-Hermon. It was the favour of these spirits (and many others) that the people of the land tried to obtain through the many sacrifices (Judg. 2:17; Jer. 7:9, 19:5). In the New Testament, the demons did not want to be sent away (Luke 8:26–39). Acts 19:35 speaks of Artemis who was the goddess of the Ephesians. Pergamum was the seat of Satan (Rev. 2:13) where the people burned incense to the emperor at the foot of his statue. Territorial spirits may be in control of a certain area or nation (Dan. 10:13). Scripture talks about Israel having an angel watching over it. So also, Satan's kingdom has a system where some spirits are in control of some areas.

Robb refers to several examples all over the world of territorial spirits controlling various areas. One is from Ernest Heimbach who is a pioneer international worker to the Hmong of Thailand. Heimbach declared there was a chief spirit that dominated the tribe using fear of sickness, death, attack by spirits, and opium to keep the Hmong under its control. Significant is the reference in Robb's work to information obtained from a letter from another IW regarding Thailand (Robb 1993, p. 176). The greatest of the guardian angels of Thailand is believed to be a spirit named Phra Siam Devadhiraj. It is this spirit which supposedly kept Thailand from being overrun by invaders (Western ones it is guessed as constant inroads were being made by the Burmese and Khmer throughout its history). The former king paid this spirit homage and worshipped it. Thailand is one of the most difficult countries to reach with the gospel in the 10/40 Window. Throughout Asia, the stories appear to be similar. Another type of spirit control in much the same way are the *nats* of Burma (which include natural phenomena) and the Hindu goddesses who protect villages and regions in India. They seem to control through disease, death, and catastrophe. Significant too is the goddess Kali who rules over West Bengal (city of Kolkata).

Other parts of the world are not immune to spirit control. In a First Nations village in Canada, an IW was attacked by a spirit that was in control of the village. He did battle with the spirit and claimed God's ownership over the village. The primary weapon against these spirits is that of intercessory prayer (Eph. 6:12). The Alliance Life gives a good example of this in Bamako, Mali. There was an area that was very resistant to the gospel. A church in this area was started in the 1980s. But there was much struggle in its growth. Members of the church struggled with impure lifestyles. People threw rocks at those who witnessed in evangelistic services. They could not buy land to build a church. Pastor Kone was called by God to lead against the demonic forces. The testimony of the church was restored. For years the church tried to get land, but nothing worked. Finally, they bought land but could not get permission to build. The papers kept vanishing when they were sent to the government offices. Two IWs listened to what God told them, and they began to pray. The leaders began to meet once a week to pray for warfare prayer. Prayer marches were organized to establish God's ownership of the land. When the believers did this, the papers began to move from one office to another. Finally, they were given permission to build. God had opened the doors in Bamako (Davis 1994, pp. 16–17)! One Swedish mission team has developed a strategy of evangelism that includes much prayer. They go to the new area for one month. They spend the whole month walking the streets, greeting the people, and then interceding for them in prayer together for hours (Bryant 1984, p. 204).

As mentioned earlier, the principalities seem to control ideas as well but only with the compliance of the people. Robb mentions the idea of collective possession which occurs when humanity gives itself up en masse to evil. Once the people of Germany started saying yes (or nothing at all) to the first requirements of the new regime, it snowballed into something horrible beyond imagination. Jews were restricted and homosexuals harassed. Even mentally challenged people were not left alone by the Nazi regime. Finally came the concentration death camps in which millions were murdered. Robb refers to the example given by Wink of Germany during World War II. The example of the Hitler Youth in Germany, the SS, and Gestapo are all historical evidence of this. Even today one can feel the malevolence at the German border near a gate arch where Nazism once was supreme. Other modern examples include Pol Pot's destruction of two million Cambodians, the genocides perpetrated by people like Idi Amin and Saddam Hussein. In America, the Theosophical Society tried to gain entrance of a guru in 1926 (Robb 1993, p. 177). His goal was to combine all religions into one, but the prayer of God's people and the spiritual state of the nation did not allow it. The guru became incoherent and was stripped of the powers that had worked in India. Unfortunately, such good spiritual barriers are now no longer functioning in America.

The control of the spirits is achieved through deception and false mindsets, says Robb. In the Western world, many have fallen prey to the "isms"—secularism, humanism, naturalism, materialism, relativism, and pluralism. They are wrong notions of reality (Gal. 4:3, Col. 2:8–9). These have taken the true God entirely out of the picture of many. Pluralism acknowledges spirituality, but not the exclusive message of the gospel and so leads astray too. The first five do not acknowledge spirituality whatsoever, and then grudgingly the last does admit it, but on the basis of equality, which is also a lie. There is only one way to God and that is through Jesus Christ.

These wrong notions of reality express themselves in many ways. The Shona people have legends of Chaminuka and Nehanda who are heroes to that culture in Zimbabwe. The spirits of these heroes are now being consulted by the government officials (Robb 1993, p. 177). There are also legends requiring animal sacrifices, festivals, and possessions of individuals to speak their will (the will of the spirits). The people need to ask permission to leave their territory and wear charms for protection. Even in Japanese culture, which is advanced technologically, there is a good deal of bondage in Shintoism. Over half of the population attend the Shinto shrines, and every child wears an amulet. Shinto priests are on hand to dedicate new buildings.

The false ideas manage to distort any perception of humanity that is good. The Bozos of Mali sacrifice animals and deformed people, recounts Robb. Those that are albinos, for example, are killed so that the harvest will be blessed by the spirits. Twins are murdered at birth in the belief that no two people can have the same spirit. The Bantu of Somalia need bloodshed in order to get a good harvest. The men will rush at each other from the sides of a field and beat each other with clubs. The blood and deaths will ensure a good harvest. The same application of negative mindsets and deception can be made to the rate of abortion in the Western world. The unborn babies are killed for the sake of convenience.

Robb mentions several ways that the control of the spirits is maintained (Robb 1993, p. 178).

1. *Animistic practises*—these attempt to manipulate the spirit world in order to control it and bring about peace and happiness. The use of shamans and charms are a part of getting

one's desires: a good job, good crops, healing, etc. Though the goal of the people is to manipulate the spirits, in the end, it is really the spirits who are using them.

2. *Through humans and mediaries*—(a) political leaders are responsible for the welfare of their people. Jeroboam (1 Kings 17:21–22) was responsible like many of the kings after him in leading the people of Israel astray. Ferdinand and Imelda Marcos were deeply involved in the occult by consulting a soothsayer. Thus, they exploited their own people who desperately needed good leadership. Corazon Aquino would not enter their residence because of the practises done there. (b) Spirit mediums, such as those in Acts 8:10, 13:6–11. These were used to turn people away from God. This was Simon's role as the people acclaimed his greatness in Acts 8. Elymas the sorcerer tried to directly oppose the apostles so that the pro-counsul would not believe at Paphos in Acts 13. There are many attempts nowadays for spiritual control over areas, recounts Robb. One of many is the story of a Chinese Christian worker who was waiting for a bus outside the grounds of a festival of a certain town. The spirits could not come into the mediums at the festival while she was waiting there (Robb 1993, p. 178). The presence of praying Christians interrupts the work and link of such people.

3. *Through places and objects* dedicated to the spirits. The spirit pillars erected in Thai villages increased the apathy of the people to the gospel, reported IW Joy Boese (Robb 1993, p. 177). The devil posts in Korea also served the same purpose, for they were placed there to protect the village and did this through the spirit called to inhabit them. When King Josiah burned the high places and shrines in ancient Israel, he broke the hold the spirits had on the people (Deut. 7:25, 26; 2 Kings 23).

4. *Through rituals of worship*—this has already been referred to in the section on the 10/40 Window. Since ritual is a part of daily life of all religions in some form, then the

repetition of each action would deepen the bondage. This worship may even include human sacrifice, which has been referred to in animistic practises. There are places in Africa which are still home to such practises; for example, a coastal island which the Lebu people of Senegal frequent. This has given the people much political, economic, and spiritual power. This is not restricted to non-Western nations; certainly in the West this happens under Satanic worship. The FBI estimates that 50 percent of the missing people in the US have been sacrificed (Robb 1993, p. 179).

5. *Through blocking God's people*—new converts of a church in Sao Tome and Principe died in a cholera epidemic that swept an area after an IW had encountered a demonic prince. This prince told the international worker to stop all activity, and the epidemic was a direct attack shortly after. Blocking God's people may simply come about through discouragement, infirmity, disunity, and discrediting ministers and ministries. Satan has a variety of attacks in the physical realm. Scripture tells of several people who experienced physical attacks from Satan (Luke 13:16, Matt. 12:22, Acts 10:38). In the C&MA, there are several IWs who have been sent home from Africa because of sickness. Some of them are convinced that these are a result of Satan's open hindrance to their presence in that part of the world. Warner tells the story of a Christian from Ghana who had aches and pains that the doctor could not cure. After dealing with personal sin in the area of sorcery, the sickness left. Many IWs suffer from physical diseases with spiritual roots. One IW had asthma. One day God told him that he was resentful against his mother for her missionary work. He prayed about it and dealt with it as sin. Once he did that, the asthma left, and he was cured.

Hindering the truth—or in this case, the evangelism efforts of others, is also an attack by the enemy. Sherman goes so far as to declare that the lack of effort in evangelism may be due to demonic influence. Christians are reluctant to evangelise for many reasons. The enemy may simply not want the truth of the gospel to be known by those under his control. We need to pray as in Luke 10:2 that the labourers would be available to preach. We need to use many methods in proclaiming the truth of the gospel (1 Cor. 15:58).

Sometimes families or mission teams can be the target of Satan's attacks as well. Any strife or disharmony can be used by Satan to interrupt the life and ministry of those involved. You must be on your guard against him and all his ways. There are some places where the international workers have a difficult time getting along with each other. This may be an area where the demons may be causing the problem and interfering with God's work.

Areas Open to Attack

Warner lists several general areas in which Satan likes to attack God's people. Satan likes to attack by taking what is already there naturally and intensifying it, making it compulsive.

1. *Appetite for food*—diseases like anorexia and bulimia are two areas that are common strongholds of satanic bondage and deception. Food becomes a focus for these people instead of God. They run to it for comfort and strength instead of to Him. The anorexic concentrates on staying thin because that is important. It is an area of control. They think about food all the time.
2. A second area of control is in the *sexual area*. Christian marriages and homes are under attack because they are strong witnesses to God's love and grace. Many pastors have fallen because they were not on guard in this area of their lives. The battle begins in the mind. If you watch what goes into your mind and take these thoughts captive to Christ, then you will be able to resist the temptations of Satan (2 Cor. 10:5). Controlling this area is done in the mind (Matt. 5:28). Following the guidelines Paul gives in Philippians 4:8 is helpful. Learn to say 'no' to the thought based on this passage.

This would help curtail a lot of immorality in Christians if they would take this verse seriously to heart. "Finally, brothers whatever is true, whatever is noble, whatever is right, whatever is pure, whatever is lovely, whatever is admirable—if anything is excellent or praiseworthy—think about these things" (NIV). The InterVarsity Press Commentary on the New Testament says that this verse takes into account the best of the Graeco-Roman heritage worthy of Paul's praise. Paul encourages the readers in Philippi to look at their culture and decide which things fit God's parameters on the list. True things find their measure in God (Rom. 1:18, 25) and the gospel (Gal. 2:5, 5:7). Something that is noble is worthy of respect. The 'pure' word would automatically be taken by the Jewish populace as something sanctified for the temple. But "lovely and admirable" are Hellenistic in origin. "Lovely" can have a broad application but 'beautiful' would definitely apply here. "Admirable" is a part of the virtues because most people would seek after it. If it is not true, right, pure, etc., say "no."

Sometimes demons can use physical objects as a way of getting to people. Idols themselves have no power (Isa. 44:9–20), but the demon they represent does. There are two types of objects: (1) *occultic/religious ones*—made for worship. These should not be brought into Christian homes and need to be destroyed. (2) *Spiritually neutral objects*—houses, buildings, etc. They can be cleansed and consecrated for God's use.

3. *Spiritual attacks* on Christians are part of life (1 Thess. 2:18, 2 Cor. 11:3). The attacks will always be on God's true character, what we think He is, and on our relationship to Christ. Thoughts such as God does not love us or won't forgive a certain sin are examples of this kind of attack. Sometimes attacks are in the mental and emotional areas. The attack is *always a battle for the mind*. Past emotional experiences can be used by demons to lead into bondage. Satan will push you beyond what you should feel. If you

are an anxious person, Satan will make you even more anxious to wear you out. If you are an angry person, you will be angry at many things and disrupt life for other people. If you are sad, Satan can make you feel depressed. I have felt this kind of depression many times. But since I learned about this spiritual warfare, I am not so depressed. If I feel depressed, I just tell the depression to go away in Jesus's name and it does. About 80 percent of my depression attacks fall into this category. I did not know that I was depressed because it was a spiritual attack; I thought it was me. Sometimes it is, but often it is Satan trying to make me feel worse than I do. If you have been through a terrible experience, say an accident with a car, you could end up being very afraid to drive and become too fearful to drive. It is normal to feel that way after an accident for a while. But if it persists and becomes uncontrollable, then it is possible that Satan has taken advantage of the situation and made it a stronghold for his terrorist attacks. There is something very good about obeying God in renouncing satanic influence. You don't have to feel like doing it. I don't even have to feel like obeying God in renouncing these feelings; I just do it, and it happens. Some people use how they feel as an excuse not to do things for God. They say, "I don't feel like praying, I don't feel like going to church," so they think it is dishonest to do these things. It's not dishonesty; it's obedience. Do what God asks you to regardless of how you feel. This is a part of maturity, a part of self-discipline, and this will help you to win the battle. Sometimes emotional breakdowns have a spiritual cause—resentments against others, for example. If Satan can make you think you're losing your mind, then he has made you ineffective for God. If Satan can stop you or hinder your work for God or your personal growth and walk with Christ, then he is winning the battle.

Sherman adds several points about the battle for the mind. He states that when you have failed, when you are down, or when tragedy strikes, that's when Satan attacks. We have to recognize the attacks of the enemy and search out our weaknesses. John 10:10 says that the devil comes to steal, to kill, and to destroy. Satan steals our days and can ruin them. Suicide in particular is certainly the devil's work. Along with that comes the self-destructive behaviour of drug and alcohol abuse. Satan can destroy us with sin and tempts us to do so with the promise of fulfillment. When we sin, we are participating with Satan.

There are six main ways that you can be open for Satan's attack (Warner 1993, p. 21). If you are not aware of these, then you may have struggles and not realize why.

1. *Ancestral sin*—if your ancestors have been involved in sin, they may pass it on to you. This can include spiritual things like worship of evil spirits or gods or being involved in an evil immoral lifestyle such as murder, alcoholism, or sexual sin. If an ancestor has been a part of these things, you may be attacked in the same areas by temptations you do not understand. You can pass on a negative spiritual inheritance just the same as you can a positive spiritual one. The demons will take advantage of your relationship to that person and harass you too. For instance, if your grandfather was an alcoholic, then one of his sons may be an alcoholic, and you may too. Even the person who says, "I will never be like that," may end up being driven into a situation where drinking may seem like a solution. Another example along the same lines, if a grandfather treats his family poorly or works very hard, he may have a son who does the same. Or maybe a grandson as it says in Exodus 20:5, 34:7. The Bible says about the sins going on down the generations because the generations are all sinful. Becoming a Christian does not cancel out the effect of your ancestor's sin. You need to take a specific stand and tell

Satan that the door for attack is no longer open; you close it in the name of Jesus Christ.

2. *Personal sin*—you can't sin and get away with it. When you sin, you give the devil a foothold in your life. This opens you up to attack. One sin usually leads to another and another until you are caught in a whole web of sin. Sherman categorizes sins in three areas: our mind, attitude, and mouth. The thoughts we have can be influenced by the negatives in our life—inferiority and condemnation of ourselves, for example. Your thoughts have to agree with God's truth. In the heart (Prov. 4:23), we are our true selves. The attitudes and emotions we have are important for spiritual warfare. (Eph. 4:26–27). Don't let the sun go down on your anger and deal with the wrong attitudes that can take root. Ephesians 4:22–24 says to put off the old self and put on the new self. We can't live in pride and rebellion and expect victory in our lives. Choose humility (1 Pet. 5:6–9) in how you live your life. Make sure you make decisions by God's leading and not feelings alone. The final area Sherman talks about is the mouth. We are supposed to be encouragers to each other. Our words can bring good or evil, life or death. The Holy Spirit can use our words as vehicles for truth, righteousness, and life; or conversely, Satan can use our words for deception, accusation, or death (Sherman 1990, p. 54). In that sense, they are very much like curses in a less direct way. We can use words in prayer to change what is happening in a sick person for healing. When we pray according to His will, mighty things can happen. Likewise, when we speak negatively, in complaints or criticisms (Prov. 18:21), we can cause harm. We need to put Psalm 141:3 in our minds: a guard over our lips or mouth and curb the negativity.

3. *Curses*—even if you don't believe in the reality of curses, they can cause trouble. A missionary family came home on furlough, and their children began misbehaving. Counselling didn't seem to help. Finally, someone asked if a

curse had been placed on the family by a witch doctor. The international worker said, yes, he had seen the witch doctor do it, but he hadn't believed in curses, so he didn't think about it. If you enter the devil's territory in missions, you open yourself up to attack. The family renounced the witch doctor's curse, and the children began behaving again. The boy stopped going with his bad friends, and the girl also returned to normal. In claiming the power of Christ, they rejected Satan.

4. *Careless exposure* in the devil's territory can be a problem. An IW family went to a shrine in Japan, and at the ceremony, the priest had prayed for the spirits to come down on the people. The IW family began having problems because they had not claimed the protection of Christ over the enemy. Whenever I go near a shrine or worship house that is not of God, I pray for protection and instantly renounce any influence of the enemy.

5. *Previous trauma* can also be a stronghold for satanic attack. A trauma is any incident which leaves a strong negative mark in your life. There are many examples of traumas: muggings, hostage, near-death accident, rapes, or a frightening experience. If you were scared by a snake very badly when you were a child, that could be a trauma, leaving you very frightened of snakes. Some people have a difficult past; they have suffered from physical, sexual, or emotional abuse. There are some families where there is a lot of trouble and anger which puts hurt into people's lives. If your father beat you up, you will have emotional and physical scars. Any strong event can leave scars in your life. If there was another student who treated you badly in school, that could leave a scar. Some people have had satanic ritual abuse. Any of these could leave you open to attack. You could become a fearful person, being afraid all the time.

6. *God's providence*—like Job in the Old Testament, God may decide to test you in some way by allowing Satan to attack you. Job came through his experience a better person,

understanding who he was and who God was. He knew God was in control.

Battle Lines

> Missionary service needs to be seen as the invasion of enemy-held territory in order to claim it for Christ. (Warner 1993, p. 22)

Missions is an act of war on Satan; we are taking people from his kingdom into God's. We should expect him to fight back when we enter his territory. When God told Israel to enter Canaan, he told them it would not be easy. The victory over the enemy was not all at once. They would have to take the land bit by bit. In each battle, God gave them something to do (Josh. 6:2–3, 4:11–12). The battle was never won on military strength alone but by faith. We must actively attack the enemy through evangelism. Evangelism is moving people from one kingdom to another, from the kingdom of darkness to the kingdom of light (Acts: 20:18). The conversion must be on a functional worldview level, or the new convert will syncretise because he is not sure where the real power is: in his old faith or in the new one. In the first two hundred years of Christianity, the early converts were instructed in the faith before baptism. At the baptism, they faced west and said, "Satan, I renounce you and all your works and all your ways." Then they would face east and say, "Lord Jesus, I give myself to You in worship and in service." One important thing to do is to get rid of all occult objects. This may involve real power demonstrations because the spirits will object to this. Even if the objects are valuable, it is important to get rid of them because they are a point of control. One family had to destroy a gold watch because it was an heirloom of an ancestor who practised witchcraft. When they destroyed it, the watch disappeared. Sometimes this can be a real witness to others and encourage them to come to God (Acts 19:20).

Many times, God will do dramatic healings as a part of establishing his church in other parts of the world. Not all healings are from God; we need to test them and make sure that the healing is of

God or not. Sometimes Satan will do healings just to get people to come under his power. Some parents brought their boy to a doctor who used New Age techniques, calling on the spirits to heal the boy. The boy got better from his illness, but afterward they began having trouble with him because he became hyperactive. They couldn't control him with medication or counselling. Finally, someone suggested prayer for healing from a spiritual point of view. He was prayed for and released from the bondage he had been put under when the doctor had cured him by calling on the spirits. The price for that was bondage to Satan. After the prayer, the boy was cured of his hyperactivity.

In the process of proclaiming the gospel, often IWs are called upon to confront those who oppose them in a demonstration very much like Elijah did with the worshippers of Baal on Mount Carmel (1 Kings 18). He called them to prove who was the true God. Which one had the real power? Would they worship God or worship the devil? It is not necessary to look for these dramatic confrontations so as to test God, but when the situation comes up, enter the battle knowing God is the true God, and He does answer prayer. This is called the power encounter, dealing with unbelievers in showing the power of God.

Encounters with the enemy may also involve deliverance on occasion. The Holy Spirit shows us how to pray (Rom. 8:26–27). In Mark's Gospel (9:29), Jesus referred to a demon that could only be driven out by prayer and fasting. This may open a particular field that is very difficult to the gospel. The OMF IWs in West Kalimantan were having difficulty getting Chinese converts; they had only five after several years of work. The leaders began getting involved in deliverance ministry, and as they did, that the number of converts went up to one thousand five hundred in a very short time. This was because they were releasing those bound by Satan through deliverance work. Robb records a similar incident that happened with Pastor David Yonggi Cho in South Korea. Early in his ministry he prayed for a woman who was paralysed and cast the demon out by the power of Christ. The church from there on began to grow very rapidly.

Intercessory prayer is one of the ways to overcome Satan. Joshua was told to take the territory of Canaan for God. It was not just a physical battle; it was spiritual. Prayer and fasting are where we should begin to lay the grounds for battle just as the Swedish mission team does (2 Chron. 20:15, 17, 21). The prayers are what make the ministry effective. God works in response to his people's prayers. In the book of Acts, prayer is mentioned thirty times; often prayer preceded a major breakthrough and growth of the church. Praying for those who have been bound by the enemy can be effective in helping them to gain freedom. There is still a personal choice to make, but they now have the freedom to choose. Love can be used to break barriers in deliverance, whether it be for individuals or nations. Praying through scripture can be helpful in declaring the truth of God in the situation. Hammond also mentions the idea of binding and loosing (Matt. 12:29). The use of 'bind' in the 'Greek' means 'to tie' as with chains. Tying Satan with prayer in God's name can be a way of binding Satan on earth as he has been bound in heaven. Satan can bind people, and we can release them in prayer (Luke 13:15–16).

Sherman records an interesting experience that happened some years ago regarding spiritual warfare and praise. The ministry team had been preaching against witchcraft in Papua New Guinea for some time, but there was no change in the hearts of the people. As the team prayed for wisdom, things begin to happen. Four different men from four different nations came to the team and gave them the same message, praise in warfare. The team began praising God and immediately saw some breakthroughs. People were baptised, being healed, and many came to Christ. A local shaman put a curse on the team evangelizing his village. The team did not pay much attention, but the leader of the team broke out with a fever and grew weaker and weaker. Three days later he was delirious and babbling with a fever. The doctor diagnosed an advanced stage of cerebral malaria. The team began fasting and praying throughout the night. Sherman went to visit the leader in ICU and rebuked the demon power of death. By the next morning, the leader was better but had no response in his eyes. More prayer was given on the situation, and the next day the sick man was better, weak but talking. Prayer has to be approached with wisdom and humility; if you aren't sure it's the enemy, ask God to show you what's going on in the situation.

A revival in which fifty thousand Koreans came to Christ in 1907 was the result of prayer. Bush recorded the results of a concentrated prayer effort in the 10/40 Window due to prayer (Bush 1999, p. 114). The Temple of Ten Thousand Buddhas in Hong Kong was closed in a dramatic way because people prayed. In 1997, Buddhists were ready for the Communist takeover of Hong Kong. They had made one of the largest outdoor Buddhas on Lantau Island, including a gigantic incense bowl. A rally of Buddhists all over Asia was to be held in the outdoor stadium on Hong Kong. But shortly after the Communists took over, the monsoon rains came and hit hard. It was one of the worst storms in the history of the area. A large landslide hit the temple, and the walls collapsed. The government ordered the temple shut because it was not safe. Every Home for Christ made an interesting observation in their literature work regarding prayer and openness to the gospel (Robb 1993, p. 181). If there was no prayer before handing out the literature, there was a response level of 10 percent. If the staff concentrated on prayer for a particular community, the response level was 55 percent. This was an incredible increase. But even more astounding was when the staff prayed as they passed out literature to each home. Then the response level was eight out of every ten homes! How much more ministry and salvation would occur if more prayer was offered in the context of work? This is the rationale behind the Praying through the Window (the 10/40 Window) series. God answers the prayers of His people.

Divine intervention occurs at times on behalf of God's people. In Nigeria, a chief was very resistant to the gospel. He built his fence on church property and would not let his people believe in Jesus. So a fire came down and burnt his fence. It also burned things in his house, but it never hurt any people. This occurred many times. Finally, he declared his people could worship God and moved his fence back.

Caution and Critique

There is, however, a caution and critique that Robb mentions in his article on prayer and spiritual warfare. Moreau also has much to say on the matter. Much has been said and written lately about the spiritual warfare in missions work—specifically the strategic level material which focuses on binding the powers over certain areas and cities. The focus of the ministry in the New Testament, says Robb, is to people, not about binding per se (Robb 1993, p. 181). The binding seems to be incidental; the apostles just dealt with the demons when they cropped up.

The other thing Robb says is that spiritual warfare on this level can be presumptuous, an unwarranted taking of credit for events that happen in the world. The explanation is not always so simple.

> Dynamic interplay between the Divine, human and demonic factors involved…so much more inscrutable. (Robb 1993, p. 181)

God's mighty working may come in response to many factors. The suffering of local Christians for example, says Robb, has played a role in events such as the fall of Communism. They were the ones who watched, prayed, and suffered for years before the Western Christians prayed. Oversimplifying deliverance is dangerous. As in Jude, ask God to do the binding and rebuking.

Guthrie raises a valid point as well in that the avenue of spiritual warfare focuses on the demons and not God (Guthrie 2000, p. 75). Christianity just becomes the new animism, to the amusement of the locals who can see right through the practises that are being hailed as the new and best way of spiritual warfare. It tends to treat God as being unable or unwilling to work without specific targeted prayers to neutralize the satanic hosts (Guthrie 2000, p. 80). The situation is not that simple. God is the Sovereign Creator of the world, and He has power over the demons. It is true He does act in response to our prayers. The Reformation focus on scripture; grace and faith could be renewed here again in this area.

The darkness must be dealt with in order for the deliverance of the captives so that they may enter the kingdom of God. The term *battle* is quite appropriate, for it is not easy to wrest the lost from Satan's grip.

> Spiritual darkness is not merely a passive absence of light...instead [it is] an aggressive attacking oppressive stronghold that is duty-bound to strangle all those within its grasp. (Sitton 1998, p. 74)

Moreau has written a paper that carefully looks at the issues involved in the wide disparity of spiritual warfare approaches today; it is called "Gaining Perspective on Territorial Spirits." In it he looks at the main aspects of what the proponents (from conservative to more confrontational) claim, the biblical authority, and then gives thorough responses. He applauds several things about the present spiritual warfare movement: the power of prayer to make changes in our world, the spirit of co-operation rather than competition, the recognition of the evil dimensions of culture, and the discernment of areas in which the church needs to repent. These are all aspects that have been under-emphasized in the church and need to be put in their proper place. The power of prayer in evangelisation is a necessary component; otherwise, Christians are just salesmen. The true spiritual nature of our world, both in negative and positive aspects, needs to be recognized in its true reality. Moreau's disagreement is largely the same as Robb's, that the "strategic level" aspects are not strongly biblically founded. It comes across as a kind of Christian animism that even the unbelievers recognize. Gaining information about the occult is dangerous, and the Bible does not condone it. The strategic level perspective in particular does not recognize the choice of people to sin as well as the demonic interference. Both, as Robb says, work together. Finally, Moreau closes with a few suggestions for refinement. First, the assumption as to causes of change cannot be proved as there are many factors involved. The emphasis needed on change should be as much on discipleship (as Anderson advocates) as warfare itself. This would result in an integrated worldview which balances the social, personal, spiritual, and cultural issues. The evil spirits should not be blamed for all the bondage in places. An excellent overview of the spiritual warfare literature is given by Moreau and should be used as reference ("North American Case Study: An Overview of Spiritual Warfare Literature").

Robb closes his paper with the scriptural injunction to sharing God's truth of salvation and not to pray only (as in prayer walking strategies) so that the spirits thus evicted do not come back to make a more evil place for themselves than before (Luke 11:24). He strongly advises that obedience to God (2 Tim. 4:7, 2 Cor. 6:4–10) is a part of defensive strategy against spiritual attack. Robb refers to Philips' assessment of how Satan takes over a nation through drawing them away from God and His Word, increased indulgence in sin, false worship and supernaturalism, and finally, tyranny and dictatorship (Robb 1993, p. 183). In Philips' opinion, the United States is in the third slot, which is both scary and dangerous.

Practical Applications for International Workers

Warner lists twelve things you can do as an IW to put these spiritual concepts into practice. These will give you a solid base to work from.

1. *Establish the practice of worship*—it is more important to have this as an attitude and lifestyle than a thing we do. Some people feel without devotions they will have a bad day. But in reality, if you have devotions, you may have a bad day because you come under spiritual attack. There is no correlation between good days and devotions. The important thing is a relationship with God. We must all be good students of God, not just the pastors. We need to meditate on the Word day and night and have our mind set on the things of God. The most important thing for Christians is worship, focusing on God first before we focus on our needs. Satan wants to distract us so that we

don't pray and worship. The sacrifice of praise is done even when we don't feel like it; that is what sacrifice is.
2. *Feed yourself* from reading good books and the Bible. Use variety in how you study and memorize the scriptures. Practise praying the scriptures back to God. God will answer those prayers in His Word because it is His desire to do so.
3. *Establish your identity in Christ*—once you know who you are, you can fight off the lies of the devil. Be secure in who God is, then people cannot shock you by what they say or do. Don't make your goals dependent on what other people do because then they can thwart what you want. Put your eyes on Christ, what He has done and what He says about you, and you will do well. Renew your mind in prayer. A second aspect of this is, don't take your hurts and traumas with you to the field. Face them before you get there. Realize that God has the resources and ability to deal with these things. God is able and powerful enough to do so.
4. *Establish the concept of authority* in your family (if married). The leadership in the home belongs with the husband. In the West, often the woman takes the spiritual leadership, but this is the husband's role. He takes the initiative in defending the family against Satan. Teach the children the spiritual concepts of identity in Christ.
5. *Authority and interdependence in ministry*—welcome the mutual accountability of others in ministry. Don't rebel against the mission or church authority. Sherman adds not to confuse authority with feeling (Sherman 1990, p. 110). The basis of our authority is in Christ in the legal sense. Man was created with free will and authority delegated to him by God. Many positions in corporations have managers, directors, and supervisors. They do their work as being in charge of relatively small groups. The president of the company still has the control over them. Man's disobedience to God meant that some of that God-given authority was lost to Satan. God rebuked everyone involved (Gen.

3:15) and proclaimed that there was enmity between mankind and Satan. Sherman gives five methods for exercising authority (Sherman 1990, p. 122). They are the name of Jesus (including our relationship to Him) and the Word of God (1 John 3:8). Third is the power of the Holy Spirit (Acts 1:8) and the fourth the blood of Jesus (Rev. 12:11). The final method is declaring truth through the acts and character of God.

6. *Cleanse and dedicate* your workplace and home to make sure there are no negative influences every time you go somewhere new. One pastor cleanses his hotel room every time he goes to one. Walk the perimeters in a prayer walk and cleanse it for God. Any bad event—murder, abortion, suicide, etc.—will allow the demons to lay claim to a place. One lady was cured of a depression because she cleansed the things in her home. Even something like water-witching is of demonic influence. This has already been referred to in the Steps to Freedom section.

7. *Understand all authority*—God has given all authority to us as His children (Matt. 28:18). When He tells us to go somewhere, He gives us the authority to do the job. A second thing in this area is to resist any attempts of Satan to scare you off God's place for you. If God has called you there, you should stay and not be scared off or lured off by Satan.

8. *Expect spiritual opposition*—be strong and courageous like Joshua (Josh. 1:6–7, 9). Joshua had a big battle ahead of him, but he stayed to fight because God promised to help him. Use the armour of God to defend yourself from attacks (2 Cor. 10:3–5).

9. *Warfare prayer* is essential to your ministry by yourself and a prayer team. Teach them to wrestle in prayer for you so that you can be strengthened by their ministry and defeat Satan's strongholds. Sherman defines the strongholds as the evils to which certain demons can be assigned (Sherman 1990, p. 98). These can be developed when people sin and

live selfishly. As a country sins, it can be controlled by that sin. Powers such as greed, homosexuality, depression, and fear can be centred in cities, but not found in other areas to the same extent. Gambling, for example, could be the sin of Las Vegas, in Nevada. This is a city well known for its gambling and casinos. The influence of these regional sins can start with temptation, becoming a weight on our will the next time we participate in that same sin. With each repetition, it dulls our conscience. The sin can become a deeply ingrained habit. Habits of sin can lead to bondage; this is the supernatural element to the problem (Sherman 1990, p. 107).

10. *Study the unique aspects of your area*—this could lead to significant breakthroughs in the spiritual battle for the country. The spiritual history of an area or a country could tell you much about the resistant people. In Haiti, for example, an IW found out that the whole country was dedicated to Satan twice in its history. No wonder they were having a hard time with spiritual fruit. So the pastors began to pray, and God was able to break through the barriers. This kind of spiritual research is important. This could include the happenings in the country too that may have led to spiritual openings for oppression and strongholds.

 Poythress brings up the topic of idols, which, although in themselves, are less than nothing (Isa. 41:24–29), but when people worship them, they give themselves to the power of demons and deceit. The scriptures (2 Thess. 2:10–12, 2 Cor. 4:4, 2 Tim. 2:25–26) declare that the idolatry is full of deceit and delusion, taken captive to do the will of the devil. This, in a sense, defines the idolatry geographically. The various people of the Old Testament had their gods (Moabites worshipped Chemosh [1 Kings 11:7], the Ammonites worshipped Molech and Chemosh [1 Kings 11:7, Judg. 11:24], and the Philistines worshipped Dagon [1 Sam. 5:2–7]). Many Baal gods had their own areas: Baal-Meon (Num. 32:38), Baal-Hermon (Judg. 3:3), and Baal-

Peor (Num. 25:3). The modern-day adherents in cities and social groups also have idolatry. The idolatry takes them captive to this sin, trying to counterfeit the truth, power, and beauty of God and His kingdom.

11. *Teach identity in Christ*—knowing the truth can set others free. Become the person you would like to have around and be there for others. Everyone is responsible for the growth of their own character. Being responsible for others' characters is God's job.
12. *Accept personal differences in the Christian community*—this includes gifting and temperaments. We may not get along with everyone or see the same, but that is a part of the church. There are many different kinds of Christians in the body of Christ.

Summary

Now we have come full circle in this book. We've started out with missions foundations: missions definition, why it's important, where it takes place and the various aspects of when it is carried out. Then biblical theology of mission focusing on God's character and nature moving through both Old and New Testaments. The example of the author in her walk and journey along the missions path is given as one way the mission call and work may be done.

Then we move to personal call and preparation of the individual worker in some more detail. Then final aspect of the foundational premises in missions rests in spiritual warfare. This goes from the personal armour of each and every believer to the battleground overseas in the context of missions. We close this book with a few appendices related to the chapters covered, the twelve apostles, the story of Otto Koning in regards to his pineapples, the one-hundred-year prayer meeting at the forerunner to Protestant Missions, and finally the doctrinal affirmation and Who Am I supplement in spiritual warfare.

Appendices

Appendix A

The Twelve Apostles

(10:1–4)

A. In Carrying Out the Great Commission

1. They were commanded to make disciples of all the nations (Matt. 28:19).
   a) We read of the early work of the apostles in Jerusalem, Judea, and Samaria in the book of Acts.
   b) We can also read Peter's letters to those throughout Asia Minor (Turkey).
2. From sources outside the Bible, we are told the following:
   a) *Peter* is thought to have travelled to Rome and possibly Babylon (cf. 1 Pet. 5:13).
   b) *Andrew* is said to have preached in Bithynia, Scythia, Greece, and among the Parthians.
   c) *James*, the brother of John, is said to have preached in India and Spain before he was beheaded by Herod.
   d) *John*, brother of James, spent time in Patmos, later in Ephesus, and is thought by some to have established the churches of Smyrna, Pergamos, Sardis, Philadelphia, Laodicea, and Thyatira.
   e) *Philip* ministered in Phrygia.

    f) *Bartholomew* is said to have taken the gospel of Matthew to India.
    g) *Thomas* is also thought to have travelled to India.
    h) *Matthew* is said to have preached fifteen years in Palestine, and then went to Ethiopia, Macedonia, Syria, Persia, Parthia, and Medea.
    i) *James, the son of Alphaeus*—little is known of any work outside Jerusalem.
    j) *Thaddaeus* is said to have preached in Syria and Edessa.
    k) *Simon the Zealot* is said to have preached the gospel in Mauritania, Africa, and even in Britain.
    l) *Matthias* is thought to have gone to Damascus. While much of the above is not known for sure, it does seem to coincide with Paul's statements concerning the spread of the gospel (Rom. 10:14–18; Col. 1:23).

B. In Giving Their Lives for the Lord

  1. The apostles suffered much for the Lord.
    a) As He warned them (John 15:18–20)
    b) As Paul described in (1 Cor. 4:9–13)
  2. But they did more than suffer discomfort; in most cases, they gave their lives.
    a) *Peter*—crucified upside down in Rome
    b) *Andrew*—imprisoned in Greece, then crucified on a cross, the two ends of which were fixed transversely in the ground (from which came the term St. Andrew's Cross)
    c) *James*—beheaded by Herod (Acts 12:1–2)
    d) *John*—the only apostle thought to avoid a violent death
    e) *Philip*—scourged, thrown into prison, and afterward crucified
    f) *Bartholomew*—said to have been placed into a sack and thrown into the sea; some say he was crucified.
    g) *Thomas*—thrust through with a spear in India

h) *Matthew*—said by some to have died a natural death; by others that he died in Ethiopia, being slain with a halberd (pike fitted with an axe head) in the city of Nadabah
i) *James, the son of Alphaeus*—stoned by the Jews for preaching Christ
j) *Thaddaeus*—unknown
k) *Simon the Zealot*—suffered martyrdom under Trajan; some think crucified in Britain
l) *Matthias*—said to have been stoned and then beheaded

Appendix B

Otto Koning

(Story excerpt)

There are also negative examples of missionary influence. The presence of a Western international worker often models Western cultural attitudes more than the gospel of Christ. Here's a modern example as shown in *The Pineapple Story*. This story took place in Dutch New Guinea. It covered a period of seven years. A Dutch IW named Otto Koning gave this example of how his model and lifestyle worked among the people he was evangelising. He owned a garden and wanted to grow fruit. But the local people had a community sharing system: everything was shared with everything else. So they took his things because that was their custom. (The idea of stealing was not in their culture.) Koning became very frustrated with this and tried especially to protect his garden. It takes about three years to get pineapples to yield fruit. After a three-year wait, the IWs found out that the natives were stealing the ripened fruit from them. They tried to reason with them, but it didn't work. They tried to close the clinic, but the people begged for medicine. They closed the trade shop. The natives went into the jungle. They got a dog to stop them from stealing the fruit. That worked, but then the natives ran back into the jungle, and so the IW couldn't minister to them. No matter what Koning did, he couldn't protect his pineapples. One day he gave it all to God instead of protecting his interests. The change in his life was dramatic. The people asked him when he'd become a Christian because now, he shared like Christ. He lived the way he'd preached. Soon many natives became Christians. The model of Christ-likeness in community became the paradigm for change, not the Western idea of the importance of money or ownership of possessions.

Appendix C

The Hundred-Year Prayer Meeting and Subsequent Missions

A new spirituality now characterized the community, with men and women being committed to bands or choruses to encourage one another in the life of God. August of 1727 is seen as the Moravian Pentecost. Zinzendorf said August 13th was "a day of the outpourings of the Holy Spirit upon the congregation; it was its Pentecost." Within two weeks of the outpouring, twenty-four men and twenty-four women covenanted to pray "hourly intercessions," thus praying every hour around the clock. They were committed to see that "The fire must be kept burning on the altar continuously; it must not go out" (Lev. 6:13). The numbers committed to this endeavor soon increased to around seventy from the community. This prayer meeting would go non-stop for the next one hundred years and is seen by many as the spiritual power behind the impact the Moravians had on the world.

From the prayer room at Herrnhut came a missionary zeal which has hardly been surpassed in church history. The spark initially came from Zinzendorf's encounter in Denmark with Eskimos who had been converted by Lutherans. The count returned to Herrnhut and conveyed his passion to see the Gospel go to the nations. As a result, many of the community went out into the world to preach the gospel, some even selling themselves into slavery in order to fulfill the great commission. This commitment is shown by a simple statistic. Typically, when it comes to world missions, the Protestant laity to missionary ratio has been 5000:1. The Moravians, however, saw a much increased ratio of 60:1. By 1776, some 226 IWs had been sent out from the community at Herrnhut. It is clear through the teaching of the so-called Father of Modern Missions, William Carey, that the Moravians had a profound impact on him in regard to their zeal for missionary activity. It is also through the missions-minded Moravians that John Wesley came to faith. The impact of this little community in Saxony which committed to seek the face of the Lord day and night has truly been immeasurable.

In 1973, David Yonggi Cho, pastor of the Yoido Full Gospel Church in Seoul, South Korea, established a prayer mountain in night and day prayer. The prayer mountain was soon attracting over a million visitors per year, as people would spend retreats in the prayer cells provided on the mountain. Cho had a commitment to continuous prayer, to faith, and to establishing small discipleship cells in his church. Perhaps as a result, Cho's church rapidly expanded to become the largest church congregation on the globe, with membership now over seven hundred eighty thousand.

On September 19, 1999, the International House of Prayer in Kansas City, Missouri, started a prayer and worship meeting that has continued for twenty-four hours a day, seven days a week ever since. With a similar vision to Zinzendorf, that the fire on the altar should never go out, there has never been a time when worship and prayer has not ascended to heaven since that date. At the same time in many other places around the world, God placed desires and plans for 24/7 prayer in the fabric of diverse ministries and in the hearts of leaders. This has resulted in establishing 24/7 houses of prayer and prayer mountains in every continent of the Earth.

Appendix D

Doctrinal Affirmation

I recognize that there is only one true and living God (Exod. 20:3) who exists as the Father, Son, and Holy Spirit; and that He is worthy of all honor, praise, and worship as the Creator, Sustainer, and Beginning and End of all things (Rev. 4:11, 5:9–10; Isa. 43:1, 7, 21).

I recognize Jesus Christ as the Messiah, the Word who became flesh and dwelt among us (John 1:1, 14). I believe that He came to destroy the works of Satan (1 John 3:8), that He disarmed the rulers and authorities and made a public display of them, having triumphed over them by the cross (Col. 2:15).

I believe that God has proven His love for me because when I was still a sinner, Christ died for me (Rom. 5:8). I believe that He delivered me from the domain of darkness and transferred me to His kingdom, and in Him I have redemption, the forgiveness of my sins (Col. 1:13–14).

I believe that I am now a child of God (1 John 3:1–3) and that I am seated with Christ in the heavenlies (Eph. 2:6). I believe that I was saved by the grace of God through faith, that it was a gift and not the result of works on my part (Eph. 2:8).

I choose to be strong in the Lord and in the strength of His might (Eph. 6:10). I put no confidence in the flesh (Phil. 3:3), for the weapons of my warfare are not of the flesh (2 Cor. 10:4). I put on the whole armour of God (Eph. 6:10–20), and I resolve to stand firm in my faith and resist the evil one.

EXPLORING THE ROOTS OF MISSIONS: PERSONAL, BIBLICAL, AND SPIRITUAL

I believe that Jesus has all authority in heaven and on earth (Matt. 28:18) and that He is the Head over all rule and authority (Col. 2:10). I believe that Satan and his demons are subject to me in Christ because I am a member of Christ's body (Eph. 1:19–23). I, therefore, obey the command to resist the devil (Jas. 4:7), and I command him in the name of Christ to leave my presence.

I believe that apart from Christ, I can do nothing (John 15:5), so I declare my dependence on Him. I choose to abide in Christ in order to bear much fruit and glorify the Lord (John 15:8). I announce to Satan that Jesus is my Lord (1 Cor. 12:3), and I reject any counterfeit gifts or works of Satan in my life.

I believe that the truth will set me free (John 8:32) and that walking in the light is the only path of fellowship (1 John 1:7). Therefore, I stand against Satan's deception by taking every thought captive in obedience to Christ (2 Cor. 10:5). I declare that the Bible is the only authoritative standard (2 Tim. 3:15–17). I choose to speak the truth in love (Eph. 4:15).

I choose to present my body as an instrument of righteousness, a living and holy sacrifice, and I renew my mind by the living Word of God in order that I may prove that the will of God is good, acceptable, and perfect (Rom. 6:13, 12:1–2).

I ask You, Heavenly Father, to fill me with Your Holy Spirit (Eph. 5:18), to lead me into all truth (John 16:13), and to empower my life so that I may live above sin and not carry out the desires of the flesh (Gal. 5:16). I crucify the flesh (Gal. 5:24) and choose to walk by the Spirit.

I renounce all selfish goals and choose the ultimate goal of love (1 Tim. 1:5). I choose to obey the greatest commandment: to love the Lord my God with all my heart, soul, and mind and to love my neighbour as myself (Matt. 22:37–39).

Appendix E

Who Am I?

Excerpt from *Victory Over the Darkness* by Neil T. Anderson, copyright © 2000, 2013, 2020. Used by permission of Bethany House, a division of Baker Publishing Group.

I am accepted…

John 1:12—I am God's child.
John 15:15—I am Christ's friend.
Romans 5:1—I have been justified.
1 Corinthians 6:17—I am united with the Lord, and I am one spirit with Him.
1 Corinthians 6: 19–20—I have been bought with a price. I belong to God.
1 Corinthians 12:27—I am a member of Christ's body.
Ephesians 1:1—I am a saint.
Ephesians 1:5—I have been adopted as God's child.
Ephesians 2:18—I have direct access to God through the Holy Spirit.
Colossians 1:14—I have been redeemed and forgiven of all my sins.
Colossians 2:10—I am complete in Christ.

I am secure…

Romans 8:1–2—I am free forever from condemnation.

EXPLORING THE ROOTS OF MISSIONS: PERSONAL, BIBLICAL, AND SPIRITUAL

Romans 8:28—I am assured that all things work together for good.
Romans 8:31ff—I am free from any condemning charges against me.
Romans 8:35ff—I cannot be separated from the love of God.
2 Corinthians 1:21–22—I have been established, anointed, and sealed by God.
Colossians 3:3—I am hidden with Christ in God.
Philippians 1:6—I am confident that the good work that God has begun in me will be perfected.
Philippians 3:20—I am a citizen of heaven.
2 Timothy 1:7—I have not been given a spirit of fear but of power, love, and a sound mind.
Hebrews 4:16—I can find grace and mercy in time of need.
1 John 5:18—I am born of God, and the evil one cannot touch me.

I am significant…

Matthew 5:13–14—I am the salt and the light of the earth.
John 15:15—I am a branch of the true vine, a channel of His life.
John 15:16—I have been chosen and appointed to bear fruit.
Acts 1:8—I am a personal witness of Christ's.
1 Corinthians 3:16—I am God's temple.
2 Corinthians 5:17ff—I am a minister of reconciliation for God.
2 Corinthians 6:1—I am God's co-worker (1 Cor. 3:9).
Ephesians 2:6—I am seated with Christ in the heavenly realm.
Ephesians 2:10—I am God's workmanship.
Ephesians 3:12—I may approach God with freedom and confidence.
Philippians 4:13—I can do all things through Christ who strengthens me.

Supplement to Who Am I

Since I am in Christ, by the grace of God…

- I have been justified, completely forgiven, and made righteous (Rom. 5:1);

- I died with Christ and died to the power of sin's rule over my life (Rom. 6:1–6);
- I have been placed into Christ by God's doing (1 Cor. 1:30);
- I have received the Spirit of God into my life that I might know the things freely given to me by God (1 Cor. 2:12);
- I have been given the mind of Christ (1 Cor. 2:16);
- I have been given the Holy Spirit as a pledge guaranteeing my inheritance to come (Eph. 1:13–14);
- Since I died, I no longer live for myself but for Christ (2 Cor. 5:14–15);
- I have been made righteous (2 Cor. 5:21);
- I have been crucified with Christ, and it is no longer I who live, but Christ lives in me. The life I am now living is Christ's life (Gal. 2:20);
- I have been blessed with every spiritual blessing (Eph. 1:3);
- I was chosen in Christ before the foundation of the world to be holy and am without blame before Him (Eph. 1:4);
- I was predestined—determined by God—to be adopted as God's son (Eph. 1:5);
- I have been made alive together with Christ (Eph. 2:5);
- I have been rescued from the domain of Satan's rule and transferred to the kingdom of Christ (Col. 1:13);
- Christ Himself is in me (Col. 1:27);
- I am firmly rooted in Christ and am now being built in Him (Col. 2:7);
- I have been spiritually circumcised. My old unregenerate nature has been removed (Col. 2:11);
- I have been buried, raised, and made alive with Christ (Col. 2:12–13);
- I died with Christ and have been raised up with Christ. My life is now hidden with Christ in God. Christ is now my life (Col. 3:1–4);
- I have been saved and set apart according to God's doing (2 Tim. 1:9, Tit. 3:5);

- Because I am sanctified and am one with the Sanctifier, He is not ashamed to call me brother (Heb. 2:11); and
- I have been given exceedingly great and precious promises by God by which I am a partaker of God's divine nature (2 Pet. 1:4).

Understanding your identity in Christ is absolutely essential to your success at living the victorious Christian life!

—Dr. Neil Anderson, *Living Free in Christ*

The more you affirm who you are in Christ the more your behaviour will begin to reflect your true identity!

—Dr. Neil Anderson, *Victory over the Darkness*

Bibliography

Acena, Carmelyn Lois. "Sorry Lord, I Can't Be a Missionary." In *Alliance Life*, edited by Maurice Irvin. Willowdale, ON: Christian and Missionary Alliance, 1994.

Anderson, Neil T. *Victory over the Darkness.* Ventura, CA: Regal Books, 1990.

———. *The Bondage Breaker.* Eugene, Oregon: Harvest House Publishers, 1993.

———. "Who Am I," "Who Am I supplement." *The Bondage Breaker*, 239–44. Eugene, Oregon: Harvest House Publishers, 1993.

Apple, Paul. "Book of Ecclesiastes." Bible Outlines. Accessed July 8, 2006. http://www.bibleoutlines.com/library/ot/ecclesiastes.html

Barclay, O. R. "Creation." In *New Dictionary of Theology*, edited by S. B. Ferguson. Downers Grove, IL: InterVarsity Press, 1988.

"Basic Dictionary of Theological Terms." Reformed Theology. Accessed September 29, 2005. http://www.reformed-theology.org/html/dictiona.htm. This article was originally found online. It is no longer accessible.

"Historical Evidence Cleansing of the Temple." Bible History, 2013. http://www.biblehistory.net/volume2/Annas.htm.

"Destroying 'the High Places.'" Biblical Unitarian. Spirit & Truth Fellowship International, 2019. https://www.biblicalunitarian.com/articles/destroying-the-high-places.

Biblical Ministries Worldwide page. https://www.biblicalministries.org/serve/opportunities/tentmaking/ 2021 Biblical Ministries Worldwide

Blue, Ken. *Authority to Heal*. Downers Grove, Illinois: InterVarsity Press, 1987.

Bonhoeffer, Dietrich. *Selections from the Writings of Dietrich Bonhoeffer*. Arranged by Orlo Strunk Jr. Great Devotional Classics, Upper Room, 1967.

Bruce, Deborah A. "Encouraging Tentmaker Missionaries." ACMC Inc. Deborah A. Bruce Research Services, February 11, 1998. Originally accessed online in 2001 but online website is no longer available.

Bruce, F. F. *Book of the Acts*. Grand Rapids, Michigan: W. B. Eerdmans Publishing Co., 1984.

Bryant, David. *In the Gap*. Ventura, CA: InterVarsity Christian Fellowship, 1984.

———. *With Concerts of Prayer*. Ventura, CA: Regal Books, 1984.

Bush, Luis. "Explaining the 10/40 Window." *The Great Commission Handbook*. Evanston, IL: Berry Publishing Services, 1993.

———. "Paradigm Shifts in the 10/40 Window." *International Journal for Frontier Missions* 16, no. 3 (Fall, 1999): 111–17. http://www.ijfm.org/PDFs_IJFM/16_3_PDFs/01_Bush_1.pdf.

Chamovitz, Daniel. "Plant Senses: Sight." *New Scientist*. 22 August 2012. Accessed May 1, 2021. https://www.newscientist.com/article/mg21528791-800-plant-senses-sight/

Christensen, Derek. "Training for Mission." Accessed August 2005. www.seedbed.info/english/papers/2.doc. Originally found online. No longer accessible.

Christie, Lance. Email conversation. Pastor of Sema Community Church, Calgary, AB, 2006.

"Cities in the world with 75,000 to 80,000 inhabitants in 2005." Accessed October 28, 2005. http://www.mongabay.com/igapo/2005_world_city_populations/2005_city_population_15.html

Copeland, Mark A. "A Harmony of the Life of Paul: Paul's Life Prior to Conversion." Executable Outlines. 2002. http://www.ccel.org/contrib/exec_outlines/paul/paul_01.htm.

———. "A Harmony of the Life of Paul: Conversion of Paul (36 A.D.)." Executable Outlines, 2002. http://www.ccel.org/contrib/exec_outlines/paul/paul_02.htm.

———. "A Harmony of the Life of Paul: Paul's Early Years of Service (36–45 A.D.)." Executable Outlines, 2002. http://www.ccel.org/contrib/exec_outlines/paul/paul_03.htm.

———. "A Harmony of the Life of Paul: First Missionary Journey and Residence in Antioch (45–49 A.D.)." Executable Outlines, 2002. http://www.ccel.org/contrib/exec_outlines/paul/paul_04.htm.

———. "A Harmony of the Life of Paul: Conference to Jerusalem and Return to Antioch. (50 A.D.)." Executable Outlines, 2002. http://www.ccel.org/contrib/exec_outlines/paul/paul_05.htm.

———. "A Harmony of the Life of Paul: Second Missionary Journey (51–54 A.D.)." Executable Outlines, 2002. http://www.ccel.org/contrib/exec_outlines/paul/paul_06.htm

———. "A Harmony of the Life of Paul: Third Missionary Journey (54–58 A.D.)." Executable Outlines, 2002. http://www.ccel.org/contrib/exec_outlines/paul/paul_07.htm

Couturier, Adam. "What Were the High Places?" *Bible Study Magazine* 4, no. 3. October 10, 2017. http://www.biblestudymagazine.com/bible-study-magazine-blog/2017/10/10/what-were-the-high-places.

Culbertson, Howard. "A Missionary Call." Accessed September 29, 2005. http://home.snu.edu/~hculbert/call.htm.

———. "Missions Statistics from the 10/40 Window." Accessed August 2005. http://home.snu.edu/~hculbert/1040.htm.

Davis, Charles III. "And the Walls Came Tumbling Up." *Alliance Life*. Willowdale, ON: Christian and Missionary Alliance, 1994.

Dillaman, Rockwell L. "Missions and Worship": Missionary Voices. Camp Hill, PA, Christian Publications, 1996.

Dougherty, E. David. "What's Happening to Missions Mobilization?" *Evangelism and Missions Information Service* 34, no. 3, 1998. https://missionexus.org/whats-happening-to-missions-mobilization/.

Duewel, Wesley L. *Touch the World through Prayer*. Grand Rapids Michigan: Francis Asbury Press, 1986.

English, Dave. "Missions for a New Millennium: Catching Up with Paul." May 1999. http://tent.goweb.no/resources/articles/missions-for-a-new-millennium

"Everything You Wanted to Know About Hinduism," https://futurestrongacademy.com/2017/10/31/everything-you-wanted-to-know-about-hinduism/ 2008-2021 Future Strong.

Freeman, Hobart E. *An Introduction to the Old Testament Prophets.* Chicago: Moody Press, 1981.

Gailer, Susanna. "MK Care: God Still Moves." Accessed October 8, 2005. http://www.alliancewomen.org/aw/adobe/mkcare.pdf. Originally online. No longer accessible.

Ginter, Gary. *Overcoming Resistance Through Tentmaking.* Address to the National Meeting of the Evangelical Missiological Society Meeting with the International Society for Frontier Missiology at Santa Clara, Cal. Nov. 20-22, 1997. Originally available online but no longer accessible.

Goheen, Bill, and Karen Niedermayer. *Faithful in Christ Jesus.* Downers Grove, Illinois: InterVarsity Press, 1984.

Gospel for Asia. "Why Native Missions." August 2005. https://www.gfa.org.

Green, Michael. *Exposing the Prince of Darkness.* Ann Arbor, Michigan: Servant Publications, 1981.

Gordon, Robert. *How Much More.* London: Marshalls Paperbacks, 1983.

Guthrie, Stan. *Missions in the Third Millennium.* Carlisle, Cumbria, UK; Waynesboro, GA: Paternoster Press, 2000.

Halley, Henry H. *Halley's Bible Handbook.* Grand Rapids, Michigan: Zondervan Publishing House, 1965.

Hammond, Frank, and Ida Mae. *Pigs in the Parlor.* Kirkwood, MO: Impact Christian Books Inc., 1973, 2010.

Hartley III, Fred A. "Missions and Prayer." *Missionary Voices.* Camp Hill, PA: Christian Publications, 1996.

Harrison, Paul. T. "Chapter 7: Households in the New Testament." The Growing Church: Studies in the Book of Acts. Accessed January 18, 2007. http://eis.net.au/~paulh/gc0hp.htm http://

eis.net.au/~paulh/gc8hp.htm. Originally found online no longer accessible.
Hiebert, Paul. *Anthropological Insights for Missionaries.* Grand Rapids, Michigan: Baker Book House, 1995.
Howard, David M. *Student Power in World Missions.* Downers Grove, IL: InterVarsity Press, 1979.
Moravian House of Prayer. A "Brief History of 24/7 Prayer." https://www.morhop.com/a-brief-history-of-247-prayer
Jones, Esther. "Animism" (unpublished). 2007.
Joshua Project. Accessed January 10, 2007. http://www.joshuaproject.net.
Kane, Herbert. *Christian Missions in Biblical Perspective.* Grand Rapids, Michigan: Baker Book House, 1976, 1989.
King, Paul L. "Restoring the Doctrine of Binding and Loosing." Alliance World Fellowship International Office, Sao Paulo, Brazil. Accessed September 30, 2020. http://awf.world/consult/the-restoration-of-the-doctrine-of-binding-and-loosing.
Kim, Samuel I. (Soon-Il). *The Unfinished Mission in Thailand: The Uncertain Christian Impact on the Buddhist Heartland.* Seoul: East-West Center for Missions Research and Development, 1980.
Kirk, J. A. "Missiology." *New Dictionary of Theology*, edited by SB Ferguson. Downers Grove, IL: InterVarsity Press, 1988.
Kolb, Robert. "Hit Men and Midwives: Christian Witness at Work and Worship," edited by D.G. Trumper. Valparaiso, IN: Institute of Liturgical Studies, 1988.
Koning, Otto. *The Pineapple Story (part 1, part 2).* Accessed March 20, 2006. https://biblicalrestorationministries.org/pineapplestory.html.
Kraft, Charles H. *Christianity with Power.* Ann Arbour, Michigan: Servant Books, 1989.
Lane, Denis. *Tuning God's New Instruments.* Singapore: World Evangelical Fellowship, 1990.
Larkin, William J. Jr. "Chapter 5: Christianity and the Religions." The Contribution of the Gospels and Acts to a Biblical Theology of Religion. No. 2 Evangelical Missiological Society Series, edited

by Edward Rommen, Harold Netland, and William Carey. Evangelical Missiological Society. Pasadena, CA: Library, 1995.

Lausanne Congress Manila July 1989. Lausanne International Congress of World Evangelization. Lausanne, Switzerland: 1974.

"Learning Thai the Easy Way." Samathidhammaram Center. Accessed March 22, 2021. https://methika.com/chanting-book/

Lee, Robert. *The Outlined Bible*. Glasgow: Pickering & Inglis, 1982.

Lee, Sandra. Prayer: "Warriors on Their Knees." Wycliffe. Accessed October 9, 2005. http://www.wycliffe.org/knam/English/resources/columns_praying.htm. Originally available online. No longer accessible.

Lester, Robert C. "The Rituals and Festivals of the Buddhist Life." Buddhist Gateway: Faith Library. Rites and Rituals. 1987. From *Religious Traditions of the World*, edited by H. Byron Earhart (San Francisco: HarperSanFrancisco, 1993). http://www.buddhistgateway.com/library/rituals/.

Lewis, C. S. *Mere Christianity*. New York, New York: Macmillan Publishing Co. Inc., 1952.

Lilback, P.A. "Covenant." *New Dictionary of Theology*, edited by S.B. Ferguson. Downers Grove, IL: InterVarsity Press, 1988.

Livingston, G. Herbert. *The Pentateuch in Its Cultural Environment*. Baker Book House, Grand Rapids, Michigan: Baker Book House, 1982.

Loewen, Jacob A. *The Bible in Cross-Cultural Perspective*. Pasadena, CA: William Carey Library, 2000.

Lord, Donald C. *Mo Bradley and Thailand*. Grand Rapids: Eerdmans, 1969.

Loss, Myron. *Culture Shock*. Winona Lake, IN: Light and Life Press, 1983.

Massey, Joshua. "God's Amazing Diversity in Drawing Muslims to Christ." *International Journal of Frontier Missions* 17, no. 1 (2000): 5–14. Accessed January 24, 2007. http://www.ijfm.org/PDFs_IJFM/17_1_PDFs/Drawing_Muslims.pdf.

McDowell, Josh. "A Ready Defense: Messianic Prophecies Fulfilled in Jesus." Accessed January 8, 2007. www.greatcom.org/resources/areadydefense/ch19/default.htm.

McKaughan, Paul. "The Church and World Missions." *The Unfinished Task*. Ventura, CA: InterVarsity Christian Fellowship, 1984.

Missionary Training Service. "Chapter 1: Why Is Church Planting Important?" 2004. http://www.missionarytraining.org/chapter_1.htm.

Moreau, Scott. "Gaining Perspective on Territorial Spirits." The Lausanne Committee for World Evangelisation. Accessed February 1, 2007. https://www.lausanne.org/content/territorial-spirits

Moreau, Scott. "North American Case Study: An Overview of Spiritual Warfare Literature." The Lausanne Committee for World Evangelization. Accessed February 1, 2007. https://www.lausanne.org/content/north-america

Morris, Bob. "Shrewd yet Innocent: Thoughts on Tentmaker Integrity." *International Journal of Frontier Missions* 15, no. 1 (1998): 5–8. Accessed April 1995. http://www.ijfm.org/PDFs_IJFM/15_1_PDFs/02_Morris.pdf.

Moyer, Bruce Campbell. "Global Partnerships: Tentmakers: A Bold New Adventure in Missions." Center for World Missions and Harding University Michigan USA, 1996–2002. https://digitalcommons.andrews.edu/cgi/viewcontent.cgi?filename=27&article=1003&context=missions-books&type=additional

Norrish, Howard. "Lone Ranger: Yes or No." *Evangelism and Missions Information Service* 26, no. 1 (1990).

Olson, C. Gordon. *What in the World Is God Doing?* Cedar Knolls, NJ: Global Gospel Publishing, 1994.

O'Rear, Michael. "Let's Focus on Strategic Towns." Global Mapping International. Accessed January 18, 2007. http://www.gmi.org/pttw4/towns.htm.

Packer, J. I. *Evangelism and the Sovereignty of God*. Downers Grove, Illinois: InterVarsity Fellowship, 1961.

Parks, Dr. Kent (6A), and Joni Eareckson Tada (6B).
    "Hidden and Forgotten People Including Those Who Are

Disabled." Lausanne Occasional Paper No. 35. Lausanne Committee for World Evangelization. Pattaya, Thailand, September 29 to October 5, 2004. Accessed January 19, 2007. https://www.lausanne.org/content/lop/hidden-forgotten-people-including-disabled-lop-35a

Penn-Lewis, Jessie. Evan Roberts. *War on the Saints*. Fort Washington, PA: The Christian Literature Crusade, 1956.

Pennoyer, Doug. "How to Build an Anti-Shock Kit." *The Great Commission Handbook*. Evanston, IL: Berry Publishing Services Inc., 1994.

Peters, George W. *A Biblical Theology of Mission*. Chicago: Moody Press, 1972.

"Philippians." *IVP New Testament Commentaries*. Bible Gateway. Accessed January 30, 2007. http://www.biblegateway.com/resources/commentaries/index.php?action=getCommentaryText&cid=8&source=1&seq=i.57.4.2.

Piper, John. *Let the Nations Be Glad*. Grand Rapids, Michigan: Baker Books, 1993.

Poythress, Vern. "Territorial Spirits: Some Biblical Perspectives." The Works of John Frame and Vern Poythress. Accessed Sept. 30, 2020. https://frame-poythress.org/territorial-spirits-some-biblical-perspectives/.

Reapsome, Jim. "Missionaries for the 21st Century." *The Great Commission Handbook*. Evanston, IL: Berry Publishing Services Inc., 1994.

Reed, Lyman. *Preparing Missionaries for Intercultural Communication*. Pasadena, CA: William Carey Library, 1985.

Remin, Rod. Canadian Theological Professor of Biblical Languages, 2005.

Richardson, Don. "A Man for All Peoples." *Journey to the Nations*, edited by Debra Sanders. Pasadena, CA: Caleb Project, 1983.

———. *Eternity in Their Hearts*. Ventura, CA: Regal Books, 1981.

Robinson, Paul F. James Vincent. *A Vision with Wings*. Chicago: Moody Press, 1992.

Robb, John. "Satan's Tactics in Building and Maintaining His Kingdom of Darkness." *International Journal of Frontier*

Missions 10, no. 4, (October 1993): 173–84. http://www.ijfm.org/PDFs_IJFM/10_4_PDFs/05_Robb.pdf.

Sherman, Dean. *Spiritual Warfare for Every Christian*. Seattle, WA: YWAM Publishing, 1990.

Siemens, Ruth. "Ruth's Story: The Story Behind GO." Global Opportunities. Accessed March 2001. http://www.globalopps.org/ruths_story.htm.

———. "Tentmaking and the Global Job Market," 1995. http://www.globalopps.org/papers/tentmaki.htm.

———, and Dave English. "The Tentmakers Preparation Checklist: Preparation Needed and How to Get It." Global Opportunities. Accessed March 2001. http://www.globalopps.org/101/tmprep.htm.

———. "Tentmaker Stories." Taken from *Tentmakers Speak by* Don Hamilton. Ventura, CA: Regal Books, 1987. Accessed March 2001. http://www.globalopps.org/stories.htm.

———. "Why Did Paul Make Tents?" Accessed March 2001. http://www.globalopps.org/papers/whydid.htm.

Sitton, David, "The Basics of Animism: Spiritual Warfare in Tribal Contexts." *International Journal of Frontier Missions* 15, no. 2 (1998): 69–74. http://www.ijfm.org/PDFs_IJFM/15_2_PDFs/02_Sitton_Article.pdf.

Smith, Alexander Garnett. *Siamese Gold: A History of Church Growth in Thailand: An Interpretive Analysis 1816–1980.* Bangkok, Thailand: Kanok Bannasan (OMF Publishers), 1982.

Stanley, Charles F. *Handle with Prayer*. Wheaton, Illinois: Victor Books, 1982.

Stedman, Ray C. "The Temple Cleanser." Message No: 7, Catalogue No: 3837. May 8, 1983. Discovery Publishing, a ministry of Peninsula Bible Church. http://www.pbc.org/library/files/html/3837.html.

Stott, John R. "Living God is a Missionary God." *Journey to the Nations*, edited by Debra Sanders. Pasadena, CA: Caleb Project, 1983.

Tenney, Merrill C. *New Testament Survey*. Grand Rapids, Michigan: Wm. B. Eerdmans Publishing Co. 1961 (1980).

"The Court of the Gentiles." Bible History. Accessed October 20, 2006. http://www.bible-history.com/jewishtemple/JEWISH_TEMPLEThe_Court_of_the_Gentiles.htm.

Thomas, Charlotte. "Take the Shock out of Culture Shock."

Thompson, A. E. *A.B. Simpson: His Life and Work*. Christian Publications Inc., 1960.

Travis, S. H. "Eschatology." New *Dictionary of Theology*. Edited by S.B. Ferguson. Downers Grove, IL: InterVarsity Press, 1988.

Troutman, Charles. *Everything You Wanted to Know about the Mission Field but Are Afraid You Won't Learn Until You Get There*. Downers Grove, IL: InterVarsity Press, 1976.

"The Gospel of Matthew: The Twelve Apostles." n.d. http://www.ccel.org/contrib/exec_outlines/matt/mt10_1.htm

Van Rheenen, Gailyn. "Worldview and Syncretism." Presented at the Symposium "Distinctively Christian, Distinctly Mongolian" in Ulaanbaatar, Mongolia, on March 11, 2003. http://missiology.org/mongolianlectures/worldviewandsyncretism.htm.

———. "Living in the Heavenly Realms." Presented at the Symposium "Distinctively Christian, Distinctly Mongolian" in Ulaan Baator, Mongolia on March 11, 2003. http://missiology.org/mongolian-lectures/heavenlyrealms.htm.

Vine, W. E. *An Expository Dictionary of New Testament Words*. Moody Press, Chicago: Oliphants Ltd., 1940 (1952).

Wagner, Peter. *On the Crest of the Wave*. Ventura, CA: Regal Books, 1983.

———. "Evangelizing the World People by People." *Journey to the Nations,* edited by Debra Sanders. Pasadena, CA: Caleb Project, 1983.

Wagner, Paul. "Taking the High Places for God." *International Journal for Frontier Missions* 10, no. 3 (July 1993): 98–102. http://www.ijfm.org/PDFs_IJFM/10_3_PDFs/Wagner.pdf.

Warner, Timothy. *Resolving Spiritual Conflicts and Cross-Cultural Ministry Workbook* (and tape series). La Habra, CA: Freedom in Christ Ministries International, 1993.

———. "Doctrinal Affirmation." *Resolving Spiritual Conflicts and Cross-Cultural Ministry Workbook.* La Habra, CA: Freedom in Christ Ministries International, 1993.

Watson, David. *I Believe in the Church.* Grand Rapids, Michigan: Wm. B. Eerdmans Publishing Company, 1978.

Weerstra, Hans M. "Christian Worldview Development." *International Journal of Frontier Missions* 14, no. 1 (1997). http://www.ijfm.org/PDFs_IJFM/14_1_PDFs/01_Weerstra.pdf.

Wells, Kenneth Elmer. *History of Protestant Work in Thailand, 1828–1958.* Bangkok: Church of Christ in Thailand, 1958.

"Whatever Happened to the Twelve Apostles?" Issue #8.

White, John. *The Fight.* Leicester, England: InterVarsity Christian Fellowship, 1984.

Willis, Avery T. *Biblical Basis of Missions.* International Mission Board, 2004. http://www.ntslibrary.com/PDF%20Books/The%20Biblical%20Basis%20of%20Missions.pdf

Willits, Brad. "Refine the Call." Accessed September 29, 2005. http://www.acu.edu/img/assets/2219/refine_the_call_willits.doc. Originally found online. Url is no longer accessible.

Winter, Ralph. "Missions Today, A Look at the Future." *The Unfinished Task.* Ventura, CA: InterVarsity Christian Fellowship, 1984.

Williams, Don. *Signs, Wonders, and the Kingdom of God.* Ann Arbor, Michigan: Servant Publications, 1989.

World Evangelical Fellowship. "Reducing Missionary Attrition." Accessed 1995. Wheaton, IL: 1996. http://www.ywam.no/misjon/artikkel/attritio.htm.

http://shop4.gospelcom.net/epages/chinstitute.storefront/en/product/1008

http://chi.gospelcom.net/GLIMPSEF/Glimpses/glmps008.shtml. Access date unknown.

About the Author

The author lives in western Canada with her husband and their dog. She loves reading, writing, photography, and painting animals. Her passion for working with internationals is evident in her classes where she teaches English to students at church once a week. She loves the challenge of working with other cultures and truly enjoyed her experiences living overseas in Asia as well as visiting Europe. Missions has been her passion since feeling God's call as a teen. She believes in prayer for supporting missions and international workers. Every tribe, every tongue, and every nation will be seen around the throne (Rev. 7:9). The author longs for that day to see all peoples rejoicing around the throne of the Lamb.